ONE

Don't Let a Democrat or College Student* Read This Book!

*Unless they attend Hillsdale College or Liberty University!

TAD ARMSTRONG

outskirts press

ONE
Don't Let a Democrat or College Student* Read This Book!
All Rights Reserved.
Copyright © 2018 Tad Armstrong
v3.0

The opinions expressed in this manuscript are solely the opinions of the author and do not represent the opinions or thoughts of the publisher. The author has represented and warranted full ownership and/or legal right to publish all the materials in this book.

This book may not be reproduced, transmitted, or stored in whole or in part by any means, including graphic, electronic, or mechanical without the express written consent of the publisher except in the case of brief quotations embodied in critical articles and reviews.

Outskirts Press, Inc.
http://www.outskirtspress.com

Paperback ISBN: 978-1-4787-9671-8
Hardback ISBN: 978-1-4787-9379-3

Library of Congress Control Number: 2018904863

Cover Photo © 2018 gettyimages.com.com. All rights reserved - used with permission.

Outskirts Press and the "OP" logo are trademarks belonging to Outskirts Press, Inc.

PRINTED IN THE UNITED STATES OF AMERICA

DEDICATION

I dedicate this work to Amos Humiston
(see Chapter Seventeen)
and to my grandchildren so far:
Gabby, Gracie, Maddy, Dean and Emerson.
May God give us the strength to preserve the
blessings of freedom for them, just as the Amos
Humistons of our nation's past gave their lives
to preserve it for us.

A lie told often enough becomes the truth.
                                Vladimir Lenin

TABLE OF CONTENTS

PREFACE i

ACKNOWLEDGMENTS v

Chapter One   ONE COURT 1

Chapter Two   ONE PRESIDENT ≈ ONE SENATE 7

Chapter Three   ONE ROBE ≈ ONE OATH 11

Chapter Four   ONE VOTE 27

Chapter Five   ONE METHOD 37

Chapter Six   ONE ROBE SHORT ON JUNE 24, 1992, ELIMINATED COMMENCEMENT PRAYERS IN PUBLIC GRADE SCHOOLS! 45

Chapter Seven   ONE ROBE LONG ON APRIL 26, 1995, PRESERVED FEDERALISM! 61

Chapter Eight   ONE ROBE SHORT ON MAY 22, 1995, KILLED THE HOPE OF CONGRESSIONAL TERM LIMITS! 85

Chapter Nine   ONE ROBE LONG ON APRIL 18, 2007, BANNED ONE FORM OF LEGALIZED SLAUGHTER! 115

Chapter Ten	ONE ROBE LONG ON JUNE 26, 2008, COULD SAVE YOUR LIFE SOMEDAY!.....	145
Chapter Eleven	ONE ROBE SHORT ON MAY 23, 2011, FREED THE GUILTY!	173
Chapter Twelve	ONE ROBE SHORT ON JUNE 26, 2013, ALTERED THE TRADITIONAL INSTITUTION OF MARRIAGE!................	199
Chapter Thirteen	ONE ROBE LONG ON MAY 5, 2014, PRESERVED PRAYER IN GREECE!	229
Chapter Fourteen	ONE ROBE SHORT ON JUNE 26, 2014, EMPOWERED THE EXECUTIVE BRANCH WHILE YOU WERE SLEEPING!.................	265
Chapter Fifteen	ONE ROBE LONG ON JUNE 30, 2014, PRESERVED RELIGIOUS FREEDOM!	317
Chapter Sixteen	ONE ROBE SHORT -ONE ROBE LONG -TEN ADDITIONAL CASES THAT, LIKE IT OR NOT, DEFINE WHAT WE PRESENTLY STAND FOR AS A NATION.........................	359
Chapter Seventeen	ONE SACRIFICE OUGHT TO BE ENOUGH!...	363
Chapter Eighteen	ONE LAST CHANCE TO SAVE AMERICA..	367
ABOUT THE AUTHOR...		377
APPENDIX		379
INDEX OF CASES		381

PREFACE

Because I believe ignorance is the greatest threat to freedom, I hope my passion to educate with this book comes through loud and clear and that this preface will entice all prospective readers to take the journey.

As I compose this last step before going to print, America is on the brink of anarchy – an utter disregard for the rule of law. Parts of our nation are presently experiencing the devastation that anarchy produces; to wit: Chicago, Ferguson, Baltimore.

Patriotic American Atheists, Jews, Christians, Muslims, and so on, have legitimate positions on either side of such matters as prayer in public school (Chapter Six), the limits of federal power (Chapter Seven), federal term limits (Chapter Eight), partial-birth abortion (Chapter Nine), gun control (Chapter Ten), cruel and unusual punishment (Chapter Eleven), gay marriage (Chapter Twelve), prayer in city government (Chapter Thirteen), recess appointment power (Chapter Fourteen), and abortifacient mandates (Chapter Fifteen). But, it is crucial for the reader to understand that, although the foregoing Supreme Court decisions do discuss policy, this book is not about any attempt to influence policy.

Rather, it is about (1) understanding the Rule of Law (the meaning of the provisions set forth in the Constitution), (2) honoring those who both seek to become president, senator or Supreme Court justice and who take their oath to support the Constitution seriously, and, (3) persuading citizens who may never have understood the importance of who becomes a Supreme Court justice to participate in the decisions that determine who gets an appointment for a robe fitting - by voting.

Numerous Supreme Court justices over the course of our Constitution's existence have, on occasion, found themselves in disagreement with policies underlying legislation or executive action, yet have felt duty-bound (oath-bound) to uphold the policies because the Constitution required them to do so. And, of course, on occasion, these same oath-bound justices have struck down legislation or executive action as unconstitutional in spite of their agreement with the policies underlying said laws or actions.

When those who are given the distinct privilege of serving on the High Court assume an arrogance of power that places their own personal views of what they believe is best for America ahead of their first duty to recognize the limits of their constitutional power, anarchy is sure to follow. See Chapter Three.

By introducing the reader to several Supreme Court decisions decided by **one vote** (some that honor the Constitution and some that flaunt its authority), the hope is that our citizenry will come to understand the importance of abiding by the Rule of Law and doing their part with their **one vote** to put presidents and senators in office who will likely fill Supreme Court vacancies with justices who favor the Rule of Law over their own lawless grab for power. The attempt is to persuade Americans to save our Country (and ourselves) with our votes in November of 2018 and beyond, for if ignorance-in-voting or apathy-in-non-voting permits just **one future Supreme Court vacancy** left by an oath-taker's death or retirement to be filled by a policy-making-oath-breaker, then America's obituary can be written. The principles of the greatest experiment in freedom the world has ever known will be tossed to the wind - the Constitution will be irrelevant - anarchy will consume us. My passion for writing this book is founded upon a belief that the Framers' vision for America is worth preserving. If you agree, I encourage you to read this book, spread its message and vote accordingly in 2018 and beyond. If you disagree, I would still love the chance to persuade.

The Nation experienced an oath-taker's death in 2016 with the shocking and untimely demise of Justice Antonin Scalia. Fortunately, Donald J. Trump was elected president – he nominated Neil Gorsuch to fill that vacancy on the High Court – and, the nomination was confirmed in the Senate. What a different nation it would be today had Hillary Clinton been in position to fill Justice Scalia's seat. While we lost a great legal scholar with Scalia's passing, we did not lose any ground in the battle to preserve the Constitution with the Gorsuch appointment.

There could easily be one to three Supreme Court vacancies in the next three to seven years. All the more reason to read this book and understand that we are on the brink of constitutional disaster if we don't get this right.

Tad Armstrong
June, 2018

ACKNOWLEDGMENTS

Thank you, Melody. Our close friends and family know how much you have sacrificed to enable me to pursue my passion to educate our citizens.

Thank you, Meghan, for proofreading and always giving me a boost of encouragement (just at the right time) to stay the course.

So many good friends have helped me along the way: Phyllis Schlafly, Anne Schlafly Cori, Jack Klobnak, Steve Klingel, Kevin Jackson, Drs. Wayne and Karladine Graves, Bill Federer, Pastor Tom Hufty, Captain Mark J. Schreiber, Pastor R.B. and Helen Hall, Pastor Tom and Debbie Graddy, Pastor Doug White, Professor Richard Huston at Greenville College, Dr. Christopher Stocklin and Jim McIntosh at Brookes Bible College, Mark Spengler, Mary Lou Ferguson, Tom and Vickie Maxwell, Pastor Camy and BJ Arnett, Judge John Knight, James Likens, Gary Goode, Pastor Myles Holmes, Pastor Stan and Delbra Pratt, Pastors Dennis and Patti Amsden, Dr. William and Diana Starr Drake, Jeff Schwarz and so many more. Thanks to all.

Thanks to all students and others associated with our ELL Constitution Clubs for the past fourteen years in Illinois (Alton, Decatur, Edwardsville, Fairview Heights, Glen Carbon, Granite City, Highland, Jerseyville, Edwardsville High School, and Marquette High School), as well as in Troy, Michigan. Consider visiting the ELL website at ellconstitutionclubs.com.

There are two groups especially close to my heart. I teach a small group (Sunday school) at my church, the First Baptist Church in Maryville, Illinois. I call them the "old geezers" because that is what they are. Believe me, I get much more than I give to these folks with so much wisdom to share. I also meet with a men's group every Saturday in Edwardsville, Illinois. Their good looks more than make up for their lack of wisdom. And, thanks and praise to God for giving me the strength to persevere in some very difficult times.

Chapter One

ONE COURT

"Presidents come and go,
but the Supreme Court goes on forever."

William Howard Taft

"Less than two weeks into his first term, President Trump nominated Neil Gorsuch for the Supreme Court. All Republican Senators and Three Democrat Senators confirmed the nomination and he was sworn in as our Nation's 112th Justice on April 10, 2017. As I hope the ensuing pages will persuade, if this President achieves nothing more, his tenure will be hailed as successful."

Tad Armstrong

This book is written to persuade the reader of the importance of preserving our United States Constitution. I must first convince you that the goal is worthy of the effort. And, assuming I do, you will then want to learn what role you can play in that preservation. Thanks for starting the journey. I hope you are still with me at the end because, if enough of you are, I am convinced that "We, the People" can still save America!

I am going to be taking you into the four corners of our nation's supreme Rule of Law. I urge you to get a copy of a pocket-sized Constitution published by either the Cato Institute or the Heritage Foundation. You can also obtain the 8½ x 11 version online at our website: ellconstitutionclubs.com.

I will be quoting the Constitution, but there is something about taking that step of authenticity by getting your own copy and reading it for yourself that brings it all to life. That simple step will help provide you with sufficient confidence in the knowledge you obtain to boldly spread the message to those in need of hearing it. They won't be hard to find.

Before we get to the Supreme Court decisions that control your life – the decisions that define America – let's gather up some delicious facts in the garden of constitutional trivia.

There are seven articles in the Constitution proper and, after ratification in 1791 of the first 10 amendments (referred to as our "Bill of Rights"), we added an additional 17 amendments for a total of 27. The Twenty-Seventh Amendment was sent to the states for proposed ratification, along with the Bill of Rights, on September 25, 1789; however, it was not ratified until May 7, 1992, over 200 years later! Go ahead. Take a look and you will understand why it took so long to become law.

Article I sets up our legislative branch of government, Article II our executive branch and Article III our judicial branch.

Take a look at some important provisions in Article III:

Article III, §1:

The judicial power of the United States shall be vested in one Supreme Court and in such inferior courts as the Congress may from time to time ordain and establish...

And Article VI:

Article VI, ¶2:

This Constitution and the laws of the United States which shall be made in pursuance thereof...shall be the supreme law of the land...

The Constitution establishes the United States Supreme Court as the highest court in the land and the Constitution as the supreme law of the land.

When Article III speaks of "inferior courts," it is referencing all federal courts that are, by definition, of lesser authority than the Supreme Court and, as is evident, these "inferior" bodies are not directly established by the Constitution but, rather, by Congress.

At present, there are 94 federal districts.[1] The federal district courts are known as trial courts because trials occur there: evidence is presented, witnesses testify and verdicts are rendered by juries when

---

1 http://uscourts.gov/FederalCourts/UnderstandingtheFederalCourts/CourtofAppeals.aspx

the parties seek a trial by jury and by judges when they do not. There is at least one federal district in each state as well as the District of Columbia, Puerto Rico, the Virgin Islands, Guam and the Northern Mariana Islands.

In the federal system, appeals are taken from these 94 district courts to one of 12 Courts of Appeals.[2] When a party feels he has not had a fair trial, he has the right of one appeal. The case is not retried; rather, the appellate court reviews the case and decides whether the trial court judgment should stand or whether it should be modified in some fashion or outright reversed or tried again in the trial court.

Although there are very narrowly defined types of cases that can be initially filed in the Supreme Court, it rarely acts as a trial court. Therefore, it functions as an appellate court in all but rare instances. The appeals come to the justices, for the most part, from a federal court of appeals or from the highest state court in a given state and it may be a surprise to learn that, for the most part, the decision to hear an appeal in the Supreme Court is discretionary with the justices. In fact, about 10,000 parties per year cry out to be heard, but only 80 or so are accepted.[3] These appeals are not based upon a "right" to be heard, but rather, on permission granted by at least four of the nine Supreme Court justices that is called a "writ of certiorari." Please don't get lost in the Latin - some terms arise so often that mention of them cannot be overlooked.

Many of the cases accepted by the Supreme Court involve issues that have been interpreted differently by the various state or federal courts, the idea being that a final decision will help establish uniformity throughout the nation.

---

2   http://uscourts.gov/FederalCourts/UnderstandingtheFederalCourts/ CourtofAppeals.aspx.
3   http:/www.supremecourt.gov/faq.aspx.

One

The U.S. Constitution established the Supreme Court but left it to Congress to decide how many justices should make up the court. The Judiciary Act of 1789 set the number at six. In 1807, Congress increased the number to seven and in 1837 the number was increased again to nine. In 1863 a tenth justice was added and just three years later the number was reduced back to seven. The last change came in 1869 when the number was bumped up to nine.

Ever since Chief Justice John Marshall's 1803 opinion in *Marbury v. Madison*,[4] the Supreme Court has been the final arbiter of constitutional interpretation. There have been a few instances of constitutional crises where presidents have disregarded a High Court ruling, but they are, thankfully, rare.

For the foregoing reasons, I am on solid ground when I say that five of the nine justices possess more secular power than any other group in the free world and, where one of them is needed to break a tie, that **one robe** that swings the vote is the most powerful of all. The only body more powerful than the Supreme Court are the American people - enough of them - coming together to amend the Constitution and overcome a result of the Court they deem to be in need of fixing. Article V outlines the process for amending the Constitution the proper way. Check it out. However, it is far easier to elect the right presidents and senators to help ensure they will put the right justices on the Court who will not likely get it wrong in the first instance! The next chapter explains that process.

---

[4] If you would like to read Marbury v. Madison, consult the Appendix for instructions.

Chapter Two

ONE PRESIDENT
≈
ONE SENATE

"The contest, for all ages, has been to rescue Liberty from the grasp of executive power."

Daniel Webster

So you want to become a member of the Supreme Court? I will speak to the qualifications you must have in Chapter Three, but assuming you can pass those with flying colors, where do you go to apply?

Well, you might let it be known to "the powers that be" that you are interested in the job, but this is an instance where the job finds you and not the other way around. This chapter discusses "the powers that be" part of the journey and, for that, we return to the Constitution.

Article II, §2, ¶2:

The President...shall nominate, and by and with the advice and consent of the Senate, shall appoint...judges of the Supreme Court...

It is clear that the president has the sole power to initiate the process to fill a vacancy on the Court by nominating you for the job. Then, if the president gets the "advice and consent of the Senate" (a simple majority in favor of the nomination) and he still wants you to have the job, he[5] "appoints" you to it. There have been a few instances where justices have served without confirmation, albeit temporarily, when the appointments were made during a recess of the Senate. Lest we forget, you could theoretically reject all of this praise and national attention anytime you wish until you have accepted an appointment. After that, your "rejection" would be termed a "resignation," but more on the length of your tenure in Chapter Three.

Shall we return to the garden of constitutional trivia?

George Washington made 11 appointments to the Court, while Franklin Roosevelt made the second highest number of appointments, nine.[6]

---

5   See political correctness disclaimer in Chapter Five.
6   Kermit L. Hall, editor, *The Oxford Guide to the Supreme Court* (Oxford, New York: Oxford University Press, 2005), 1152.

ONE

Justice Thurgood Marshall, the first black justice, was sworn in on October 2nd, 1967. Justice Sandra Day O'Connor, the first female justice, was sworn in on September 21st, 1981. At age 32, Justice Joseph Story was the youngest justice and, at age 90, Justice Oliver Wendell Holmes was the oldest justice to sit on the Court.[7]

Four presidents never had an opportunity to appoint a justice: William Henry Harrison, Zachary Taylor, Andrew Johnson and Jimmy Carter.[8]

Twelve nominees have been officially rejected by the Senate,[9] the most recent being Robert H. Bork in 1987 by a vote of 58 to 42.[10]

We will take a closer look at the current members on the Court in Chapter Eighteen.

---

[7] Kermit L. Hall, editor, *The Oxford Guide to the Supreme Court* (Oxford, New York: Oxford University Press, 2005), 1151-52.
[8] Kermit L. Hall, editor, *The Oxford Guide to the Supreme Court* (Oxford, New York: Oxford University Press, 2005), 1152.
[9] http://historynewsnetwork.org/article/13194.
[10] Kermit L. Hall, editor, *The Oxford Guide to the Supreme Court* (Oxford, New York: Oxford University Press, 2005), 1134.

Chapter Three

ONE ROBE
≈
ONE OATH

"Don't interfere with anything in the Constitution. That must be maintained, for it is the only safeguard of our liberties."

Abraham Lincoln

Getting the Job

To date (June of 2018) there have been 113 justices (including 17 chief justices) in the Supreme Court's history – 109 men and four women.

What are the requirements to be considered for a seat on the High Court? Well, other than being nominated by the president and then being confirmed by a majority of the Senate, there are none.[11] That's right. Technically, you do not have to be an American citizen and can even be a convicted felon. You do not have to be a lawyer or have any experience as a judge. In other words, the Framers left the selection of the justices completely to the good judgment of the president and the Senate. It's a safe bet, however, that an impressive resume is a must.

Unfortunately, the televised Senate confirmation hearings prior to a vote to confirm or reject a nominee are a joke. I said as much in my op-ed piece covering the Elena Kagan hearings, republished here with permission of the *St. Louis Post-Dispatch*.

> "Elena Kagan and the Rule of Law"
>
> Interrogation is irrelevant to the outcome and extraordinarily unfair to all nominees.
>
> St. Louis Post-Dispatch
> Tad Armstrong
> Wednesday, July 7, 2010
>
> The rules of "cloture" and "nuclear option" aside and assuming all 100 members are present, it would take 41 senators to filibuster a vote to confirm Elena

---

[11] http://www.supremecourt.gov/faq.aspx#faqgi2.

ONE

Kagan as the 112th justice of the Supreme Court. It seems rather odd that 41 senators could impede the will of 59 colleagues, especially since it only takes a simple majority to complete President Obama's plan to ensure that the make-up of the Court loses no ground in the relentless pursuit of unlimited (and unconstitutional) power. Guess how many senators are Republicans?

In general, I prefer majority rule in a legislative body. But, because confirmation of the wrong nominee to the Court is of such singular importance to our nation, my advice to the 41 is to filibuster.

A president's most important duty is to nominate replacements on the Court. Keep that in mind the next time you vote for a president. One unelected justice (if they are one of only five votes cast in the many five to four decisions involving such issues as national security, individual freedom, how your children are educated, abortion and immigration) wields more power (for a lifetime) than a four- to eight-year president and all of the short-term members of Congress combined.

Nevertheless, the Senate has determined that, although we vet a presidential candidate with two years of public scrutiny (or used to) before voting, 17 hours of softball interrogation is sufficient before voting on what is arguably the most powerful individual secular position on the face of the Earth.

What did "We, the People" get for our 17 hours? Precious little. But, we didn't expect to learn anything, did we? The process has turned into little more than free face time for senatorial grandstanding.

Some say Ms. Kagan "wowed them by her performance." I agree. She is quick on her feet, highly skilled at dodging questions and obviously intelligent. But, a requisite level of intelligence is a given for any nominee and the post she seeks does not list quickness afoot (justices take the time they need to render decisions) or question-dodging in the job description. History has taught nominees that if they actually want the job, they must either deny having opinions in the face of having them or lie. Well, I suppose Justice Sonia Sotomayor could have "changed her mind" between her confirmation hearing less than one year ago and her dissent in the recent Chicago gun rights case. You be the "judge."

Seriously, if candor is the recipe for failure, interrogation is both irrelevant to the outcome and extraordinarily unfair to all nominees. Victory awaits those who, instead, can "perform."

The only evidence worth considering are the facts revealed by an independent investigation into the nominee's past. And, the only question worth investigating is whether that past is predictive of a willingness to abide by an oath to support the Constitution (otherwise known as the "rule of law") or whether it is predictive of a plan "to mold and steer the law in order to promote ethical values and achieve certain social ends" (otherwise known as the "rule-of-whatever-floats-your-boat".) Ms. Kagan approves of the latter. I do not. Nominees who believe in the activist approach to judging missed their calling, for Congress is where the job of "molding the law to achieve social ends" properly resides – not the judiciary.

One

What would I like to see in a Supreme Court justice? I would not require prior judicial experience, but I do not see how one can judge the law without being a lawyer. Humility is a must, for the best judge is one who understands she is not perfect. And, nothing against ivy, but we could use a few graduates from law schools planted within a mile of a good corn crop and who either have had experience in running their own business or have labored by the sweat of their brow on the way to their law degree. And, finally, their past actions (not present promises) must establish that they know what it means to take an oath to support the Constitution before inheriting the awesome obligation to preserve it - not to mold it.

On second thought, because I do not believe more than five of the 41 have the fortitude to hang together while awaiting a nominee who believes in the "rule of law" before handing over the most powerful job on Earth to someone who does not, we might as well get to a vote and let the Kagan party begin. The American people will get precisely what they asked for – this time.

Tad Armstrong is an Edwardsville (Illinois) lawyer and founder of ELL Constitution Clubs.

Elena Kagan was confirmed in the Senate (63-37) shortly after the foregoing op-ed went to press.

As it turns out, all justices in the Court's history were lawyers, but over a third of them had never been federal or state judges, including such potentially more familiar names as John Marshall, Earl Warren, William Rehnquist, Felix Frankfurter, and Louis Brandeis.

Keeping the Job

The Constitution does have a few things to say about keeping the job.

> **Article III, §1:**
>
> **The judges, both of the supreme and inferior courts, shall hold their offices during good behaviour...**

Translation: all federal judges hold their positions for life; that is, until they retire, resign, die or become impeached (and then convicted) for "bad behaviour."

> **Article I, §2, ¶5:**
>
> **The House of Representatives...shall have the sole power of impeachment.**

> **Article I, §3, ¶6-7:**
>
> **The Senate shall have the sole power to try all impeachments...No person shall be convicted without the concurrence of two thirds of the members present.**
>
> **Judgment in cases of impeachment shall not extend further than removal from office, and disqualification to hold and enjoy any office of honor, trust or profit under the United States: but the party convicted shall nevertheless be liable and subject to indictment, trial, judgment and punishment, according to law.**

Article II, §4:

...All civil officers of the United States shall be removed from office on impeachment for, and conviction of, treason, bribery or other high crimes and misdemeanors.

Let's clear up some misunderstood terminology. The House of Representatives is the only body that can bring charges of impeachment. Impeachment, then, is not a conviction; rather, it is a formal accusation of wrongdoing and must be supported by a majority vote in the House. After impeachment charges are brought, the trial is before the Senate.

While it should be readily clear that Article II, §4 "treason, bribery or other high crimes and misdemeanors" qualify as Article III, §1 "bad behaviour," the standard for judges is much higher than other offices. Bad behaviour is very broad indeed.

Only one Supreme Court justice, Samuel Chase, has been impeached. He was impeached in 1804 and was tried and acquitted in 1805. The motivation for impeachment was political and, although a majority of the Senate found him guilty on three of eight articles of impeachment, none of the votes rose to the required two thirds necessary to convict.[12]

Doing the Job

Now we are getting to the heart of the matter of this thing we call judicial review. Let's spend some very serious time with a few provisions of Article VI.

---

12 http://www.senate.gov/artandhistory/history/minute/Senate_Tries_Justice.htm.

> **Article VI, ¶3:**
>
> **The Senators ... before mentioned ... and all ... judicial Officers ... of the United States ... shall be bound by Oath or Affirmation, to support this Constitution...**

Keep in mind that this book is about the role of presidents and senators in selecting Supreme Court justices and, of course, the role of the justices themselves. Thus, the selected constitutional provisions are limited to the foregoing roles. Article VI, §3 describes the oath to be taken by senators and judicial officers (judges) to "support" the Constitution.

The president's oath is a bit different.

> **Article II, §1, ¶8:**
>
> **Before [the President] enter on the Execution of his Office, he shall take the following Oath or Affirmation:- "I do solemnly swear (or affirm) that I will faithfully execute the Office of President of the United States, and will to the best of my Ability, preserve, protect and defend the Constitution of the United States.**

While the actual oaths taken by senators, justices and the president may include additional language, they must include the respective language stated in these provisions and any added language cannot contradict the required language.

It is no stretch to conclude that presidents who have a duty to preserve, protect and defend the Constitution are obligated to nominate justices to the High Court whom they believe will likely preserve,

ONE

protect and defend the Constitution, just as senators who have a duty to support the Constitution are obligated to confirm only those nominees whom they believe will also support the Constitution in their roles as justices.

> **We the people are the rightful masters of both Congress and the courts, not to overthrow the Constitution but to overthrow the men who pervert the Constitution.**
>
> **Abraham Lincoln**

First, let me be clear. I am borrowing Lincoln's admonition to encourage us to engage in an "overthrowing" via the use of the ballot box. Aside from the obvious, there are an abundance of reasons not to "overthrow" via the use of force. A more subtle reason is that without knowledge and wisdom, the sword could never bring meaningful and lasting victory. The battle for the mind is less risky to life and limb, but much more difficult to win than the taking of a hill. Without the educated consensus of the people, our form of government has no chance of surviving alongside freedom.

Second, in order to vote out the men and women who pervert the Constitution, we must first meet the challenge of understanding the Constitution. Only then will we be able to discern when it is being perverted and by whom. Please do not embarrass yourself by protesting the perversion of your free speech rights, your religious freedom or your right to peaceable assembly until you gain the knowledge necessary to understand the meaning of free speech, freedom of religion and peaceable assembly as intended by the Framers. Free speech does not include the freedom to blare your message over a loudspeaker at 2:00 a.m. in your neighborhood. Religious freedom does not find a safe harbor should you decide that paying taxes is against your faith. And, peaceable assembly does not include setting up your meeting place in the middle of an intersection, regardless of how peaceful you may be. These are obvious reminders that no freedom is absolute. The outside limits of these freedoms are challenged every day in our courts.

When one studies the Constitution, the Federalist Papers, other founding documents and Supreme Court cases, the meaning and intent of the Framers, in most instances, becomes clear. Armed with this knowledge, "We the People" can then collectively determine for ourselves whether Congress in legislating or the courts in interpreting are doing so in tune with the Constitution or in opposition to its principles. Let's go ahead and add the executive branch to Lincoln's warning to determine whether presidents and those who seek to become president are executing or would execute the law in accord with the Constitution.

In the case of the president, what does his oath "to preserve, protect and defend the Constitution to the best of his ability" mean? And, in the case of senators and justices, what does their oath "to support" the Constitution mean? Is there any significant difference?

These are not difficult questions for those of us who believe in the rule of law. First, there is no meaningful difference between the oaths and, second, their meaning is simple: the Constitution, inclusive of all proper Article V amendments, is the supreme rule of law that we all must live by. That is, oath-takers are (or should be) compelled to follow the Constitution as written and intended as best they can.

The consent of the governed begins with the ratification of the Constitution and its amendments. With rare exception, I believe that any president or senator or representative who believes the oath they take permits them to stray from the original intent of our founding document and its amendments and who act on such belief, are enemies of the people. They utterly disrespect over one million of our warriors who gave their lives to preserve the rule of law. They disrespect "the people" (you and me) by exceeding their power without our consent. It disgusts me to no end. They are not "good people" with differing ideologies – they are enemies of freedom! If you value freedom, they are enemies of you!

You may be surprised, then, that I leave room for the "rare exception" noted in the previous paragraph. I do believe that it may be entirely appropriate for presidents, for example, to exceed their constitutional limitations when preserving our national security. President Lincoln comes to mind for some of his actions taken during the Civil War. After all, we do expect our Commander in Chief to win, do we not? However, that is where the genius of the Founders comes into play, for it is the singular and critical role of the judiciary to stand firm against such attempts.

Far too many presume it is the proper function of a judge in this republic to act with the wisdom of a King Solomon when ruling and, therefore, when dispensing justice. That is true when trial judges, for example, make decisions about where a child of a broken home should live in the best interest of that child. But, that is not what Supreme Court justices do. They interpret the law.

Their constitutional role is not to do what they deem is best for the nation, unless you understand that what is best for the nation is to rule within the confines of the Constitution. Those justices that favor a "living, breathing" Constitution truly believe they have the power to amend its provisions without bothering to require Congress and the States to do so according to the requirements of Article V. Amending the Constitution the proper way was not designed to be easy. Amending it by judicial fiat is, no doubt, easier – it is also a direct contradiction of the will of the people. It is destructive of freedom, democracy and our Republic.

The beauty of our Republic is that, with one slightly modified exception noted below, majority rule is not the rule of law unless that majority acts within its constitutional limits. The Constitution is our safeguard against the tyranny of the majority. The Framers were well aware that power corrupts. That is why we have so many checks and balances – to prevent out-of-control power. They believed that our constitutional framework should not be allowed to be changed by a simple majority. But, if the need for change becomes serious enough that two thirds of Congress and three fourths of the state legislatures approve of the change, then it can be constitutionally altered through the Article V provisions.

The oath-breaker justices investigate poll results, trends, and laws of other nations, then use those findings as support for their decisions. Clearly, when it suits their version of what America ought to be (not what the Constitution says it is) they use the tyranny of a poll or trend to effectively amend the Constitution by judicial fiat. I submit this evolving methodology of far too many justices is the root cause of our nation's downfall.

This oath-breaking methodology is used to strike down otherwise constitutional legislation just as it is used to uphold otherwise unconstitutional legislation. Before we explore several important cases in detail, I will provide an example of the former.

In the 1965 case of *Griswold v. Connecticut*, seven justices voted to strike down a Connecticut statute that made it a crime for "any person to use a drug or instrument to prevent conception" and for "any person to assist, abet, or counsel another to do so." Please understand that the proper role of the Court was not to determine whether contraception is a good idea or should be criminalized; rather, it was whether Connecticut's decision to criminalize it was constitutional.

ONE

In dissent, Justice Black said:

> "I do not base my view that this Connecticut law is constitutional on a belief that the law is wise or that its policy is a good one. It is every bit as offensive to me as it is to my Brethren...
>
> "The Court talks about a constitutional 'right of privacy' as though there is some constitutional provision or provisions forbidding any law ever to be passed which might abridge the 'privacy' of individuals. But there is not...
>
> "I get nowhere in this case by talk about a constitutional 'right of privacy' as an emanation from one or more constitutional provisions. I like my privacy as well as the next one, but I am nevertheless compelled to admit that government has a right to invade it unless prohibited by some specific constitutional provision. For these reasons I cannot agree with the Court's judgment and the reasons it gives for holding this Connecticut law unconstitutional...
>
> "The due process argument which my Brothers Harlan and White adopt here is based on the premise that this Court is vested with power to invalidate all state laws that it considers to be arbitrary, capricious, unreasonable, or oppressive, or on this Court's belief that a particular state law under scrutiny has no 'rational or justifying' purpose, or is offensive to a 'sense of fairness and justice.' If these formulas based on 'natural justice' are to prevail, they require judges to determine what is or is not constitutional on the basis of their own appraisal of what laws are unwise or unnecessary. The power to make such decisions is of course that of a legislative body.

"Surely it has to be admitted that no provision of the Constitution specifically gives such blanket power to courts to exercise such a supervisory veto over the wisdom and value of legislative policies and to hold unconstitutional those laws which they believe unwise or dangerous…I do not believe that we are granted power by…any…constitutional provision …to measure constitutionality by our belief that legislation is arbitrary, capricious or unreasonable, or accomplishes no justifiable purpose, or is offensive to our own notions of 'civilized standards of conduct.' Such an appraisal of the wisdom of legislation is an attribute of the power to make laws, not of the power to interpret them…

"I realize that many good and able men have eloquently spoken and written, sometimes in rhapsodical strains, about the duty of this Court to keep the Constitution in tune with the times. The idea is that the Constitution must be changed from time to time and that this Court is charged with a duty to make those changes. For myself, I must with all deference reject that philosophy. The Constitution makers knew the need for change and provided for it. Amendments suggested by the people's elected representatives can be submitted to the people or their selected agents for ratification. That method of change was good for our Fathers, and being somewhat old-fashioned I must add it is good enough for me. And so, I cannot rely on…any mysterious and uncertain natural law concept as a reason for striking down this state law…

"We have returned to the original constitutional proposition that courts do not substitute their social

ONE

and economic beliefs for the judgment of legislative bodies, who are elected to pass laws."

In a separate dissenting opinion, Justice Stewart said:

"Since 1879 Connecticut has had on its books a law which forbids the use of contraceptives by anyone. I think this is an uncommonly silly law...As a philosophical matter, I believe the use of contraceptives in the relationship of marriage should be left to personal and private choice, based upon each individual's moral, ethical, and religious beliefs. As a matter of social policy, I think professional counsel about methods of birth control should be available to all, so that each individual's choice can be meaningfully made. But we are not asked in this case to say whether we think this law is unwise... We are asked to hold that it violates the United States Constitution and that I cannot do...

"At the oral argument in this case we were told that the Connecticut law does not 'conform to current community standards.' But it is not the function of this Court to decide cases on the basis of community standards. We are here to decide cases 'agreeably to the Constitution and laws of the United States.' It is the essence of judicial duty to subordinate our own personal views, our own ideas of what legislation is wise and what is not. If, as I should surely hope, the law before us does not reflect the standards of the people of Connecticut, the people of Connecticut can freely exercise their...rights to persuade their elected representatives to repeal it. That is the constitutional way to take this law off the books."

There you have it – two clear examples of what we should be looking for in a Supreme Court justice.

Justices Black and Stewart respect the power of the People, through their representatives, to decide matters of policy through legislation or, if necessary, through Article V amendments to the Constitution. The other seven justices in the *Griswold* case took it upon themselves to decide for the rest of us what the policy should be for all 50 States.

Chapter Four

ONE VOTE

"The best argument against democracy is a five-minute conversation with the average voter."

Winston Churchill

It is often referred to as the franchise or suffrage or a plebiscite. Do you even have a right to it? Really? Just exactly where do you find such a right and how powerful is it? Is a non-vote just as powerful as a vote?

As we learned in Chapter Two, the president nominates and the Senate confirms or rejects nominations for those who seek to become members of the Supreme Court. Your vote, as it relates to the folks who determine the make-up of the High Court (the president and the senators), is discussed in this Chapter Four.

In Chapter Three I said: "It is no stretch to conclude that presidents who have a duty to preserve, protect and defend the Constitution are obligated to nominate justices to the High Court whom they believe will likely defend the Constitution, just as senators who have a duty to defend the Constitution are obligated to confirm only those nominees whom they believe will also defend the Constitution in their roles as justices."

Your Vote for President

What does the Constitution say about how we choose a president? Without going into great detail, here are a few selected provisions that form the basis for the "electoral method" we use.

> **Article II, §1:**
>
> **Each State shall appoint, in such Manner as the Legislature thereof may direct, a Number of Electors, equal to the whole number of Senators and Representatives to which the State may be entitled in the Congress…[The Twenty-Third Amendment added a provision to include electors from the District of Columbia.]**

One

> The Congress may determine the Time of chusing the Electors, and the Day on which they shall give their Votes; which Day shall be the same throughout the United States.
>
> **Twelfth Amendment**: (ratified June 15, 1804)
>
> The Electors shall meet in their respective states, and vote by ballot for President...; they shall name in their ballots the person voted for as President...and they shall make distinct lists of all persons voted for as President...and of the number of votes for each, which lists they shall sign and certify, and transmit sealed to the seat of the government of the United States, directed to the President of the Senate; The President of the Senate shall, in the presence of the Senate and House of Representatives, open all the certificates and the votes shall then be counted;- The person having the greatest number of votes for President, shall be the President, if such number be a majority of the whole number of Electors appointed ...[The provisions go on to provide the rules applicable should no one candidate receive a majority of the electoral votes].

Every state has two senators. The number of representatives any given state has varies with the census taken every ten years. A total of 435 representatives in the House are divided amongst the states by population (with each state entitled to at least one representative). D.C. is currently entitled to 3 electors.

100 senators + 435 representatives + 3 electors from D.C. = 538. Since a majority of electoral votes are necessary to elect a president without invoking rules that take over when that does not occur, 270

electoral votes is the magic number: 538 ÷ 2 = 269. 269 + 1 = 270, a majority of 538.

Most states invoke a winner-take-all system whereby the state sends all of its electors for the winner of the popular vote to the electoral college. A few states modify that rule somewhat.

There you have it. You vote - not for the president - but for electors who vote for the president. And, get this, they are not legally required to vote for the person they purported to be "for" when you voted for them. Do not fear, for that has rarely occurred in our nation's history. But the Framers got this method right, in my estimation. What would happen, for example, if a party's chosen candidate became involved in a scandal of such magnitude on the eve of the electoral college vote, but after the general election, that putting him in office would be a disaster for the American people?

The method receives much criticism when the electoral college winner turns out to be the popular vote loser, but that has happened only five times in our nation's history:

1824: John Quincy Adams was selected by the House of Representatives. Andrew Jackson won the popular vote but received less than a majority of the electoral votes.

1876: Rutherford B. Hayes won just enough electoral votes to become president, in spite of losing the popular vote to Samuel Tilden.

1888: Benjamin Harrison became president with a substantial margin of victory in the electoral vote count even though Grover Cleveland won the popular vote.

2000: Although Al Gore won the popular vote, George W. Bush became president when Florida's 25 electoral votes pushed him one vote over the required 270.

2016: Hillary Clinton won the popular vote, but Donald Trump's electoral college margin of victory was significant: 304 to 227. Colin Powell (3), John Kasich, Ron Paul, Bernie Sanders and Faith Spotted Eagle won a total of 7 electoral votes, making up the total of 538.

I favor the electoral method because without this system, New York, Los Angeles, Chicago and other major metropolitan areas would control presidential elections. There would be no need for a presidential candidate to pay any attention to the interests of the citizens of small states. In my estimation, the entire nation is better represented with the electoral system.

Your Vote for Senators

What does the Constitution say about how we choose our senators? You might be surprised to learn that originally, each state's senators were chosen by the respective state's legislature. That was changed by the Seventeenth Amendment which states in part as follows.

> **<u>Seventeenth Amendment</u>: (ratified April 8, 1913)**
>
> **The Senate of the United States shall be composed of two Senators from each State, elected by the people thereof...**

Therefore, your vote for senator is not a vote for an elector sent somewhere to someday perhaps vote for your candidate. Your vote goes directly for the person you name. The states determine for themselves how much of the vote it takes to win. For example, some states might require more than 50% of the vote to win and, when no candidate fits that bill, a run-off election ensues.

But, What Does the Constitution Say About Your Right to Vote?

Here are the provisions that inform your "right" to vote.

> **Fifteenth Amendment, §1**: (ratified February 3, 1870)
>
> **The right of the citizens of the United States to vote shall not be denied or abridged by the United States or by any State on account of race, color, or previous condition of servitude.**
>
> **Nineteenth Amendment**: (ratified August 18, 1920)
>
> **The right of the citizens of the United States to vote shall not be denied or abridged by the United States or by any State on account of sex.**
>
> **Twenty-Fourth Amendment, §1**: (ratified January 23, 1964)
>
> **The right of the citizens of the United States to vote in any primary or other election for President... [or] for electors for President [or] for Senator...**

> shall not be denied or abridged by the United States or by any State by reason of failure to pay any poll tax or any other tax.
>
> **Twenty-Sixth Amendment, §1**: (ratified July 1, 1971)
>
> **The right of the citizens of the United States who are eighteen years of age or older, to vote shall not be denied or abridged by the United States or by any State on account of age.**

The most we can say about these provisions is that neither the federal government nor any state government can deny or abridge the right of U.S. citizens to vote for federal candidates on account of race, color, previous condition of servitude, sex, failure to pay any poll tax or any other tax, or age as long as the citizen is eighteen years of age or older. The grant of a right to vote at all, however, is an implied one.

How Much Does Your Vote (Or Non-Vote) Count?

The last time I looked, your vote counts only once. Lest you underestimate the **power of one**, take a look at these very close elections:[13]

> In 1948, Lyndon Johnson defeated Coke Stevenson by 87 votes out of 988,295 votes cast for the Texas senatorial primary!
>
> In 1974, Republican Louis Wyman defeated Democrat John Durkin for senator from New Hampshire by 2 votes out of 223,363 votes cast!

---

13 http://degreed.com/blog/top-10-closest-elections-in-us-history/.

In 1984, Democrat Frank McCloskey defeated Republican Rick McIntyre for a House of Representatives seat from Indiana by 4 votes out of 233,286 votes cast!

In 2000, Republican George W. Bush defeated Democrat Al Gore for president because he won the Florida electoral vote by 537 votes out of 5,962,657 votes cast!

In 2004, Democrat Christine Gregoire defeated Republican Dino Rossi for Governor of Washington by 133 votes out of 2,800,000 votes cast!

In 2005, Republican Bob McDonnell defeated Democrat Creigh Deeds for Virginia attorney general by 323 votes out of 1,943,403 votes cast!

In 2008, Democrat Al Franken defeated Republican Norm Coleman for the U.S. Senate from Minnesota by 312 votes out of 2,887,646 votes cast!

In 2008, Republican Mike Kelly defeated Democrat Karl Kassel for a House of Representatives seat from Alaska by 1 vote out of 10,035 votes cast!

In 2012, Rick Santorum defeated Mitt Romney in the Iowa Republican Primary by 34 votes out of 121,503 votes cast!

It is no exaggeration to suggest that your vote – yes, your measly little lonely singular vote – could decide the next leader of the free world. And, I contend that our current president and potentially our next president, together with his/her cadre of senators, will likely have the opportunity to tilt the make-up of the Supreme Court either back to our constitutional foundation or away from our form of government so far that America will not be recognizable.

Please don't be fooled. If you believe in our constitutional system, your non-vote (your failure to get up off the couch and get yourself down to the voting booth) counts just as much as a vote against our Constitution. If you believe in preserving our constitutional form of government, you **must** vote. If you do not hold such a belief, please stay home.

Chapter Five

ONE METHOD

"I know no safe depository of the ultimate powers of the society but the people themselves; and if we think them not enlightened enough to exercise their control with a wholesome discretion, the remedy is not to take it from them, but to inform their discretion by education. This is the true corrective of abuses of constitutional power."

Thomas Jefferson

The Source Material

In today's society with a myriad of internet outlets and a sold-out mainstream media who has forsaken their solemn obligation to report the news, it is a real challenge to find the truth.

I could present the material in the ensuing chapters by simply writing "about" the selected Supreme Court decisions, but why should you believe me, if that is all I present to you, any more than you would a newspaper article or television report?

Instead, my method goes straight to the source, the very opinions of the Supreme Court. While this method might prove a bit more challenging to the non-lawyer, who said freedom would come at no cost? Yes, I am asking you to earn your share of freedom the easy way, for most of you will never have to dodge bullets on a battlefield as others have done for you.

To this point, you have explored some of the structure of the Constitution and have added enough constitutional facts of interest to your arsenal of knowledge to win a few points at your next trivia fundraiser.

It's time to get serious – time to save this nation. Here are the rules – here is the method I choose to impart the knowledge you will need to do your part.

Method of Selection

Chapters Six through Fifteen each discuss one Supreme Court decision that, in my estimation, conveys the grave importance of whom we select as president and senators, for it is they who select the members of the Supreme Court when vacancies arise.

ONE

My parameters for the cases I chose were simple enough. First, I wanted the cases to be relatively recent. I chose to limit my selections as coming from either the Rehnquist Court or the Roberts Court. William Rehnquist became an associate justice of the Supreme Court in 1972, having been nominated by President Nixon. He was elevated to chief justice in 1986 by the nomination of President Reagan and died in office in 2005. His successor as chief justice, John Roberts, was new to the Court. He was nominated by President George W. Bush, was confirmed by the Senate in 2005 and presently serves at that post. My list of cases eligible for this book, then, were decided no earlier than 1986.

Second, my selected cases (with one technical exception - see Chapter Fourteen) had to be decided by **one vote** - by a vote of five to four - in order to stress the awesome power **one vote** can have on the High Court.

Third, each case had to have been of great importance to the continued survival of our constitutional republic. I chose five cases that, in my opinion, were **one robe short** of the mark. In other words, these cases fell short (by **one vote**) of preserving our constitutional heritage and ideals. I also chose five cases that, in my opinion, proved to be **one robe long** – cases whose result honored the oaths taken by five of the justices in preserving our Constitution.

In Chapter Sixteen, I provide an additional ten cases in summary fashion, all decided by a five to four vote (five **one robe long** and five **one robe short**).

Describing the Case Name

The "style" or name of a case is always presented as you would see it on the official decision of the Supreme Court to impress upon you that, except as otherwise defined, what you are going to read are the actual words of the respective justices. We tend to run on the watered-down fuel of headlines and sound bites. Even if we read every newspaper article and listen intently to radio and television, the Fourth Estate has failed us miserably. Media outlets that report fairly, ethically, and accurately are few and far between. That is why the actual words of the justices themselves are so very important. You can trust what you read in these decisions and, if you do not, go to the original opinion and verify. I will use our first case "style" as an example to explain each line:

LEE v. WEISMAN
SUPREME COURT OF THE UNITED STATES
505 U.S. 577
June 24, 1992
[5 – 4]

The first line names one of the parties on each side of the case, the second line names the court, the third line provides the "citation" (technical location where you can find the original decision), the fourth line provides the date of the decision, and the fifth line provides the vote count. Because there were nine justices on the Court for every decision we explore, the score will always add to nine. The number on the left represents the number of justices favoring the victorious outcome - the number on the right reflects the number of justices who disagreed with the majority outcome.

Rules of My Game Within the Body of a Case

I can save you a great deal of time by summarizing some parts of a decision. Believe it or not, occasionally the Court can get a bit redundant. So, in those instances, when the decision takes four pages to say what can be said without a loss of substance in a single sentence

ONE

or paragraph, I provide that summary in [brackets]. Otherwise, everything you read that is not in brackets represents the actual words of the Court.

When there is something of particular importance to learn, my comments appear in a textbox.

Occasionally, much of what the Court has to say is irrelevant to the constitutional issues we are studying. Therefore, when you see an ellipsis (…), that means the intervening material has been excised from the presentation. I assure you nothing of substance has been deleted and, as always, if you wish to test me on that score, consult the original case in its entirety. If the Court takes 25 pages to discuss an issue of evidence that is unrelated to any constitutional question and since we are, after all, studying the Constitution, what is the point?

And, finally, I sometimes provide **bold formatting** or <u>underlining</u> to emphasize something worth remembering.

My Constitution clubs are named ELL Constitution Clubs, standing for Earn It, Learn It or Lose It. Therefore, I describe the foregoing process of making a case easier to read as ELLionizing. You may see that term from time to time.

Please note that in many instances, the Court provides a good bit of history. Often, it is provided to reveal the "original intent" of the Framers for the provision in the Constitution that is being interpreted.

Use of An Asterisk

When you see one asterisk (*) behind the name of a case (for example, *Lemon v. Kurtzman** in the next chapter), that means you can read that case on my ELL Constitution Club website should you choose to do so. The complete list of cases mentioned in this book that are also on the website can be found in the Appendix, as well as the keys to finding both the website and the case. There will only be an asterisk behind such a case the first time it is mentioned within a chapter.

Opinion/Concurrence/Dissent

Each case will begin with the "Opinion" and the names of the author of the opinion (first-named justice) and all justices in agreement with the result and reasoning of the author. These justices are in the majority (at least five, but potentially all nine).

When you read a concurring opinion (or Concurrence), again, its author is mentioned first followed by those justices who agree. These are the justices who agree with the outcome, but disagree with the reasoning of the Opinion or simply have something more or different they wish to say.

When you read a dissenting opinion (or Dissent), its author (and any of those who agree) present the reasoning in support of the losing proposition (a result contrary to the winning majority).

And, finally, although not always true in context, when a concurring or dissenting opinion refers to the "Court," that normally has reference to the majority opinion in the case being discussed. Occasionally, it may refer to a different Court in a different case. Let the context be your guide.

ONE

Conclusion

There you have it. These are the rules of engagement. Settle in for some valuable knowledge that will likely knock your previously-ignorant-and/or-apathetic socks off.

Ignorant: lacking knowledge or information as to a particular subject or fact.[14] This is one of my favorite words. I use it often. It must be understood. Although many use this word incorrectly to hold someone in disrespect, it is not necessarily a pejorative term. Most of us are completely ignorant of most of the body of human knowledge collected to date. Try your hand at Jeopardy. Or, for the less-than-mechanically-inclined, try diagnosing and then repairing your car.

Now, if you are provided an opportunity to gain the knowledge you must have in order to preserve our Union and fail to take it, then you might be fair game for criticism. But, simply put, if you do not understand that the adjective "ignorant" is not normally meant to demean, then you are simply "ignorant" of the term "ignorance." I can't help you.

And, a one-time warning is provided: I have no time for political correctness! Perhaps you can tell. For example, I will assume that if you are female, you realize that, in context, when I use the pronoun "he," I am also referring to "she" and vice-versa. I am not going to take the time or space to say "he and/or she" or use the word "person." If that offends you, then you likely care more about yourself than you do about preserving freedom. Sorry. Once again, I can't help you.

Enough said! Hold on to your seat! Here we go!

---

14 Def. 2. *The American College Dictionary.* 1969. Print.

Chapter Six

ONE ROBE SHORT ON JUNE 24, 1992, ELIMINATED COMMENCEMENT PRAYERS IN PUBLIC GRADE SCHOOLS!

Always be joyful. Keep on praying.
No matter what happens, always be thankful, for this is God's will for you who belong to Jesus Christ.

1 Thessalonians 5:16-18

On June 24, 1992, commencement exercises for high school seniors (and lower grade school graduation ceremonies) were "sanitized" by a margin of **one robe**. Yes, we fell **one robe short** of affirming the validity of government-sponsored (public school-sponsored) prayer at these meaningful and memorable steps taken in the life of a newly born adult in the land of the free. The Framers of the Constitution would clearly be appalled. I believe this next case has a rather silly result, but all is not lost. See my "comment" section at the end of this chapter.

For now, let's explore the prayers that five justices of the Supreme Court just could not tolerate in Providence, Rhode Island, while keeping in mind that our vote for president and our vote for our senators helps decide who it will be that makes these decisions - constitutional conservatives or the whatever-they-think-is-best-for-us-regardless-of-what-we-think-is-best-for-us jurists. I introduce you to *Lee v. Weisman**.

LEE v. WEISMAN
SUPREME COURT OF THE UNITED STATES
505 U.S. 577
June 24, 1992
[5 – 4]

OPINION: Kennedy/ Blackmun/ Stevens/ O'Connor/ Suitor ... School principals in the public school system of the city of Providence, Rhode Island, are permitted to invite members of the clergy to offer invocation and benediction prayers as part of the formal graduation ceremonies for middle schools and for high schools. The question before us is whether [this practice] is consistent with the Religion Clauses of the First [and Fourteenth] Amendments. [Deborah Weisman, then age 14, graduated from Nathan Bishop

ONE

Middle School, a public school in Providence, at a formal ceremony in June, 1989. For many years it has been the policy of the Providence School Committee and the Superintendent of Schools to permit principals to invite members of the clergy to give invocations and benedictions at middle school and high school graduations…Daniel Weisman, Deborah's father, objected; however,…the school principal, Robert E. Lee, nevertheless invited a rabbi to deliver prayers at the graduation exercises for Deborah's class. Rabbi Leslie Gutterman, of the Temple Beth El in Providence, accepted. Deborah's father also objected to high school graduation ceremonies as Deborah would likely graduate from high school in this District in a few years.]

It has been the custom of Providence school officials to provide invited clergy with a pamphlet entitled "Guidelines for Civic Occasions," prepared by the National Conference of Christians and Jews. The Guidelines recommend that public prayers at nonsectarian civic ceremonies be composed with "inclusiveness and sensitivity," though they acknowledge that "prayer of any kind may be inappropriate on some civic occasions." The principal gave Rabbi Gutterman the pamphlet before the graduation and advised [that his prayers]…should be nonsectarian. Rabbi Gutterman's prayers were as follows:

--- INVOCATION ---
God of the Free, Hope of the Brave:
For the legacy of America where diversity is celebrated and the rights of minorities are protected, we thank You.
May these young men and women grow up to enrich it.
For the liberty of America, we thank You.

May these new graduates grow up to guard it.
For the political process of America in which all its citizens may participate, for its court system where all may seek justice, we thank You.
May those we honor this morning always turn to it in trust.
For the destiny of America, we thank You.
May the graduates of Nathan Bishop Middle School so live that they might help to share it.
May our aspirations for our country and for these young people, who are our hope for the future, be richly fulfilled. AMEN.

--- BENEDICTION ---

O God, we are grateful to You for having endowed us with the capacity for learning which we have celebrated on this joyous commencement.
Happy families give thanks for seeing their children achieve an important milestone.
Send Your blessings upon the teachers and administrators who helped prepare them.
The graduates now need strength and guidance for the future.
Help them to understand that we are not complete with academic knowledge alone.
We must each strive to fulfill what You require of us all: To do justly, to love mercy, to walk humbly.
We give thanks to You, Lord, for keeping us alive, sustaining us and allowing us to reach this special, happy occasion. AMEN.

ONE

...Attendance at graduation ceremonies is voluntary.

The school board...argued that these short prayers and others like them at graduation exercises are of profound meaning to many students and parents throughout this country who consider that due respect and acknowledgment for divine guidance and for the deepest spiritual aspirations of our people ought to be expressed at an event as important in life as a graduation...

The District Court held that [the] practice of including invocations and benedictions in public school graduations violated the Establishment Clause...and it [ordered the school to cease] the practice. The court applied the three-part...test set forth in *Lemon v. Kurtzman**. [That is,] to satisfy the Establishment Clause a governmental practice must (1) reflect a clearly secular purpose; (2) have a primary effect that neither advances nor inhibits religion; and (3) avoid excessive government entanglement with religion. The District Court held that [the school] violated the second part of the test, and so did not address either the first or the third. The court decided...that the effects test of *Lemon* is violated whenever government action "creates an identification of the state with a religion, or with religion in general" or when "the effect of the governmental action is to endorse one religion over another, or to endorse religion in general." The court determined that the practice of including invocations and benedictions, even so-called nonsectarian ones, in public school graduations creates an identification of governmental power with religious practice, endorses religion. and violates the Establishment Clause...[The Court of Appeals affirmed. So do we. The practice violates all 3 parts of the *Lemon* test.]

> So, barring a constitutional amendment or a reversal of this decision, these five justices have determined that the Constitution dictates the exclusion of government-sponsored prayer from commencement exercises in public grade schools!

DISSENT: Scalia/Rehnquist/White/Thomas…Our interpretation of the Establishment Clause should "comport with what history reveals was the contemporaneous understanding of its guarantees."…Thus, "the existence from the beginning of the nation's life of a practice, while not conclusive of its constitutionality…, is a fact of considerable import in the interpretation" of the Establishment Clause… From our nation's origin, prayer has been a prominent part of governmental ceremonies and proclamations [and presidential inaugurations and Thanksgiving]…

In addition to this general tradition of prayer at public ceremonies, there exists a more specific tradition of invocations and benedictions at public school graduation exercises. By one account, the first public high school graduation ceremony took place in Connecticut in July 1868…when "15 seniors from the Norwich Free Academy marched in their best Sunday suits and dresses into a church hall and waited through majestic music and long prayers."…The invocation and benediction have long been recognized to be "as traditional as any other parts of the school graduation program and are widely established."

The Court presumably would separate graduation invocations and benedictions from other instances of public "preservation and transmission of religious beliefs" on the ground that they involve "psychological coercion." I find it a sufficient embarrassment that our Establishment Clause jurisprudence regarding holiday displays… has come to require scrutiny more commonly associated with interior decorators than with the judiciary. But interior decorating is a rock-hard science compared to psychology practiced by amateurs… The Court has gone beyond the realm where judges know what they are doing.

ONE

> Justice Scalia's interior decorator comment is a direct reference to *Lynch v. Donnelly** and *Allegheny County v. ACLU**.
>
> These are two holiday Christmas display cases. Check them out on our website. See the Appendix for instructions.

The Court's argument that state officials have "coerced" students to take part in the invocation and benediction at graduation ceremonies…is incoherent…

The Court declares that students' "attendance and participation in the invocation and benediction are in a fair and real sense obligatory."…According to the Court, students at graduation who want "to avoid the fact or appearance of participation" in the invocation and benediction are psychologically obligated by "public pressure, as well as peer pressure,…to stand as a group or, at least, maintain respectful silence" during those prayers. This assertion – the very linchpin of the Court's opinion – is almost as intriguing for what it does not say as for what it says. It does not say, for example, that students are psychologically coerced to bow their heads, [fold their hands in prayer], pay attention to the prayers, utter "Amen," or in fact pray…It claims only that students are psychologically coerced "to stand…or, at least, to maintain respectful silence."

…The Court's notion that a student who simply sits in respectful silence during the invocation and benediction (when all others are standing) has somehow joined – or would somehow be perceived as having joined – in the prayers is nothing short of ludicrous. We indeed live in a vulgar age. But surely our social conventions have not coarsened to the point that anyone who does not stand on his chair and shout obscenities can reasonably be deemed to have assented to everything said in his presence. Since the Court does not dispute that

51

students exposed to prayer at graduation ceremonies retain (despite "subtle coercive pressures") the free will to sit, there is absolutely no basis for the Court's decision. It is fanciful enough to say that "a reasonable dissenter, 'standing head erect in a class of bowed heads,' could believe that the group exercise signified her own participation or approval of it." It is beyond the absurd to say that she could entertain such a belief while pointedly declining to rise.

But let us assume the very worst, that the nonparticipating graduate is "subtly coerced"...to stand! Even that half of the disjunctive does not remotely establish a "participation" (or an "appearance of participation") in a religious exercise. The Court acknowledges that "in our culture standing...can signify adherence to a view or simple respect for the views of others."...But if it is a permissible inference that one who is standing is doing so simply out of respect for the prayers of others that are in progress, then how can it possibly be said that a "reasonable dissenter...could believe that the group exercise signified her own participation or approval?" Quite obviously, it cannot. I may add, moreover, that maintaining respect for the religious observances of others is a fundamental civic virtue that government (including the public schools) can and should cultivate – so that even if it were the case that the displaying of such respect might be mistaken for taking part in the prayer, I would deny that the dissenter's interest in avoiding even the false appearance of participation constitutionally trumps the government's interest in fostering respect for religion generally.

The opinion manifests that the Court itself has not given careful consideration to its test of psychological coercion. For if it had, how could it observe, with no hint of concern or disapproval, that students stood for the Pledge of Allegiance, which immediately preceded Rabbi Gutterman's invocation? The government can, of

ONE

course, no more coerce political orthodoxy than religious orthodoxy. Moreover, since the Pledge...has been revised...to include the phrase "under God," recital of the Pledge would appear to raise the same Establishment Clause issue as the invocation and benediction...Must the Pledge therefore be barred from the public schools (both from graduation ceremonies and from the classroom)? In *West Virginia v. Barnette** we held that a public school student could not be compelled to recite the Pledge; we did not even hint that she could not be compelled to observe respectful silence – indeed, even to stand in respectful silence – when those who wished to recite it did so...

I also find it odd that the Court concludes that the high school graduates may not be subjected to this supposed psychological coercion, yet refrains from addressing whether "mature adults" may. I had thought that the reason graduation from high school is regarded as so significant an event is that it is generally associated with transition from adolescence to young adulthood. Many graduating seniors, of course, are old enough to vote. Why, then, does the Court treat them as though they were first-graders? Will we soon have a jurisprudence that distinguishes between mature and immature adults?

The other "dominant fact" identified by the Court is that "state officials direct the performance of a formal religious exercise" at school graduation ceremonies. "Directing the performance of a formal religious exercise" has a sound of liturgy to it, summoning up images of the principal directing acolytes where to carry the cross, or showing the rabbi where to unroll the Torah...All the record shows is that principals...have invited clergy to deliver invocations and benedictions at graduations; and that Principal Lee invited Rabbi Gutterman, provided him a two-page pamphlet, prepared by the National Conference of Christians and Jews, giving general advice on inclusive prayer for civic occasions, and advised him that his prayers at graduation should be nonsectarian. How these facts can fairly be transformed into the charges that Principal Lee "directed and controlled the content of Rabbi Gutterman's prayer," that school officials "monitor prayer" and attempted to "compose official prayers" and that the "government involvement with religious activity in this case is persuasive," is difficult to fathom. The Court identifies nothing in the record remotely suggesting that school officials have ever drafted, edited, screened, or censored graduation prayers, or that Rabbi Gutterman was a mouthpiece of the school officials...

The deeper flaw in the Court's opinion…lies…in the Court's making violation of the Establishment Clause hinge on such a precious question. The coercion that was a hallmark of historical establishments of religion was coercion of religious orthodoxy and of financial support by force of law and threat of penalty. Typically, attendance at the state church was required; only clergy of the official church could lawfully perform sacraments; and dissenters…faced an array of civil disabilities…

The Establishment Clause was adopted to prohibit such an establishment of religion at the federal level (and to protect state establishments of religion from federal interference). I will further acknowledge for the sake of argument that, as some scholars have argued, by 1790 the term "establishment" had acquired an additional meaning – "financial support of religion generally, by public taxation" – that reflected the development of "general or multiple" establishments, not limited to a single church. But that would still be an establishment coerced by force of law. And I will further concede that our constitutional tradition, from the Declaration of Independence and the first inaugural address of Washington, quoted earlier, down to the present day, has, with a few aberrations, ruled out of order government-sponsored endorsement of religion – even when no legal coercion is present, and indeed even when no ersatz, "peer-pressure" psycho-coercion is present – where the endorsement is sectarian, in the sense of specifying details upon which men and women who believe in a benevolent, omnipotent Creator and Ruler of the world are known to differ (for example, the divinity of Christ). But there is simply no support for the proposition that the officially sponsored nondenominational invocation and benediction read by Rabbi Gutterman – with no one legally coerced to recite them – violated the Constitution of the United States. To the contrary, they are so characteristically American they could have come from the pen of George Washington or Abraham Lincoln himself.

Thus, while I have no quarrel with the Court's general proposition that the Establishment Clause "guarantees that government may not coerce anyone to support or participate in religion or its exercises," I see no warrant for expanding the concept of coercion beyond acts backed by threat of penalty – a brand of coercion that, happily, is readily discernible to those of us who have made a career of reading the disciples of Blackstone [an English legal scholar] rather than of Freud. The Framers were indeed opposed to coercion of religious worship by the national government; but, as their own sponsorship of nonsectarian prayer in public events demonstrates, they understood that "speech is not coercive; the listener may do as he likes."

…The Court relies on our school prayer cases, *Engel** and *Abington**. But…, they do not support…the Court's psycho-journey…*Engel* and *Abington* do not constitute an exception to the rule…that public ceremonies may include prayer; rather, they simply do not fall within the scope of the rule (for obvious reason that school instruction is not a public ceremony)…

We have made clear our understanding that school prayer occurs within a framework in which legal coercion to attend school (i.e., coercion under threat of penalty) provides the ultimate backdrop. In *Abington*, for example, we emphasized that the prayers were "prescribed as part of the curricular activities of students who are required by law to attend school." *Engel's* suggestion that the school prayer program at issue there – which permitted students to "remain silent or be excused from the room" – involved indirect coercive pressure should be understood against this back-drop of legal coercion. The question whether the opt-out procedure in *Engel* sufficed to dispel the coercion resulting from the mandatory attendance requirement is quite different from the question whether forbidden coercion exists in an environment utterly devoid of legal compulsion. And finally, our school prayer cases turn in part on the fact that the classroom is inherently an instructional setting, and daily prayer there – where parents are not present to counter the students' emulation of teachers as role models and the children's susceptibility to peer pressure – might be thought to raise special concerns regarding state interference with the liberty of parents to direct the religious upbringing of their children: "Families entrust public schools with the education of their children, but condition their trust on the understanding that the classroom will not purposely be used to advance religious views that may conflict with the private beliefs of the student and his or her family." Voluntary prayer at graduation – a one-time ceremony at which parents, friends, and relatives are present – can hardly be thought to raise the same concerns…

Given the odd basis for the Court's decision, invocations and benedictions will be able to be given at public school graduations next June, as they have been for the past century and a half, so long as school authorities make clear that anyone who abstains from screaming in protest does not necessarily participate in the prayers. All that is seemingly

ONE

needed is an announcement, or perhaps a written insertion at the beginning of the graduation program, to the effect that, while all are asked to rise for the invocation and benediction, none is compelled to join them, nor will be assumed, by rising, to have done so. That obvious fact recited, the graduates and their parents may proceed to thank God, as Americans have always done, for the blessings He has generously bestowed on them and on their country...

The Founders of our Republic knew the fearsome potential of sectarian religious belief to generate civil dissension and civil strife. And they also knew that nothing, absolutely nothing, is so inclined to foster among religious believers of various faiths a toleration – no, an affection – for one another than voluntarily joining in prayer together, to the God whom they all worship and seek. Needless to say, no one should be compelled to do that, but it is a shame to deprive our public culture of the opportunity, and indeed the encouragement, for people to do it voluntarily. The Baptist or Catholic who heard and joined in the simple and inspiring prayers of Rabbi Gutterman on this official and patriotic occasion was inoculated from religious bigotry and prejudice in a manner that cannot be replicated. To deprive our society of that important unifying mechanism, in order to spare the non-believer what seems to me the minimal inconvenience of standing or even sitting in respectful nonparticipation, is as senseless in policy as it is unsupported in law...

SUMMARY: Technically, five justices ruled that because an official prayer at graduation (1) does not reflect a clearly secular purpose, (2) does not have a primary effect that neither advances nor inhibits religion, and (3) excessively entangles government with religion, it has no place in our schools, at least in our high schools and grade schools. Are commencement prayers at college graduation ok? So far they are because those graduates are adults. Aren't most high school graduates adults? Oh, well, we lost this one by **one robe**.

COMMENT: As I informed in Chapter Eight (Prayer) of my book, It's OK To Say "God,"[15] let us not make the mistake of taking this decision beyond its limited holding. The Supreme Court has not "taken prayer out of public school." If you believe it has or if you just assume it has, please, please stop repeating that falsehood to others.

The truth, according to Justice O'Connor in her concurring opinion in *Wallace v. Jaffree** (1985), is that "nothing in the Constitution prohibits public school students from voluntarily praying at any time before, during or after the school day."

As Justice Scalia points out, it is sad when a majority of the Court fails to recognize the simple value in paying respect to the views of others. Out of some childish fear that a non-believer may feel coerced into standing during a commencement prayer or that someone may falsely conclude that a non-believer actually believes because they stand, we have crafted a constitutional principle - a principle that most high schoolers would likely write off as silly nonsense.

Perhaps people of faith should start a movement - literally, a "move" (after receiving a diploma on the stage at school) to a local church for prayer and a sermon customized for the next generation. What do you think? Might work quite well - might even become a tradition!

PLEA: Speak to your fellow Christians about voting. Gasp! Can we do that at church? Of course. Are you willing to let even your

---
[15] Armstrong, Tad. *It's OK To Say "God."* WestBow Press, 2011. Print.

ONE

friends know how important this is? We are the problem. Vote for candidates that believe in the Constitution. That is the only way we will fill those seats on the High Court with justices who take their oath seriously to support the Constitution. That is the only way we will preserve freedom in this nation.

Chapter Seven

ONE ROBE LONG ON APRIL 26, 1995, PRESERVED FEDERALISM!

This is one of the more important cases in this book. Most Americans are tired of the ever-widening reach of the federal government's tentacles. Of course, the limits of federal authority have never changed. They are firmly established in the Constitution. However, the interpretation of that reach by the judiciary has exceeded the Founders' intent in far too many instances.

This next case finally set some limits to the power of the Feds. Its importance has little to do with either the Second Amendment or the wisdom of a law that forbids guns within a zone around public schools. It has everything to do with who has the ultimate authority to make such laws: state and local governments or the federal government.

Every time we turn around, some federal politician wants to fix a local problem with a national law. My own Senator Dick Durbin (D-IL) has introduced federal legislation to protect kids from getting concussions on the football field. Perhaps a law is needed for that, I don't know, but it should not come from Washington. Our coaches, school boards, cities and states can take care of coaching football. It just makes one want to shout loud enough for them to hear in D.C.: "leave us alone"!

So, what is federalism and why is it so important to the preservation of our American brand of freedom?

Federalism is a system of government whereby the same geographic area is controlled by two separate governments. In our nation, that means the Feds govern the nation within its sphere and each state governs itself within its sphere. The tension between state rights and nationalism was designed to promote a healthy check on the power of each.

ONE

In theory, neither Congress nor the president has any power not granted to them by the Constitution. Each respective state, except for some powers denied to them by the Constitution, retains all other powers not granted to the Feds.

The power of Congress to pass laws, then, is limited by the Constitution. And, if Congress exceeds its bounds, its work-product is unconstitutional and void - well, at least when the Supreme Court eventually gets around to saying it is in a litigated challenge. *United States v. Lopez** is a 1995 victory for freedom that survived by just **one robe.** I am especially proud that this victory came out of a case from Texas, the freedom-loving state of my birth.

UNITED STATES V. LOPEZ

SUPREME COURT OF THE UNITED STATES
514 U.S. 549
April 26, 1995
[5-4]

OPINION: Rehnquist/O'Connor/Scalia/Kennedy/Thomas ... In the Gun-Free School Zones Act of 1990, Congress made it a federal offense "for any individual knowingly to possess a firearm at a place that the individual knows, or has reasonable cause to believe, is a school zone." The Act neither regulates a commercial activity nor contains a requirement that the possession be connected in any way to interstate commerce. We hold that the Act exceeds the authority of Congress "to regulate Commerce...among the several States..."

Unless logic is to be utterly disregarded, I fail to see how any justice could possibly disagree with the majority in this case, yet it is a 5-4 decision. I wonder how James Madison would react to the dissenting views?

On March 10, 1992, [Lopez], who was then a 12th-grade student, arrived at Edison High School in San Antonio, Texas, carrying a concealed .38 caliber handgun and five bullets. Acting upon an anonymous tip, school authorities confronted [Lopez], who admitted that he was carrying the weapon. He was arrested and charged under Texas law with firearm possession on school premises. The next day, the state charges were dismissed after federal agents charged [Lopez]…with violating the [federal] Gun-Free School Zones Act of 1990.

> Let us not forget that Texas had at least some type of criminal statute in force to take care of Mr. Lopez. Why was the state charge dismissed? Why was the federal charge pursued? Perhaps the Feds wanted to take a constitutional spin with these facts to see whether the federal act would hold up to a constitutional challenge. Perhaps the Federal penalty was more in line with what the "Feds" wanted to see. Who knows?

A federal grand jury indicted [Lopez] on one count of knowing possession of a firearm at a school zone, in violation [of the Act]… The District Court…found him guilty…and sentenced him to six months' imprisonment and two years' supervised release. On appeal, [Lopez] challenged his conviction based on his claim that [the Act] exceeded Congress' power to legislate under the Commerce Clause. The Court of Appeals…agreed and reversed his conviction…We granted certiorari and…now affirm the Court of Appeals.

> The Federal District Court found Lopez guilty of violating the federal statute. From here on out I will refer to it as the Act. Lopez appealed his conviction to the Federal Court of Appeals. He did not likely contest what had happened and may have even admitted to violating the Act. However, he was challenging the authority of Congress to pass the Act.

ONE

> He stood up to Congress and effectively said: "Enough already - the Constitution doesn't give Congress power to legislate gun free school zones in Texas." The Court of Appeals agreed with Lopez. Then, the federal government appealed that decision to the Supreme Court and, in the end, five of nine justices agreed with Lopez. Victory – by **one robe**!
>
> When the Court grants "certiorari" that means that, in the discretion of at least four of the nine justices, the Court agrees to hear a requested appeal.

We start with first principles. The Constitution creates a Federal Government of enumerated powers. See Art. I §8.

> Article I, §8 begins: "The Congress shall have the power to…" I encourage you to pull it out and take a look. You will find a list of limited powers granted to Congress.

As James Madison wrote, "the powers delegated by the proposed Constitution to the federal government are few and defined. Those which are to remain in the State governments are numerous and indefinite." This constitutionally mandated division of authority was adopted by the Framers to ensure protection of our fundamental liberties. "Just as the separation and independence of the coordinate branches of the Federal Government serve to prevent the accumulation of excessive power in any one branch, a healthy balance of power between the States and the Federal Government will reduce the risk of tyranny and abuse from either front."

> Since every federal law must be founded upon some power granted in the Constitution, the feds contend Congress gets its power to pass gun-free school zone laws from the Commerce Clause (Article I, §8). That clause states in pertinent part:
>
> "Congress shall have power to regulate commerce among the several states."

...[In *Gibbons v. Ogden**, the] Court...acknowledged that limitations on the commerce power are inherent in the very language of the Commerce Clause: "...The enumeration pre-supposes something not enumerated; and that something, if we regard the language, or the subject of the sentence, must be the exclusively internal commerce of a State."

...[Three cases, *NLRB v. Jones & Laughlin Steel, United States v. Darby**, and *Wickard v. Filburn**] ushered in an era of Commerce Clause jurisprudence that greatly expanded the previously defined authority of Congress under that Clause. In part, this was a recognition of the great changes that had occurred in the way business was carried on in this country. Enterprises that had once been local or at most regional in nature had become national in scope. But the doctrinal change also reflected a view that earlier Commerce Clause cases artificially had constrained the authority of Congress to regulate interstate commerce.

But even these modern-era precedents...confirm that this power is subject to outer limits. In *Jones & Laughlin Steel*, the Court warned that the scope of the interstate commerce power "must be considered in the light of our dual system of government and may not be extended so as to embrace effects upon interstate commerce so indirect and remote that to embrace them, in view of our complex society, would effectually obliterate the distinction between what is national and what is local and create a completely centralized government."...Since that time, the Court has heeded that warning and undertaken to decide whether a rational basis existed for concluding that a regulated activity sufficiently affected interstate commerce...

We have identified three broad categories of activity that Congress may regulate under its commerce power. First, Congress may regulate the use of the channels of interstate commerce. Second, Congress is empowered to regulate and protect the instrumentalities of interstate commerce, or persons or things in interstate commerce, even though the threat may come only from intrastate activities…Finally, Congress' commerce authority includes the power to regulate those activities having a substantial relation to interstate commerce - those activities that substantially affect interstate commerce…

We conclude, consistent with the great weight of our case law, that the proper test requires an analysis of whether the regulated activity "substantially affects" interstate commerce.

We now turn to consider the power of Congress, in the light of this framework, to enact [this Gun Free School Zone Act]. The first two categories of authority may be quickly disposed of: [The Act] is not a regulation of the use of the channels of interstate commerce, nor is it an attempt to prohibit the interstate transportation of a commodity through the channels of commerce; nor can [it] be justified as a regulation by which Congress has sought to protect an instrumentality of interstate commerce or a thing in interstate commerce. Thus, if [it] is to be sustained, it must be under the third category as a regulation of an activity that substantially affects interstate commerce…

Where economic activity substantially affects interstate commerce, legislation regulating that activity will be sustained…

[The Act] is a criminal statute that by its terms has nothing to do with "commerce" or any sort of economic enterprise, however broadly one might define those terms. [It] is not an essential part of a larger regulation of economic activity, in which the regulatory scheme could be undercut unless the intrastate activity were regulated. It cannot, therefore, be sustained under our cases upholding regulations of activities that arise out of or are connected with a commercial transaction, which viewed in the aggregate, substantially affects interstate commerce. Second, [the Act] contains no jurisdictional element which would ensure, through case-by-case inquiry, that the firearm possession in question affects interstate commerce…

Although as part of our independent evaluation of constitutionality under the Commerce Clause we of course consider legislative findings, and indeed even congressional committee findings, regarding effect on interstate commerce, the Government concedes that "neither the statute nor its legislative history contains express congressional findings regarding the effects upon interstate commerce of gun possession in a school zone." We agree with the Government that Congress normally is not required to make formal findings as to the substantial burdens that an activity has on interstate commerce…But to the extent that congressional findings would enable us to evaluate the legislative judgment that the activity in question substantially affected interstate commerce, even though no such substantial effect was visible to the naked eye, they are lacking here…

The Government's essential contention…is that we may determine here that [the Act] is valid because possession of a firearm in a local school zone does indeed substantially affect interstate commerce. The Government argues [1] that possession of a firearm in a school zone may result in violent crime and [2] that violent crime can be expected to affect the functioning of the national economy in two ways. [3] First, the costs of violent crime are substantial, and, through the mechanism of insurance, those costs are spread throughout the population. [4] Second, violent crime reduces the willingness of individuals to travel to areas within the country that are perceived to be unsafe. [5] The Government also argues that the presence of guns in schools poses a substantial threat to the educational process by threatening the learning environment. A handicapped educational process, in turn, will result in a less productive citizenry. [6] That, in turn, would have an adverse effect on the nation's economic well-being. As a result, the Government argues that Congress could rationally have concluded that [the Act] substantially affects interstate commerce.

> If the foregoing convoluted "reasoning" were to hold up, literally nothing could ever elude the regulatory power of Congress.

We pause to consider the implications of the Government's arguments. The Government admits, under its "costs of crime" reasoning, that Congress could regulate not only all violent crime, but all activities that might lead to violent crime, regardless of how tenuously they relate to interstate commerce. Similarly, under the Government's "national productivity" reasoning, Congress could regulate any activity that it found was related to the economic productivity of individual citizens: family law (including marriage, divorce, and child custody), for example. Under the…theories [of the] Government…, it is difficult to perceive any limitation of federal power, even in areas such as criminal law enforcement or education where States historically have been sovereign. Thus, if we were to accept the Government's arguments, we are hard pressed to posit any activity by an individual that Congress is without power to regulate.

> Most assuredly, unlimited power in Congress was not the intent of the Framers.

Although JUSTICE BREYER argues that acceptance of the Government's rationales would not authorize a general federal police power, he is unable to identify any activity that the States may regulate but Congress may not. JUSTICE BREYER posits that there might be some limitations on Congress' commerce power, such as family law or certain aspects of education. These suggested limitations, when viewed in light of the dissent's expansive analysis, are devoid of substance.

JUSTICE BREYER focuses, for the most part, on the threat that firearm possession in and near schools poses to the educational process and the potential economic consequences flowing from that threat. Specifically, the dissent reasons that (1) gun-related violence is a serious problem; (2) that problem, in turn, has an adverse effect on classroom learning; and (3) that adverse effect on classroom learning, in turn, represents a substantial threat to trade and commerce. This analysis would be equally applicable, if not more so, to subjects such as family law and direct regulation of education.

For instance, if Congress can, pursuant to its Commerce Clause power, regulate activities that adversely affect the learning environment, then it also can regulate the educational process directly. Congress could determine that a school's curriculum has a "significant" effect on the extent of classroom learning. As a result, Congress could mandate a federal curriculum for local elementary and secondary schools because what is taught in local schools has a significant "effect on classroom learning," and that, in turn, has a substantial effect on interstate commerce.

> Are you getting a feel about how important it is to maintain at least five conservative justices on the High Court? You have heard of Common Core. If the liberal reasoning wins out, a national curriculum in our public schools (Common Core) would survive a constitutional challenge.

One

JUSTICE BREYER rejects our reading of precedent and argues that "Congress…could rationally conclude that schools fall on the commercial side of the line." Again, JUSTICE BREYER's rationale lacks any real limits because, depending on the level of generality, any activity can be looked upon as commercial. Under the dissent's rationale, Congress could just as easily look at child rearing as "falling on the commercial side of the line" because it provides a "valuable service – namely, to equip children with the skills they need to survive in life and, more specifically, in the workplace." We do not doubt that Congress has authority under the Commerce Clause to regulate numerous commercial activities that substantially affect interstate commerce and also affect the educational process. That authority, though broad, does not include the authority to regulate each and every aspect of local schools.

Admittedly, a determination whether an intrastate activity is commercial or noncommercial may in some cases result in legal uncertainty. But, so long as Congress' authority is limited to those powers enumerated in the Constitution, and so long as those enumerated powers are interpreted as having judicially enforceable outer limits, congressional legislation under the Commerce Clause always will engender "legal uncertainty." …The Constitution mandates this uncertainty by withholding from Congress a plenary police power that would authorize enactment of every type of legislation. Congress has operated within this framework of legal uncertainty ever since this Court determined that it was the Judiciary's duty "to say what the law is." *Marbury v. Madison**…

The possession of a gun in a local school zone is in no sense an economic activity that might, through repetition elsewhere, substantially affect any sort of interstate commerce…

To uphold the Government's contentions here, we would have to pile inference upon inference in a manner that would bid fair to convert congressional authority under the Commerce Clause to a general police power of the sort retained by the States. Admittedly, some of our prior cases have taken long steps down that road, giving great deference to congressional action. The broad language in these opinions has suggested the possibility of additional expansion, but we decline here to proceed any further. To do so would require us to conclude that the Constitution's enumeration of powers does not presuppose something not enumerated, and that there never will be a distinction between what is truly national and what is truly local. This we are unwilling to do...The Court of Appeals is *Affirmed.*

CONCURRENCE: Kennedy/O'Connor...This case requires us to consider our place in the design of the Government and to appreciate the significance of federalism in the whole structure of the Constitution.

Of the various structural elements in the Constitution, separation of powers, checks and balances, judicial review, and federalism, only concerning the last does there seem to be much uncertainty respecting the existence, and the content, of standards that allow the Judiciary to play a significant role in maintaining the design contemplated by the Framers. Although the resolution of specific cases has proved difficult, we have derived from the Constitution workable standards to assist in preserving separation of powers and checks and balances. These standards are by now well accepted. Judicial review is also established beyond question (*Marbury v. Madison*) and though we may differ when applying its principles, its legitimacy is undoubted. Our role in preserving the federal balance seems more tenuous.

ONE

There is irony in this, because of the four structural elements in the Constitution just mentioned, federalism was the unique contribution of the Framers to political science and political theory. Though on the surface the idea may seem counterintuitive, it was the insight of the Framers that freedom was enhanced by the creation of two governments, not one. "In the compound republic of America, the power surrendered by the people is first divided between two distinct governments, and then the portion allotted to each subdivided among distinct and separate departments. Hence a double security arises to the rights of the people. The different governments will control each other, at the same time that each will be controlled by itself." The Federalist No. 51…

If, as Madison expected, the Federal and State Governments are to control each other and hold each other in check by competing for the affections of the people, those citizens must have some means of knowing which of the two governments to hold accountable for the failure to perform a given function…Were the Federal Government to take over the regulation of entire areas of traditional state concern, areas having nothing to do with the regulation of commercial activities, the boundaries between the spheres of federal and state authority would blur and political responsibility would become illusory… The resultant inability to hold either branch of the government answerable to the citizens is more dangerous even than devolving too much authority to the remote central power. To be sure, one conclusion that could be drawn from The Federalist Papers is that the balance between national and state power is entrusted in its entirety to the political process. Madison's observation that "the people ought not surely to be precluded from giving most of their confidence where they may discover it to be most due," The Federalist No. 46, can be interpreted to say that the essence of responsibility for a shift in power from the State to the Federal Government rests upon a political judgment, though he added assurance that "the State governments could have little to apprehend, because it is only within a certain sphere that the federal power can, in the nature of things, be advantageously administered." Whatever the judicial role, it is axiomatic that Congress does have substantial discretion and control over the federal balance.

For these reasons, it would be mistaken and mischievous for the political branches to forget that the sworn obligation to preserve and protect the Constitution in maintaining the federal balance is their own in the first and primary instance. In the Webster-Hayne Debates and the debates over the Civil Rights Acts, some Congresses have accepted responsibility to confront the great questions of the proper federal balance in terms of lasting consequences for the constitutional design. The political branches of the Government must fulfill this grave constitutional obligation if democratic liberty and the federalism that secures it are to endure.

> In other words, the legislative and executive branches have as much responsibility as does the judicial branch to respect the boundaries between state and federal authority crafted by the Framers of our government.

At the same time, the absence of structural mechanisms to require those officials to undertake this principled task, and the momentary political convenience often attendant upon their failure to do so, argue against a complete renunciation of the judicial role. Although it is the obligation of all officers of the Government to respect the constitutional design, the federal balance is too essential a part of our constitutional structure and plays too vital a role in securing freedom for us to admit inability to intervene when one or the other level of Government has tipped the scales too far…

ONE

The statute before us upsets the federal balance to a degree that renders it an unconstitutional assertion of the commerce power, and our intervention is required. As THE CHIEF JUSTICE explains, unlike the earlier cases to come before the Court here neither the actors nor their conduct have a commercial character, and neither the purposes nor the design of the statute have an evident commercial nexus. The statute makes the simple possession of a gun within 1,000 feet of the grounds of the school a criminal offense. In a sense any conduct in this interdependent world of ours has an ultimate commercial origin or consequence, but we have not yet said the commerce power may reach so far. If Congress attempts that extension, then at the least we must inquire whether the exercise of national power seeks to intrude upon an area of traditional state concern.

> Nexus: connection.

An interference of these dimensions occurs here, for it is well established that education is a traditional concern of the States. The proximity to schools, including of course schools owned and operated by the States or their subdivisions, is the very premise for making the conduct criminal. In these circumstances, we have a particular duty to ensure that the federal-state balance is not destroyed...

While it is doubtful that any State, or indeed any reasonable person, would argue that it is wise policy to allow students to carry guns on school premises, considerable disagreement exists about how best to accomplish that goal. In this circumstance, the theory and utility of our federalism are revealed, for the States may perform their role as laboratories for experimentation to devise various solutions where the best solution is far from clear.

If a State or municipality determines that harsh criminal sanctions are necessary and wise to deter students from carrying guns on school premises, the reserved powers of the States are sufficient to enact those measures. Indeed, over 40 States already have criminal laws outlawing the possession of firearms on or near school grounds.

Other, more practicable means to rid the schools of guns may be thought by the citizens of some States to be preferable for the safety and welfare of the schools those States are charged with maintaining. These might include inducements to inform on violators where the information leads to arrests or confiscation of the guns; programs to encourage the voluntary surrender of guns with some provision for amnesty; penalties imposed on parents or guardians for failure to supervise the child; fining parents who allow students to possess a firearm at school; misdemeanor for parents to allow students to possess a firearm at school; laws providing for suspension or expulsion of gun-toting students or programs for expulsion with assignment to special facilities; automatic year-long expulsion for students with guns and intense semester-long reentry program.

The statute now before us forecloses the States from experimenting and exercising their own judgment in an area to which States lay claim by right of history and expertise, and it does so by regulating an activity beyond the realm of commerce in the ordinary and usual sense of that term. The tendency of this statute to displace state regulation in areas of traditional state concern is evident from its territorial operation. There are over 100,000 elementary and secondary schools in the United States. Each of these now has an invisible federal zone extending 1,000 feet beyond the (often irregular) boundaries of the school property. In some communities no doubt it would be difficult to navigate without infringing on those zones. Yet throughout these areas, school officials would find their own programs for the prohibition of guns in danger of displacement by the federal authority unless the State chooses to enact a parallel rule.

This is not a case where the etiquette of federalism has been violated by a formal command from the National Government directing the State to enact a certain policy…or to organize its governmental functions in a certain way…While the intrusion on state sovereignty may not be as severe in this instance as in some of our recent Tenth Amendment cases, the intrusion is nonetheless significant. Absent a stronger connection or identification with commercial concerns that are central to the Commerce Clause, that interference contradicts the federal balance the Framers designed and that this Court is obliged to enforce…

CONCURRENCE: Thomas…[Not Provided.]

DISSENT: Stevens…Guns are both articles of commerce and articles that can be used to restrain commerce. Their possession is the consequence, either directly or indirectly, of commercial activity.

Say goodbye to federalism. Say goodbye to states' rights and all of the enumerated (and limiting) Congressional powers. If Justice Stevens had prevailed, say hello to a national police power. Apparently he actually believes that mere possession of any item of tangible property is sufficient to come within Congressional regulation of "commerce among the several states." For, even if one has not purchased the item (whatever it is) in his possession, but received it as a gift, surely it has been the subject of some "indirect" commercial activity at some time in its past, or so his theory goes. Mere possession of something, then, gets us beyond the question of whether the federal government has the appropriate "commerce power" to regulate it. Once you are there, as we have seen, the connection to "other states," according to the dissenting views, is practically a given.

In my judgment, Congress' power to regulate commerce in firearms includes the power to prohibit possession of guns at any location because of their potentially harmful use...

> He certainly is consistent. Justice Stevens would allow Congress to regulate possession of anything potentially harmful that is located anywhere! There is no limit!

It necessarily follows that Congress may also prohibit their possession in particular markets. The market for the possession of handguns by school-age children is, distressingly, substantial ... Whether or not the national interest in eliminating that market would have justified federal legislation in 1789, it surely does today.

> I am not going to take the time to research either the state of public schooling in 1789 or possession of handguns by school-age children in 1789 because whether or not there would have been "justification" for federal legislation in 1789 is irrelevant to the issues here.

> However, I am willing to bet that in 1789 school-age children owned guns, knew how to use guns and did so responsibly, all with the knowledge and guidance of their parents.

DISSENT: Souter...In reviewing congressional legislation under the Commerce Clause, we defer to what is often a merely implicit congressional judgment that its regulation addresses a subject substantially affecting interstate commerce "if there is any rational basis for such a finding."...If that congressional determination is within the realm of reason, "the only remaining question for judicial inquiry is whether 'the means chosen by Congress are reasonably adapted to the end permitted by the Constitution.'"...

ONE

> Remarkable! What Justice Souter has just described amounts to no standard at all.

DISSENT: Breyer/Stevens/Souter/Ginsburg…The issue in this case is whether the Commerce Clause authorizes Congress to enact a statute that makes it a crime to possess a gun in, or near, a school. In my view, the statute falls well within the scope of the commerce power as this Court has understood that power over the last half century.

In reaching this conclusion, I apply three basic principles of Commerce Clause interpretation. First, the power to "regulate Commerce…among the several States" encompasses the power to regulate local activities insofar as they significantly affect interstate commerce…

Second, in determining whether a local activity will likely have a significant effect upon interstate commerce, a court must consider, not the effect of an individual act (a single instance of gun possession), but rather the cumulative effect of all similar instances (*i.e.,* the effect of all guns possessed in or near schools)…

Third, the Constitution requires us to judge the connection between a regulated activity and interstate commerce, not directly, but at one remove. Courts must give Congress a degree of leeway in determining the existence of a significant factual connection between the regulated activity and interstate commerce – both because the Constitution delegates the commerce power directly to Congress and because the determination requires an empirical judgment of a kind that a legislature is more likely than a court to make with accuracy. The traditional words "rational basis" capture this leeway. Thus, the specific question before us, as the Court recognizes, is not whether the "regulated activity sufficiently affected interstate commerce," but, rather, whether Congress could have had "*a rational basis*" for so concluding...Applying these principles to the case at hand, we must ask whether Congress could have had a *rational basis* for finding a significant (or substantial) connection between gun-related school violence and interstate commerce ...As long as one views the commerce connection, not as a "technical legal conception," but as "a practical one," the answer to this question must be yes. Numerous reports and studies – generated both inside and outside government – make clear that Congress could reasonably have found the empirical connection that its law, implicitly or explicitly, asserts.

> Enjoy as you sit back and watch the Search for the Empirical Connection! (Sounds like a movie title.) Have a few laughs and ask this question, "If this is what judges do, do we need them?" Perhaps I am being too harsh – perhaps not respectful enough. See what you think. Here goes!

For one thing, reports, hearings, and other readily available literature make clear that the problem of guns in and around schools is widespread and extremely serious. These materials report, for example, that four percent of American high school students...carry a gun to school at least occasionally; that 12 percent of urban high school students have had guns fired at them; that 20 percent of those students have been threatened with guns; and that, in any 6-month period, several hundred thousand schoolchildren are victims of violent crimes in or near their schools. And, they report that this widespread violence in schools throughout the nation significantly interferes with the quality of education in those schools...Based on reports such as these, Congress obviously could have thought that guns and learning are mutually exclusive. Congress could therefore have found a substantial educational problem – teachers unable to teach, students unable to learn – and concluded that guns near schools contribute substantially to the size and scope of that problem.

> Okay. Follow the bouncing ball of logic. Justice Breyer says: Guns are not conducive to learning. The problem of guns at schools is widespread and "substantial." He goes on…

Having found that guns in schools significantly undermine the quality of education in our nation's classrooms, Congress could also have found, given the effect of education upon interstate and foreign commerce, that gun-related violence in and around schools is a commercial, as well as a human, problem. Education, although far more than a matter of economics, has long been inextricably intertwined with the nation's economy. When this nation began, most workers received their education in the workplace, typically (like Benjamin Franklin) as apprentices. As late as the 1920's, many workers still received general education directly from their employers – from large corporations, such as General Electric, Ford, and Goodyear, which created schools within their firms to help both the worker and the firm. (Throughout most of the 19th century fewer than one percent of all Americans received secondary education through attending a high school.) As public school enrollment grew in the early 20th century, the need for industry to teach basic educational skills diminished. But, the direct economic link between basic education and industrial productivity remained. Scholars estimate that nearly a quarter of America's economic growth in the early years of this century is traceable directly to increased schooling; that investment in "human capital" (through spending on education) exceeded investment in "physical capital" by a ratio of almost two to one; and that the economic returns to this investment in education exceeded the returns to conventional capital investment.

> He postulates: "As the overall level of education rises, the economy of the country grows." Wow. This is really deep.

In recent years the link between secondary education and business has strengthened, becoming both more direct and more important. Scholars on the subject report that technological changes and innovations in management techniques have altered the nature of the workplace so that more jobs now demand greater educational skills…

> Next he reaches the truly astounding conclusion that "education is more important today than ever before."

Increasing global competition also has made primary and secondary education economically more important…

The economic links I have just sketched seem fairly obvious. Why then is it not equally obvious, in light of those links, that a widespread, serious, and substantial physical threat to teaching and learning *also* substantially threatens the commerce to which that teaching and learning is inextricably tied? That is to say, guns in the hands of six percent of inner-city high school students and gun-related violence throughout a city's schools must threaten the trade and commerce that those schools support. The only question, then, is whether the latter threat is (to use the majority's terminology) "substantial." The evidence of (1) the *extent* of the gun-related violence problem, (2) the *extent* of the resulting negative effect on classroom learning and (3) the *extent* of the consequent negative commercial effects, when taken together, indicate a threat to trade and commerce that is "substantial." At the very least, Congress could rationally have concluded that the links are "substantial."

> Hopefully, you see that Justice Breyer's "analysis" will always lead to affirming commerce power in Congress for whatever they pass, right? Somehow, four Supreme Court justices have found "unlimited power" in the list of limited powers of Article I, §8. Don't forget that Texas has its own gun-free school zone statute to protect its schools in the manner Texans determine to be best for Texans. Leave Texas and other states alone!

...For these reasons, I would reverse the judgment of the Court of Appeals. Respectfully, I dissent.

> Cell phones, gum, T-shirts that carry teenage messages, knives, tattoos, lunch boxes with sharp edges, Twinkies, etc., etc., "have a detrimental effect on education" and, therefore, a negative effect on the economy. Is there no end to the "national police"? And, lest we forget, we are not dealing with the wisdom of this legislation. We are dealing with the power to enact it.

SUMMARY: The congressional attempt to impose criminal sanctions for matters solely within the domain of state and local government failed. Thankfully, five of nine justices finally placed a limit on the commerce power that will hopefully stand as a benchmark for years to come.

COMMENT: Doesn't this case make it clear that the liberal justices put their own policy agenda ahead of the Constitution? They wanted to control guns and it mattered not to them that Congress exceeded its power to do so. Their interpretation of the commerce clause literally does away with the concept of limited federal power embodied in Article I, §8. They had to get downright silly in their argument in order to stretch the commerce power this far.

PLEA: We don't need justices on the High Court to tell us that merely possessing something, anything, that Congress seeks to control brings it within the commerce power. This case should have been unanimous in striking down the Gun-Free School Zones Act of 1990. If you want big government out of your life, you must educate your neighbors and vote for presidents who care about the Constitution and for senators who will take their oath seriously. Your **one vote** can make a difference – it could make "the" difference.

Chapter Eight

ONE ROBE SHORT ON MAY 22, 1995, KILLED THE HOPE OF CONGRESSIONAL TERM LIMITS!

Federal congressional term limits have been discussed off and on for several years around the nation. Of course, the Twenty-Second Amendment provides for term limits for the office of the president. We know government is broken, especially the government we send to Washington, D.C. We know our Founders never intended federal legislators to be career politicians and many of us want to vote them all out, but just can't seem to vote out our own.

I'm not sure whether term limits for representatives or senators is a good idea, but many would like to give it a try. Perhaps we should do so on the theory that we couldn't possibly do worse than what we have in place now. But, how can that be accomplished?

Could it come about through a congressional act passed by each House and signed by the president? Even if we assume it could, let's face reality. Neither our representatives nor our senators in Washington would ever pass such a statute – a statute that limits their own power. That is just not going to happen.

There is a way to amend the Constitution without Congress through a state-initiated convention, but it has never been done before.

Would it be possible, however, for a state to get the job done? Could a state, by its own statute or its own constitution, forbid federal representatives or senators who have already served a chosen number of terms from being on subsequent ballots in that state?

If that is possible, wouldn't it be truly American for each state to decide for itself (through its own citizens, of course) whether the people of that state want to give term limits a try? In 1992 the voters of Arkansas amended their constitution to accomplish that very goal. Most of our citizenry does not likely know that the following

ONE

Supreme Court decision closed the door on a state-led movement to accomplish congressional term limits and, for all practical purposes, a federal movement, as well. **One robe short** in this 1995 decision means that the only way we will ever have legislative term limits in the federal government is to either amend the Constitution through a constitutional convention called by the states or **add one robe** to the Court when a vacancy occurs, hoping to reverse this decision.

Only your vote can accomplish either. This decision is a bit more difficult than most to understand, but it is too important to leave out of this book. Let's take a look at *U.S. Term Limits, Inc. v. Thornton.**

U.S. TERM LIMITS, INC. V. THORNTON

SUPREME COURT OF THE UNITED STATES
514 U.S. 779
May 22, 1995
[5 - 4]

OPINION: Stevens/ Kennedy/ Souter/ Ginsburg/ Breyer...The Constitution sets forth qualifications for membership in the Congress of the United States.

> **Article I, §2, cl. 2...provides:**
>
> "No Person shall be a Representative who shall not have attained to the Age of twenty five Years, and been seven Years a Citizen of the United States, and who shall not, when elected, be an Inhabitant of that State in which he shall be chosen."

Article I, §3, cl. 3...provides:

"No Person shall be a Senator who shall not have attained to the Age of thirty Years, and been nine Years a Citizen of the United States, and who shall not, when elected, be an Inhabitant of that State for which he shall be chosen."

> In order to be a representative in the House, one needs to be at least 25 years of age, an inhabitant of the state when elected and a United States citizen for at least seven years. In like manner, in order to be a senator, one needs to be at least 30, an inhabitant of the state when elected and a United States citizen for at least nine years. Please note that these offices do not require "natural born citizenship" and, therefore, a "naturalized citizen" would qualify for either office.

Today's cases present a challenge to [Amendment 73 of] the Arkansas State Constitution that prohibits the name of an otherwise-eligible candidate for Congress from appearing on the general election ballot if that candidate has already served three terms in the House of Representatives or two terms in the Senate. The Arkansas Supreme Court held that the amendment violates the Federal Constitution. We agree...Such a state-imposed restriction is contrary to the "fundamental principle of our representative democracy"...that "the people should choose whom they please to govern them." Allowing individual States to adopt their own qualifications for congressional service would be inconsistent with the Framers' vision of a uniform National Legislature representing the people of the United States...

ONE

> Did I understand that correctly? Yes, the Court is actually saying that an amendment to the Arkansas Constitution providing for term limits and adopted by the people of Arkansas violates a most fundamental principle of our representative democracy that "the people should choose whom they please to govern them." Do you see a contradiction? Please be patient and wait until you have read the dissent to weigh in on this outcome.

Source of the Power

Contrary to petitioners' assertions, the power to add qualifications is not part of the original powers of sovereignty that the Tenth Amendment reserved to the States...As Justice Story recognized, "the states can exercise no powers whatsoever, which exclusively spring out of the existence of the national government, which the constitution does not delegate to them...No state can say that it has reserved what it never possessed."

...With respect to setting qualifications for service in Congress, no such right existed before the Constitution was ratified. The contrary argument overlooks the revolutionary character of the Government that the Framers conceived. Prior to the adoption of the Constitution, the States had joined together under the Articles of Confederation. In that system, "the States retained most of their sovereignty, like independent nations bound together only by treaties." After the Constitutional Convention convened, the Framers were presented with, and eventually adopted a variation of, "a plan not merely to amend the Articles of Confederation but to create an entirely new National Government with a National Executive, National Judiciary, and a National Legislature." In adopting that plan, the Framers envisioned a uniform national system, rejecting the notion that the nation was a collection of States, and instead creating a direct link between the National Government and the people of the United States...In that National Government, representatives owe primary allegiance not to the people of a State, but to the people of the nation. As Justice Story observed, each Member of Congress is "an officer of the union, deriving his powers and qualifications from the constitution, and neither created by, dependent upon, nor controllable by, the states...Those officers owe their existence and functions to the united voice of the whole, not of a portion, of the people." Representatives and senators are as much officers of the entire union as is the president. States thus "have just as much right, and no more, to prescribe new qualifications for a representative, as they have for a president...It is no original prerogative of state power to appoint a representative, a senator, or president for the union."

We believe that the Constitution reflects the Framers' general agreement with the approach later articulated by Justice Story. For example, Art. I, §5, cl. 1, provides: "Each House shall be the Judge of the Elections, Returns and Qualifications of its own Members." The text of the Constitution thus gives the representatives of <u>all</u> the people the final say in judging the qualifications of the representatives of <u>any one State</u>. For this reason, the dissent falters when it states that "the people of Georgia have no say over whom the people of Massachusetts select to represent them in Congress."

Two other sections of the Constitution further support our view of the Framers' vision. First, consistent with Story's view, the Constitution provides that the salaries of representatives should "be...paid out of the Treasury of the United States," Art. I, §6, rather than by individual States. <u>The salary provisions reflect the view that representatives owe their allegiance to the people, and not to the States</u>. Second, the provisions governing elections reveal the Framers' understanding

ONE

that powers over the election of federal officers had to be delegated to, rather than reserved by, the States…

In short, as the Framers recognized, electing representatives to the National Legislature was a new right, arising from the Constitution itself. The Tenth Amendment thus provides no basis for concluding that the States possess reserved power to add qualifications to those that are fixed in the Constitution. Instead, any state power to set the qualifications for membership in Congress must derive not from the reserved powers of state sovereignty, but rather from the delegated powers of national sovereignty. <u>In the absence of any constitutional delegation to the States of power to add qualifications to those enumerated in the Constitution, such a power does not exist</u>...

The Convention and Ratification Debates

…The provisions in the Constitution governing federal elections confirm the Framers' intent that States lack power to add qualifications…

In light of the Framers' evident concern that States would try to undermine the National Government, they could not have intended States to have the power to set qualifications. Indeed, one of the more anomalous consequences of petitioners' argument is that it accepts federal supremacy over the procedural aspects of determining the times, places, and manner of elections while allowing the States carte blanche with respect to the substantive qualifications for membership in Congress.

Carte blanche: free rein

The dissent nevertheless contends that the Framers' distrust of the States with respect to elections does not preclude the people of the States from adopting eligibility requirements to help narrow their own choices. As the dissent concedes, however, the Framers were unquestionably concerned that the States would simply not hold elections for federal officers, and therefore the Framers gave Congress the power to "make or alter" state election regulations. Yet under the dissent's approach, the States could achieve exactly the same result by simply setting qualifications for federal office sufficiently high that no one could meet those qualifications. <u>In our view, it is inconceivable that the Framers would provide a specific constitutional provision to ensure that federal elections would be held while at the same time allowing States to render those elections meaningless by simply ensuring that no candidate could be qualified for office</u>. Given the Framers' wariness over the potential for state abuse, we must conclude that the specification of fixed qualifications in the constitutional text was intended to prescribe uniform rules that would preclude modification by either Congress or the States.

We find further evidence of the Framers' intent in Art. 1, §5, cl. 1, which provides: "Each House shall be the Judge of the Elections, Returns and Qualifications of its own Members." That Art. I, §5, vests a federal tribunal with ultimate authority to judge a Member's qualifications is fully consistent with the understanding that those qualifications are fixed in the Federal Constitution, but not with the understanding that they can be altered by the States...

We also find compelling the complete absence in the ratification debates of any assertion that States had the power to add qualifications. In those debates, the question whether to require term limits, or "rotation," was a major source of controversy. The draft of the

One

Constitution that was submitted for ratification contained no provision for rotation...Opponents of ratification condemned the absence of a rotation requirement, noting that "there is no doubt that senators will hold their office perpetually; and in this situation, they must of necessity lose their dependence, and their attachments to the people." Even proponents of ratification expressed concern about the "abandonment in every instance of the necessity of rotation in office." At several ratification conventions, participants proposed amendments that would have required rotation.

> "Rotation" was a form of term limits whereby candidates for office were not limited to the number of terms they served, but were required to sit-it-out every few years.

The Federalists' responses to those criticisms and proposals addressed the merits of the issue, arguing that rotation was incompatible with the people's right to choose. As we noted above, Robert Livingston argued:

> "The people are the best judges who ought to represent them. To dictate and control them, to tell them whom they shall not elect, is to abridge their natural rights. This rotation is an absurd species of ostracism."

Similarly, Hamilton argued that the representatives' need for reelection rather than mandatory rotation was the more effective way to keep representatives responsive to the people, because "when a man knows he must quit his station, let his merit be what it may, he will turn his attention chiefly to his own emolument."

Regardless of which side has the better of the debate over rotation, it is most striking that nowhere in the extensive ratification debates have we found any statement by either a proponent or an opponent of rotation that the draft constitution would permit States to require rotation for the representatives of their own citizens. If the participants in the debate had believed that the States retained the authority to impose term limits, it is inconceivable that the Federalists would not have made this obvious response to the arguments of the pro-rotation forces. The absence in an otherwise freewheeling debate of any suggestion that States had the power to impose additional qualifications unquestionably reflects the Framers' common understanding that States lacked that power...

Democratic Principles

...Finally, state-imposed restrictions...violate a third idea central to this basic principle: that <u>the right to choose representatives belongs not to the States, but to the people</u>...The Framers ...conceived of a Federal Government directly responsible to the people, possessed of direct power over the people, and chosen directly, not by States, but by the people. The Framers implemented this ideal most clearly in the provision...that calls for the Members of the House of Representatives to be "chosen every second Year by the People of the several States." Art. I, §2, cl. 1. Following the adoption of the Seventeenth Amendment in 1913, this ideal was extended to elections for the Senate. The Congress of the United States, therefore, is not a confederation of nations in which separate sovereigns are represented by appointed delegates, but is instead a body composed of representatives of the people. As Chief Justice John Marshall observed: "The government of the Union, then,...is, emphatically, and truly, a government of the people. In form and in substance it emanates from them. Its powers are granted by them, and are to be exercised directly on them, and for their benefit."

ONE

...Permitting individual States to formulate diverse qualifications for their representatives would result in a patchwork of state qualifications, undermining the uniformity and the national character that the Framers envisioned and sought to ensure...Such a patchwork would also sever the direct link that the Framers found so critical between the National Government and the people of the United States.

State Practice

Petitioners attempt to overcome this formidable array of evidence against the States' power to impose qualifications by arguing that the practice of the States immediately after the adoption of the Constitution demonstrates their understanding that they possessed such power. One may properly question the extent to which the States' own practice is a reliable indicator of the contours of restrictions that the Constitution imposed on States, especially when no court has ever upheld a state-imposed qualification of any sort. But petitioners' argument is unpersuasive even on its own terms. At the time of the Convention, "almost all the State Constitutions required members of their Legislatures to possess considerable property." Despite this near uniformity, only one State, <u>Virginia</u>, placed similar restrictions on <u>Members of Congress, requiring that a representative be a "freeholder."</u> Just 15 years after imposing a property qualification, Virginia replaced that requirement with a provision requiring that representatives be only "qualified according to the Constitution of the United States." Moreover, several States, including New Hampshire, Georgia, Delaware, and South Carolina, revised their Constitutions at around the time of the Federal Constitution. In the revised Constitutions, each State retained property qualifications for its own state elected officials yet placed no property qualification on its congressional representatives.

The contemporaneous state practice with respect to term limits is similar. At the time of the Convention, States widely supported term limits in at least some circumstances. The Articles of Confederation contained a provision for term limits. As we have noted, some members of the Convention had sought to impose term limits for Members of Congress. In addition, many States imposed term limits on state officers, four placed limits on delegates to the Continental Congress, and several States voiced support for term limits for Members of Congress. Despite this widespread support, no State sought to impose any term limits on its own federal representatives. Thus, a proper assessment of contemporaneous state practice provides further persuasive evidence of a general understanding that the qualifications in the Constitution were unalterable by the States.

In sum, the available historical and textual evidence, read in light of the basic principles of democracy underlying the Constitution, reveal the Framers' intent that neither Congress nor the States should possess the power to supplement the exclusive qualifications set forth in the text of the Constitution.

Petitioners argue that, <u>even if</u> States may not add qualifications, Amendment 73 is constitutional because it is not such a qualification, and because Amendment 73 is a permissible exercise of state power to regulate the "<u>Times, Places and Manner of holding Elections.</u>" <u>We reject these contentions</u>.

...§3...provides that certain senators and representatives shall not be certified as candidates and shall not have their names appear on the ballot. They may run as write-in candidates and, if elected, they may serve. Petitioners contend that only a legal bar to service creates an impermissible qualification, and that Amendment 73 is therefore consistent with the Constitution...

In our view, an amendment with the avowed purpose and obvious effect of evading the requirements of the Qualifications Clauses by handicapping a class of candidates cannot stand. To argue otherwise is to suggest that the Framers spent significant time and energy in debating and crafting Clauses that could be easily evaded. More importantly, allowing States to evade the Qualifications Clauses by "dressing eligibility to stand for Congress in ballot access clothing" trivializes the basic principles of our democracy that underlie those Clauses. Petitioners' argument treats the Qualifications Clauses not as the embodiment of a grand principle, but rather as empty formalism...

Petitioners make the related argument that Amendment 73 merely regulates the "Manner" of elections, and that the amendment is therefore a permissible exercise of state power under Article I, §4, cl. 1 (the Elections Clause), to regulate the "Times, Places and Manner" of elections. We cannot agree.

A necessary consequence of petitioners' argument is that Congress itself would have the power to "make or alter" a measure such as Amendment 73…That the Framers would have approved of such a result is unfathomable...

The Framers intended the Elections Clause to grant States authority to create procedural regulations, not to provide States with license to exclude classes of candidates from federal office…

We hold that a state amendment is unconstitutional when it has the likely effect of handicapping a class of candidates and has the sole purpose of creating additional qualifications indirectly. Thus, the dissent's discussion of the evidence concerning the possibility that a popular incumbent will win a write-in election is simply beside the point…

We are, however, firmly convinced that allowing the several States to adopt term limits for congressional service would effect a fundamental change in the constitutional framework. Any such change must come not by legislation adopted either by Congress or by an individual State, but rather - as have other important changes in the electoral process - through the amendment procedures set forth in Article V...The judgment is affirmed.

CONCURRENCE: Kennedy...[Not Provided.]

DISSENT: Thomas/Rehnquist/O'Connor/Scalia...It is ironic that the Court bases today's decision on the right of the people to "choose whom they please to govern them." Under our Constitution, there is only one State whose people have the right to "choose whom they please" to represent Arkansas in Congress. The Court holds, however, that neither the elected legislature of that State nor the people themselves (acting by ballot initiative) may prescribe any qualifications for those representatives. The majority therefore defends the right of the people of Arkansas to "choose whom they please to govern them" by invalidating a provision that won nearly 60% of the votes cast in a direct election and that carried every congressional district in the State...

Nothing in the Constitution deprives the people of each State of the power to prescribe eligibility requirements for the candidates who seek to represent them in Congress. The Constitution is simply silent on this question. And where the Constitution is silent, it raises no bar to action by the States or the people.

I

Because the majority fundamentally misunderstands the notion of "reserved" powers, I start with some first principles. Contrary to the majority's suggestion, the people of the States need not point to any affirmative grant of power in the Constitution in order to prescribe qualifications for their representatives in Congress, or to authorize their elected state legislators to do so.

A

Our system of government rests on one overriding principle: all power stems from the consent of the people. To phrase the principle in this way, however, is to be imprecise about something important to the notion of "reserved" powers. The ultimate source of the Constitution's authority is the consent of the people of each individual State, not the consent of the undifferentiated people of the nation as a whole.

The ratification procedure erected by Article VII makes this point clear. The Constitution took effect once it had been ratified by the people gathered in convention in nine different States. But the Constitution went into effect only "between the States so ratifying the same," Art. VII; it did not bind the people of North Carolina until they had accepted it. In Madison's words, the popular consent upon which the Constitution's authority rests was "given by the people, not as individuals composing one entire nation, but as composing the distinct and independent States to which they respectively belong." The Federalist No. 39.

When they adopted the Federal Constitution, of course, the people of each State surrendered some of their authority to the United States (and hence to entities accountable to the people of other States as well as to themselves). They affirmatively deprived their States of certain powers (Art. I, §10) and they affirmatively conferred certain powers upon the Federal Government (Art. I, §8).

> Article I, §10, disempowers states from certain functions and gives them powers only after getting consent from Congress for other functions. Article I, §8, provides a list of powers given to Congress. I urge you to get out your pocket Constitution and read them. They will stick with you if you do.

Because the people of the several States are the only true source of power, however, the Federal Government enjoys no authority beyond what the Constitution confers: the Federal Government's powers are limited and enumerated. In the words of Justice Black, "the United States is entirely a creature of the Constitution. Its power and authority have no other source."

In each State, the remainder of the people's powers - "the powers not delegated to the United States by the Constitution, nor prohibited by it to the States," Amdt. 10 - are either delegated to the state government or retained by the people.

> The Tenth Amendment is a very short and potent tool for state empowerment. Take a look at it.

The Federal Constitution does not specify which of these two possibilities obtains; it is up to the various state constitutions to declare which powers the people of each State have delegated to their state government. As far as the Federal Constitution is concerned, then, the States can exercise all powers that the Constitution does not withhold from them. The Federal Government and the States thus face different default rules: where the Constitution is silent about the exercise of a particular power - that is, where the Constitution does not speak either expressly or by necessary implication - the Federal Government lacks that power and the States enjoy it.

ONE

These basic principles are enshrined in the Tenth Amendment, which declares that all powers neither delegated to the Federal Government nor prohibited to the States "are reserved to the States respectively, or to the people." With this careful last phrase, the Amendment avoids taking any position on the division of power between the state governments and the people of the States: it is up to the people of each State to determine which "reserved" powers their state government may exercise. But the Amendment does make clear that powers reside at the state level except where the Constitution removes them from that level. All powers that the Constitution neither delegates to the Federal Government nor prohibits to the States are controlled by the people of each State.

To be sure, when the Tenth Amendment uses the phrase "the people," it does not specify whether it is referring to the people of each State or the people of the nation as a whole. But the latter interpretation would make the Amendment pointless: there would have been no reason to provide that where the Constitution is silent about whether a particular power resides at the state level, it might or might not do so. In addition, it would make no sense to speak of powers as being reserved to the undifferentiated people of the nation as a whole, because the Constitution does not contemplate that those people will either exercise power or delegate it. The Constitution simply does not recognize any mechanism for action by the undifferentiated people of the nation. Thus, the amendment provision of Article V calls for amendments to be ratified not by a convention of the national people, but by conventions of the people in each State or by the state legislatures elected by those people. Likewise, the Constitution calls for Members of Congress to be chosen State by State, rather than in nationwide elections. Even the selection of the president - surely the most national of national figures - is accomplished by an electoral college made up of delegates chosen by the various States, and candidates can lose a presidential election despite winning a majority of the votes cast in the nation as a whole…

In short, the notion of popular sovereignty that undergirds the Constitution does not erase state boundaries, but rather tracks them. The people of each State obviously did trust their fate to the people of the several States when they consented to the Constitution; not only did they empower the governmental institutions of the United States, but they also agreed to be bound by constitutional amendments that they themselves refused to ratify. See Art. V (providing that proposed amendments shall take effect upon ratification by three-quarters of the States). At the same time, however, the people of each State retained their separate political identities. As Chief Justice Marshall put it, "no political dreamer was ever wild enough to think of breaking down the lines which separate the States, and of compounding the American people into one common mass." *McCulloch v. Maryland.*

Any ambiguity in the Tenth Amendment's use of the phrase "the people" is cleared up by the body of the Constitution itself. Article I begins by providing that the Congress of the United States enjoys "all legislative Powers herein granted," §1, and goes on to give a careful enumeration of Congress' powers, §8. It then concludes by enumerating certain powers that are *prohibited* to the States. The import of this structure is the same as the import of the Tenth Amendment: if we are to invalidate Arkansas' Amendment 73, we must point to something in the Federal Constitution that deprives the people of Arkansas of the power to enact such measures.

B

The majority disagrees that it bears this burden. But its arguments are unpersuasive.

One

1

The majority begins by announcing an enormous and untenable limitation on the principle expressed by the Tenth Amendment. According to the majority, the States possess only those powers that the Constitution affirmatively grants to them or that they enjoyed before the Constitution was adopted; the Tenth Amendment "could only 'reserve' that which existed before." From the fact that the States had not previously enjoyed any powers over the particular institutions of the Federal Government established by the Constitution, the majority derives a rule precisely opposite to the one that the Amendment actually prescribes: "The states can exercise no powers whatsoever, which exclusively spring out of the existence of the national government, which the constitution does not delegate to them."

The majority's essential logic is that the state governments could not "reserve" any powers that they did not control at the time the Constitution was drafted. But it was not the state governments that were doing the reserving. The Constitution derives its authority instead from the consent of *the people* of the States. Given the fundamental principle that all governmental powers stem from the people of the States, it would simply be incoherent to assert that the people of the States could not reserve any powers that they had not previously controlled.

The Tenth Amendment's use of the word "reserved" does not help the majority's position. If someone says that the power to use a particular facility is reserved to some group, he is not saying anything about whether that group has previously used the facility. He is merely saying that the people who control the facility have designated that group as the entity with authority to use it. The Tenth Amendment is similar: the people of the States, from whom all

103

governmental powers stem, have specified that all powers not prohibited to the States by the Federal Constitution are reserved "to the States respectively, or to the people."

The majority is therefore quite wrong to conclude that the people of the States cannot authorize their state governments to exercise any powers that were unknown to the States when the Federal Constitution was drafted. Indeed, the majority's position frustrates the apparent purpose of the Amendment's final phrase. The Amendment does not pre-empt any limitations on state power found in the state constitutions, as it might have done if it simply had said that the powers not delegated to the Federal Government are reserved to the States. But the Amendment also does not prevent the people of the States from amending their state constitutions to remove limitations that were in effect when the Federal Constitution and the Bill of Rights were ratified...

2

The majority also sketches out what may be an alternative (and narrower) argument...The majority suggests that it would be inconsistent with the notion of "national sovereignty" for the States or the people of the States to have any reserved powers over the selection of Members of Congress. The majority apparently reaches this conclusion in two steps. First, it asserts that because Congress as a whole is an institution of the National Government, the individual Members of Congress "owe primary allegiance not to the people of a State, but to the people of the nation." Second, it concludes that because each Member of Congress has a nationwide constituency once he takes office, it would be inconsistent with the Framers' scheme to let a single State prescribe qualifications for him.

Political scientists can debate about who commands the "primary allegiance" of Members of Congress once they reach Washington.

ONE

From the framing to the present, however, the *selection* of the representatives and senators from each State has been left entirely to the people of that State or to their state legislature...The very name "congress" suggests a coming together of representatives from distinct entities. In keeping with the complexity of our federal system, once the representatives chosen by the people of each State assemble in Congress, they form a national body and are beyond the control of the individual States until the next election. But the selection of representatives in Congress is indisputably an act of the people of each State, not some abstract people of the nation as a whole...

In short, while the majority is correct that the Framers expected the selection process to create a "direct link" between members of the House of Representatives and the people, the link was between the representatives from each State and the people of that State; the people of Georgia have no say over whom the people of Massachusetts select to represent them in Congress. This arrangement must baffle the majority, whose understanding of Congress would surely fit more comfortably within a system of nationwide elections. But the fact remains that when it comes to the selection of Members of Congress, the people of each State have retained their independent political identity. As a result, there is absolutely nothing strange about the notion that the people of the States or their state legislatures possess "reserved" powers in this area.

The majority seeks support from the Constitution's specification that Members of Congress "shall receive a Compensation for their Services, to be ascertained by Law, and paid out of the Treasury of the United States." Art. I, §6, cl. 1. But the fact that Members of Congress draw a federal salary once they have assembled hardly means that the people of the States lack reserved powers over the selection of their representatives. Indeed, the historical evidence about the compensation provision suggests that the States' reserved powers may even extend beyond the selection stage. The majority itself indicates that if the Constitution had made no provision for congressional compensation, this topic would have been "left to state legislatures." Likewise, Madison specifically indicated that even with the compensation provision in place, the individual States still enjoyed the reserved power to supplement the federal salary.

As for the fact that a State has no reserved power to establish qualifications for the office of president, it surely need not follow that a State has no reserved power to establish qualifications for the Members of Congress who represent the people of that State. Because powers are reserved to the States "respectively," it is clear that no State may legislate for another State: even though the Arkansas legislature enjoys the reserved power to pass a minimum-wage law for Arkansas, it has no power to pass a minimum-wage law for Vermont. For the same reason, Arkansas may not decree that only Arkansas citizens are eligible to be president of the United States; the selection of the president is not up to Arkansas alone, and Arkansas can no more prescribe the qualifications for that office than it can set the qualifications for Members of Congress from Florida. But none of this suggests that Arkansas cannot set qualifications for Members of Congress from Arkansas.

In fact, the Constitution's treatment of presidential elections actively contradicts the majority's position. While the individual States have no "reserved" power to set qualifications for the office of president, we have long understood that they do have the power (as far as the Federal Constitution is concerned) to set qualifications for their presidential electors - the delegates that each State selects to represent it in the electoral college that actually chooses the nation's chief executive. Even respondents do not dispute that the States may establish qualifications for their delegates to the electoral college, as long as those qualifications pass muster under other constitutional provisions (primarily the First and Fourteenth Amendments). As the majority cannot argue that the Constitution affirmatively grants this power, the power must be one that is "reserved" to the States. It necessarily follows that the majority's understanding of the Tenth Amendment is incorrect, for the position of presidential elector surely "springs out of the existence of the national government."

3

In a final effort to deny that the people of the States enjoy "reserved" powers over the selection of their representatives in Congress, the majority suggests that the Constitution expressly delegates to the States certain powers over congressional elections. Such delegations of power, the majority argues, would be superfluous if the people of the States enjoyed reserved powers in this area.

Only one constitutional provision - the Times, Places and Manner Clause of Article I, §4 - even arguably supports the majority's suggestion. It reads:

> "The Times, Places and Manner of holding Elections for Senators and Representatives, shall be prescribed in each State by the Legislature thereof; but the Congress may at any time by Law make or alter such Regulations, except as to the Places of chusing Senators."

Contrary to the majority's assumption, however, this Clause does not delegate any authority to the States. Instead, it simply imposes a duty upon them. The majority gets it exactly right: by specifying that the state legislatures "shall" prescribe the details necessary to hold congressional elections, the Clause "expressly requires action by the States." This command meshes with one of the principal purposes of Congress' "make or alter" power: to ensure that the States hold congressional elections in the first place, so that Congress continues to exist. As one reporter summarized a speech made by John Jay at the New York ratifying convention: "Every government was imperfect, unless it had a power of preserving itself. Suppose that, by design or accident, the states should *neglect to appoint representatives;* certainly there should be some constitutional remedy for this evil. The obvious meaning of the paragraph was, that, if this neglect should take place, Congress should have power, by law, to support the government, and prevent the dissolution of the Union. Jay believed this was the design of the federal Convention." Constitutional provisions that impose affirmative duties on the States are hardly inconsistent with the notion of reserved powers.

Of course, the second part of the Times, Places and Manner Clause does grant a power rather than impose a duty. As its contrasting uses of the words "shall" and "may" confirm, however, the Clause grants power exclusively to Congress, not to the States. If the Clause did not exist at all, the States would still be able to prescribe the times, places, and manner of holding congressional elections; the deletion of the provision would simply deprive Congress of the power to override these state regulations.

The majority also mentions Article II, §1, cl. 2: "Each State shall appoint, in such Manner as the Legislature thereof may direct, a Number of Presidential Electors, equal to the whole Number of Senators and Representatives to which the State may be entitled in the Congress..." But this Clause has nothing to do with congressional elections, and in any event it too imposes an affirmative obligation on the States. In fact, some such bare-bones provision was essential in order to coordinate the creation of the electoral college. As mentioned above, moreover, it is uncontested that the States enjoy the reserved power to specify qualifications for the presidential electors who are chosen pursuant to this Clause.

Respondent Thornton seeks to buttress the majority's position with Article I, §2, cl. 1, which provides: "The House of Representatives shall be composed of Members chosen every second Year by the People of the several States, and the Electors in each State shall have the Qualifications requisite for Electors of the most numerous Branch of the State Legislature."

According to respondent Thornton, this provision "grants States authority to prescribe the qualifications of voters" in congressional elections. If anything, however, the Clause *limits* the power that the States would otherwise enjoy. Though it does leave States with the ability to control who may vote in congressional elections, it has the effect of restricting their authority to establish special requirements that do not apply in elections for the state legislature.

Our case law interpreting the Clause affirmatively supports the view that the States enjoy reserved powers over congressional elections. We have treated the Clause as a one-way ratchet: while the requirements for voting in congressional elections cannot be more onerous than the requirements for voting in elections for the most numerous branch of the state legislature, they can be less so. If this interpretation of the Clause is correct, it means that even with the Clause in place, States still have partial freedom to set special voting requirements for congressional elections. As this power is not granted in Article I, it must be among the "reserved" powers.

II

I take it to be established, then, that the people of Arkansas do enjoy "reserved" powers over the selection of their representatives in Congress. Purporting to exercise those reserved powers, they have agreed among themselves that the candidates covered by §3 of Amendment 73 - those whom they have already elected to three or more terms in the House of Representatives or to two or more terms in the Senate - should not be eligible to appear on the ballot for reelection, but should nonetheless be returned to Congress if enough voters are sufficiently enthusiastic about their candidacy to write in their names. Whatever one might think of the wisdom of this arrangement, we may not override the decision of the people of Arkansas unless something in the Federal Constitution deprives them of the power to enact such measures.

The majority settles on "the Qualifications Clauses" as the constitutional provisions that Amendment 73 violates. Because I do not read those provisions to impose any unstated prohibitions on the States, it is unnecessary for me to decide whether the majority is correct to identify Arkansas' ballot-access restriction with laws fixing true term limits or otherwise prescribing "qualifications" for congressional office. As I discuss in Part A below, the Qualifications Clauses are merely straightforward recitations of the minimum eligibility requirements that the Framers thought it essential for every Member of Congress to meet. They restrict state power only in that they prevent the States from *abolishing* all eligibility requirements for membership in Congress.

Because the text of the Qualifications Clauses does not support its position, the majority turns instead to its vision of the democratic principles that animated the Framers. But the majority's analysis goes to a question that is not before us: whether Congress has the power to prescribe qualifications for its own members. As I discuss in Part B, the democratic principles that contributed to the Framers' decision to withhold this power from Congress do not prove that the Framers also deprived the people of the States of their reserved authority to set eligibility requirements for their own representatives.

ONE

In Part C, I review the majority's more specific historical evidence. To the extent that they bear on this case, the records of the Philadelphia Convention affirmatively support my unwillingness to find hidden meaning in the Qualifications Clauses, while the surviving records from the ratification debates help neither side. As for the post-ratification period, five States supplemented the constitutional disqualifications in their very first election laws. The historical evidence thus refutes any notion that the Qualifications Clauses were generally understood to be exclusive. Yet the majority must establish just such an understanding in order to justify its position that the Clauses impose unstated prohibitions on the States and the people. In my view, the historical evidence is simply inadequate to warrant the majority's conclusion that the Qualifications Clauses mean anything more than what they say.

A

...At least on their face, then, the Qualifications Clauses do nothing to prohibit the people of a State from establishing additional eligibility requirements for their own representatives...

B

Although the Qualifications Clauses neither state nor imply the prohibition that it finds in them, the majority infers from the Framers' "democratic principles" that the Clauses must have been generally understood to preclude the people of the States and their state legislatures from prescribing any additional qualifications for their representatives in Congress. But the majority's evidence on this point establishes only two more modest propositions: (1) the Framers did not want the Federal Constitution itself to impose a broad set of disqualifications for congressional office, and (2) the Framers did not want the Federal Congress to be able to supplement the few disqualifications that the Constitution does set forth. The logical conclusion is simply that the Framers did not want the people of the States and their state legislatures to be constrained by too many qualifications imposed at the national level. The evidence does not support the majority's more sweeping conclusion that the Framers intended to bar the people of the States and their state legislatures from adopting additional eligibility requirements to help narrow their own choices…

C

In addition to its arguments about democratic principles, the majority asserts that more specific historical evidence supports its view that the Framers did not intend to permit supplementation of the Qualifications Clauses. But when one focuses on the distinction between congressional power to add qualifications for congressional office and the power of the people or their state legislatures to add such qualifications, one realizes that this assertion has little basis…

III

It is radical enough for the majority to hold that the Constitution implicitly precludes the people of the States from prescribing any eligibility requirements for the congressional candidates who seek their votes. This holding, after all, does not stop with negating the term limits that many States have seen fit to impose on their senators and representatives. Today's decision also means that no State may disqualify congressional candidates whom a court has found to be mentally incompetent who are currently in prison or who have past vote-fraud convictions. Likewise, after today's decision, the people of each State must leave open the possibility that they will trust someone with their vote in Congress even though they do not trust him with *a* vote in the election for Congress. See, *e.g.,* R.I.Gen.Laws § 17-14-1.2 (1988) (restricting candidacy to people "qualified to vote")…

Today's decision reads the Qualifications Clauses to impose substantial implicit prohibitions on the States and the people of the States.

ONE

I would not draw such an expansive negative inference from the fact that the Constitution requires Members of Congress to be a certain age, to be inhabitants of the States that they represent, and to have been United States citizens for a specified period. Rather, I would read the Qualifications Clauses to do no more than what they say. I respectfully dissent.

SUMMARY: Whether Congress could pass an ordinary statute to require term limits was not the issue in *Thornton*; however, it was discussed and the Court clearly stated that Congress does not have power under the Constitution, short of amendment, to do so. That is what we call dicta, meaning that because the commentary was not directly related to the issue before the court (the Arkansas constitutional attempt at term limits for Congress), it does not rise to the level of precedent or law. Dicta is, therefore, interesting but not binding. However, we also know that Congress would never pass such a statute or start the ball rolling to amend the Constitution on an issue that would limit their own power, so it is all but a foregone conclusion that the constitutionality of a congressional attempt at term limits will never reach the Supreme Court.

Short of a future constitutional convention to adopt term limits, this case, then, effectively puts the issue to rest. We were **one robe short** of getting it done through state law.

PLEA: If you are still interested in federal term limits for Congress, then you will have to get on the band wagon for a state initiated constitutional convention...or **vote** for the candidates that will get us **one more robe** on the High Court. That is much easier to accomplish and may someday get this case reversed. It is up to you. Don't let your vote defeat term limits forever.

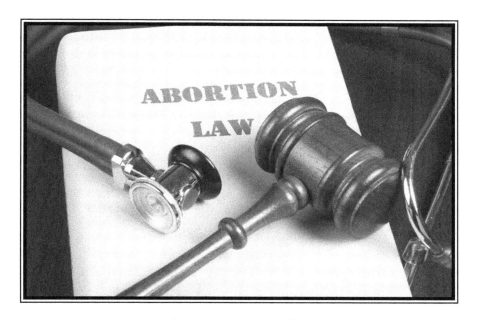

Chapter Nine

ONE ROBE LONG ON APRIL 18, 2007, BANNED ONE FORM OF LEGALIZED SLAUGHTER!

In 2000, by a **one robe** margin, one form of abortion almost too horrific to describe was allowed to stand by the Supreme Court in *Stenberg v. Carhart**. That procedure is known as partial-birth abortion.

Congress reacted to that decision with the Partial–Birth Abortion Ban Act of 2003. Although President Clinton had vetoed two prior attempts by Congress to put an end to this form of slaughter, President Bush signed this one into law.

This is a difficult read, not because it is an intellectual challenge - it is not - rather, it is difficult because our nation's callous regard for human life is so alarming. It reveals the awesome power of **one robe** and, therefore, the awesome power of your **one vote**.

Let's review *Gonzales v. Carhart*. Though it is a victory, it is difficult to believe we have to fight so hard for such little gain. For now, I suppose we must rejoice over any step we can achieve that moves us toward sanity, even if ever so slightly.

GONZALES v. CARHART
SUPREME COURT OF THE UNITED STATES
550 U.S. 124
April 18, 2007
[5 - 4]

OPINION: Kennedy/Roberts/Scalia/Thomas/Alito…These cases require us to consider the validity of the Partial–Birth Abortion Ban Act of 2003 (Act), a federal statute regulating abortion procedures…The Act refers to the Court's opinion in *Stenberg v. Carhart*, which also addressed the subject of abortion procedures used in the later stages of pregnancy. Compared to the state statute at issue in

ONE

Stenberg, the Act is more specific concerning the instances to which it applies and in this respect more precise in its coverage. We conclude the Act should be sustained against the objections lodged by the broad, facial attack brought against it.

> Facial attack: a challenge to a statute because it is unconstitutional as to all plaintiffs.

> An "as applied" challenge argues the statute is unconstitutional as applied to the actual plaintiff and his circumstances, not necessarily to all plaintiffs.

> *Stenberg v. Carhart* was a Supreme Court decision rendered in 2000 that found a Nebraska statute banning partial-birth abortion to be unconstitutional - you guessed it - by a 5 to 4 margin. Throughout this opinion, the Court will be referring to the federal response to *Stenberg*, the Partial–Birth Abortion Ban Act of 2003, as the "Act." It was a congressional attempt to remedy the problems the Court had with Nebraska's attempt. And, yes, the Carhart in this case is the same Carhart in the *Stenberg* case. He calls himself a doctor and government recognizes his license to practice medicine. He kills babies for a living.

In No. 05–380 (*Carhart*) respondents are LeRoy Carhart, William G. Fitzhugh, William H. Knorr, and Jill L. Vibhakar, doctors who perform second-trimester abortions. These doctors filed their complaint against the Attorney General of the United States in the United States District Court for the District of Nebraska. They challenged the constitutionality of the Act and sought a permanent injunction against its enforcement. In 2004,...the District Court granted a permanent injunction that prohibited the Attorney General from enforcing the Act in all cases but those in which there was no dispute the fetus was viable. The Court of Appeals for the Eighth Circuit affirmed. We granted certiorari.

> Certiorari: the act of granting permission to hear an appeal.

In No. 05–1382 (*Planned Parenthood*) respondents are Planned Parenthood Federation of America, Inc., Planned Parenthood Golden Gate, and the City and County of San Francisco. The Planned Parenthood entities sought to enjoin enforcement of the Act in a suit filed in the United States District Court for the Northern District of California…In 2004, the District Court… enjoined the Attorney General from enforcing the Act. The Court of Appeals for the Ninth Circuit affirmed. We granted certiorari.

> The previous two paragraphs introduce you to these consolidated cases being heard together because of their identical issues. Viability is a medical term. For a fetus to be viable, it must be capable of living outside the womb by either natural or artificial means.

I
A

The Act [bans a particular procedure to] end fetal life, so it is necessary here, as it was in *Stenberg,* to discuss abortion procedures in some detail. Three United States District Courts heard extensive evidence describing the procedures. In addition to the two courts involved in the instant cases the District Court for the Southern District of New York also considered the constitutionality of the Act. It found the Act unconstitutional and the Court of Appeals for the Second Circuit affirmed…We refer to the District Courts' exhaustive opinions in our own discussion of abortion procedures.

ONE

> Three District Courts and three Courts of Appeal struck this Act down. Thankfully, five Supreme Court justices saw it differently. Note that Planned Parenthood is a party to one of the cases. Their goal is to kill as many babies as possible. The rest of this opinion is very difficult for anyone who cares about life to read. But, it must be read. We cannot continue to bury our heads in the sand.

Abortion methods vary depending to some extent on the preferences of the physician and, of course, on the term of the pregnancy and the resulting stage of the unborn child's development. Between 85 and 90 percent of the approximately 1.3 million abortions performed each year in the United States take place in the first three months of pregnancy, which is to say in the first trimester. The most common first-trimester abortion method is **vacuum aspiration** (otherwise known as **suction curettage**) in which the physician vacuums out the embryonic tissue. Early in this trimester an alternative is to use medication, such as mifepristone (commonly known as RU–486), to terminate the pregnancy. The Act does not regulate these procedures.

Of the remaining abortions that take place each year, most occur in the second trimester. The surgical procedure referred to as "**dilation and evacuation**" or "**D & E**" is the usual abortion method in this trimester. Although individual techniques for performing D & E differ, the general steps are the same.

A doctor must first dilate the cervix at least to the extent needed to insert surgical instruments into the uterus and to maneuver them to evacuate the fetus. The steps taken to cause dilation differ by physician and gestational age of the fetus…

After sufficient dilation the surgical operation can commence. The woman is placed under general anesthesia or conscious sedation.

The doctor…inserts grasping forceps through the woman's cervix and into the uterus to grab the fetus. The doctor grips a fetal part with the forceps and pulls it back through the cervix and vagina, continuing to pull even after meeting resistance from the cervix. The friction causes the fetus to tear apart. For example, a leg might be ripped off the fetus as it is pulled through the cervix and out of the woman. The process of evacuating the fetus piece by piece continues until it has been completely removed. A doctor may make 10 to 15 passes with the forceps to evacuate the fetus in its entirety, though sometimes removal is completed with fewer passes. Once the fetus has been evacuated, the placenta and any remaining fetal material are suctioned or scraped out of the uterus. The doctor examines the different parts to ensure the entire fetal body has been removed.

Some doctors, especially later in the second trimester, may kill the fetus a day or two before performing the surgical evacuation.

They inject digoxin or potassium chloride into the fetus, the umbilical cord, or the amniotic fluid. Fetal demise may cause contractions and make greater dilation possible. Once dead, moreover, the fetus' body will soften, and its removal will be easier. Other doctors refrain from injecting chemical agents, believing it adds risk with little or no medical benefit.

> You may have thought the foregoing procedures were the ones banned by the Act of Congress being challenged. Wrong! The foregoing procedures are allowed! We are just now getting to the "more" inhumane procedures.

The abortion procedure that was the impetus for the numerous bans on "partial-birth abortion," including the Act, is a variation of this standard D & E (hereinafter **Dilation and Extraction**). The medical community has not reached unanimity on the appropriate name for this D & E variation. It has been referred to as "**intact D & E**," "**dilation and extraction**" (**D & X**), and "**intact D & X**." For discussion purposes this D & E variation will be referred to as intact D & E. The main difference between the two procedures is that in intact D & E a doctor extracts the fetus intact or largely intact with only a few passes. There are no comprehensive statistics indicating what percentage of all D & Es are performed in this manner...

In an intact D & E procedure the doctor extracts the fetus in a way conducive to pulling out its entire body, instead of ripping it apart. One doctor, for example, testified: "If I know I have good dilation and I reach in and the fetus starts to come out and I think I can accomplish it, the abortion with an intact delivery, then I use my forceps a little bit differently. I don't close them quite so much, and I just gently draw the tissue out attempting to have an intact delivery, if possible."

Rotating the fetus as it is being pulled decreases the odds of dismemberment. A doctor also "may use forceps to grasp a fetal part, pull it down, and re-grasp the fetus at a higher level - sometimes using both his hand and a forceps - to exert traction to retrieve the fetus intact until the head is lodged in the cervix."

Intact D & E gained public notoriety when, in 1992, Dr. Martin Haskell gave a presentation describing his method of performing the operation. In the usual intact D & E the fetus' head lodges in the cervix, and dilation is insufficient to allow it to pass. Haskell explained the next step as follows:

> "At this point, the right-handed surgeon slides the fingers of the left hand along the back of the fetus and 'hooks' the shoulders of the fetus with the index and ring fingers (palm down).

"While maintaining this tension, lifting the cervix and applying traction to the shoulders with the fingers of the left hand, the surgeon takes a pair of blunt curved Metzenbaum scissors in the right hand. He carefully advances the tip, curved down, along the spine and under his middle finger until he feels it contact the base of the skull under the tip of his middle finger.

"The surgeon then forces the scissors into the base of the skull or into the foramen magnum. **Having safely entered the skull**, he spreads the scissors to enlarge the opening.

> Josef Mengele was also recognized by the Third Reich as a licensed medical doctor. "Having safely entered the skull" of a living child? Sounds like something Dr. Mengele would enjoy. Folks, we have lost our way.

"The surgeon removes the scissors and introduces a suction catheter into this hole and evacuates the skull contents. With the catheter still in place, he applies traction to the fetus, removing it completely from the patient."

This is an abortion doctor's clinical description. Here is another description from a nurse who witnessed the same method performed on a 26.5-week fetus and who testified before the Senate Judiciary Committee:

> Witness this nurse's description of partial-birth abortion.

"Dr. Haskell went in with forceps and grabbed the baby's legs and pulled them down into the birth canal. Then he delivered the baby's body and the

> arms - everything but the head. The doctor kept the head right inside the uterus...
>
> "The baby's little fingers were clasping and unclasping, and his little feet were kicking. Then the doctor stuck the scissors in the back of his head, and the baby's arms jerked out, like a startle reaction, like a flinch, like a baby does when he thinks he is going to fall.
>
> "The doctor opened up the scissors, stuck a high-powered suction tube into the opening, and sucked the baby's brains out. Now the baby went completely limp...
>
> "He cut the umbilical cord and delivered the placenta. He threw the baby in a pan, along with the placenta and the instruments he had just used."

Dr. Haskell's approach is not the only method of killing the fetus once its head lodges in the cervix, and "the process has evolved" since his presentation. Another doctor, for example, squeezes the skull after it has been pierced "so that enough brain tissue exudes to allow the head to pass through." Still other physicians reach into the cervix with their forceps and crush the fetus' skull. Others continue to pull the fetus out of the woman until it disarticulates at the neck, in effect decapitating it. These doctors then grasp the head with forceps, crush it, and remove it.

Some doctors performing an intact D & E attempt to remove the fetus without collapsing the skull. Yet one doctor would not allow delivery of a live fetus younger than 24 weeks because "the objective of his procedure is to perform an abortion," not a birth. The doctor thus answered in the affirmative when asked whether he would "hold the fetus' head on the internal side of the cervix in order to collapse the skull" and kill the fetus before it is born. Another doctor testified he crushes a fetus' skull not only to reduce its size but also to ensure the fetus is dead before it is removed. For the staff to have to deal with a fetus that has "some viability to it, some movement of limbs," according to this doctor, "is always a difficult situation."

D & E and intact D & E are not the only second-trimester abortion methods. Doctors also may abort a fetus through medical induction. The doctor medicates the woman to induce labor, and contractions occur to deliver the fetus. Induction, which unlike D & E should occur in a hospital, can last as little as 6 hours but can take longer than 48. It accounts for about 5 percent of second-trimester abortions before 20 weeks of gestation and 15 percent of those after 20 weeks. Doctors turn to two other methods of second-trimester abortion, hysterotomy and hysterectomy, only in emergency situations because they carry increased risk of complications. In a hysterotomy, as in a cesarean section, the doctor removes the fetus by making an incision through the abdomen and uterine wall to gain access to the uterine cavity. A hysterectomy requires the removal of the entire uterus. These two procedures represent about 0.07 percent of second-trimester abortions.

B

After Dr. Haskell's procedure received public attention, with ensuing and increasing public concern, bans on "partial-birth abortion" proliferated. By the time of the *Stenberg* decision, about 30 States had enacted bans designed to prohibit the procedure. In 1996, Congress also acted to ban partial-birth abortion. **President Clinton vetoed** the congressional legislation, and the Senate failed to override the veto. Congress approved another bill banning the procedure in 1997, but **President Clinton again vetoed it**. In 2003, after this

ONE

Court's decision in *Stenberg,* Congress passed the Act at issue here. On November 5, 2003, **President Bush signed the Act into law.** It was to take effect the following day.

> Don't ever say your vote doesn't matter. This paragraph tells me all I need to know about President Clinton. I have no respect for him as a leader. Hmmm! President Bush, however, got the job done!

The Act responded to *Stenberg* in two ways. First,...Congress found, among other things, that "a moral, medical, and ethical consensus exists that the practice of performing a partial-birth abortion...is a gruesome and inhumane procedure that is never medically necessary and should be prohibited."

Second, and more relevant here, the Act's language differs from that of the Nebraska statute struck down in *Stenberg*. The operative provisions of the Act provide in relevant part:

> "(a) Any physician who...knowingly performs a partial-birth abortion and thereby kills a human fetus shall be fined...or imprisoned not more than 2 years, or both. This subsection does not apply to a partial-birth abortion that is necessary to save the life of a mother whose life is endangered by a physical disorder, physical illness, or physical injury, including a life-endangering physical condition caused by or arising from the pregnancy itself...
>
> "(1) the term 'partial-birth abortion' means an abortion in which the person performing the abortion—
>
> "(A) deliberately and intentionally vaginally delivers a living fetus until, in the case of a head-first presentation, the entire fetal head is outside the body

of the mother, or, in the case of breech presentation, any part of the fetal trunk past the navel is outside the body of the mother, for the purpose of performing an overt act that the person knows will kill the partially delivered living fetus; and

"(B) performs the overt act, other than completion of delivery, that kills the partially delivered living fetus...

"(e) A woman upon whom a partial-birth abortion is performed may not be prosecuted under this section, for a conspiracy to violate this section, or for an offense under section 2, 3, or 4 of this title based on a violation of this section..."

C

The District Court in [this case] concluded the Act was unconstitutional for two reasons. First, it determined the Act was unconstitutional because it lacked an exception allowing the procedure where necessary for the <u>health</u> of the mother. Second, the District Court found the Act deficient because it covered not merely intact D & E but also certain other D & Es.

> Until this case, any procedure that caused less discomfort to the mother was permissible as being necessary "for her health."

The Court of Appeals for the Eighth Circuit addressed only the lack of a health exception. The court began its analysis with what it saw as the appropriate question - "whether 'substantial medical authority' supports the medical necessity of the banned procedure." This was the proper framework, according to the Court of Appeals, because "when a lack of consensus exists in the medical community, the Constitution requires legislatures to err on the side of protecting

ONE

women's health by including a health exception." The court rejected the Attorney General's attempt to demonstrate changed evidentiary circumstances since *Stenberg* and considered itself bound by *Stenberg's* conclusion that a health exception was required. It invalidated the Act.

This is the first case to uphold the elimination of a "health exception" for the mother in an abortion statute. Heretofore, if there was any reason why a procedure could be advantageous to a woman, the fetus automatically lost.

D

The District Court in *Planned Parenthood* concluded the Act was unconstitutional "because it (1) posed an undue burden on a woman's ability to choose a second trimester abortion; (2) was unconstitutionally vague; and (3) required a health exception as set forth by....*Stenberg*."

The Court of Appeals for the Ninth Circuit agreed. Like the Court of Appeals for the Eighth Circuit, it concluded the absence of a health exception rendered the Act unconstitutional. The court interpreted *Stenberg* to require a health exception unless "there is *consensus in the medical community* that the banned procedure is never medically necessary to preserve the health of women." Even after applying a deferential standard of review to Congress' factual findings, the Court of Appeals determined "substantial disagreement exists in the medical community regarding whether" the procedures prohibited by the Act are ever necessary to preserve a woman's health.

The Court of Appeals concluded further that the Act placed an undue burden on a woman's ability to obtain a second-trimester abortion…

II

The principles set forth in the joint opinion in *Planned Parenthood v. Casey** did not find support from all those who join the instant opinion. Whatever one's views concerning the *Casey* joint opinion, it is evident a premise central to its conclusion - that the government has a legitimate and substantial interest in preserving and promoting fetal life - would be repudiated were the Court now to affirm the judgments of the Courts of Appeals.

Casey involved a challenge to *Roe v. Wade**. The opinion contains this summary:

> "It must be stated at the outset and with clarity that *Roe's* essential holding, the holding we reaffirm, has three parts. First is a recognition of the right of the woman to choose to have an abortion before viability and to obtain it without undue interference from the State. Before viability, the State's interests are not strong enough to support a prohibition of abortion or the imposition of a substantial obstacle to the woman's effective right to elect the procedure. Second is a confirmation of the State's power to restrict abortions after fetal viability, if the law contains exceptions for pregnancies which endanger the woman's life or health. And third is the principle that the State has legitimate interests from the outset of the pregnancy in protecting the health of the woman and the life of the fetus that may become a child. These principles do not contradict one another; and we adhere to each."

Though all three holdings are implicated in the instant cases, it is the third that requires the most extended discussion; for we must determine whether the Act furthers the legitimate interest of the

Government in protecting the life of the fetus that may become a child.

To implement its holding, *Casey* rejected both *Roe's* rigid trimester framework and the interpretation of *Roe* that considered all previability regulations of abortion unwarranted. On this point *Casey* overruled the holdings in two cases because they undervalued the State's interest in potential life.

We assume the following principles for the purposes of this opinion. Before viability, a State "may not prohibit any woman from making the ultimate decision to terminate her pregnancy." It also may not impose upon this right an undue burden, which exists if a regulation's "purpose or effect is to place a substantial obstacle in the path of a woman seeking an abortion before the fetus attains viability." On the other hand, "regulations which do no more than create a structural mechanism by which the State, or the parent or guardian of a minor, may express profound respect for the life of the unborn are permitted, if they are not a substantial obstacle to the woman's exercise of the right to choose." *Casey*, in short, struck a balance. The balance was central to its holding. We now apply its standard to the cases at bar.

III

We begin with a determination of the Act's operation and effect. A straightforward reading of the Act's text demonstrates its purpose and the scope of its provisions: It regulates and proscribes, with exceptions or qualifications to be discussed, performing the intact D & E procedure...

We conclude that the Act is [constitutional.]

A

The Act punishes "knowingly performing" a "partial-birth abortion" [and] defines the unlawful abortion in explicit terms.

First, the person performing the abortion must "vaginally deliver a living fetus." The Act does not restrict an abortion procedure involving the delivery of an expired fetus. The Act, furthermore, is inapplicable to abortions that do not involve vaginal delivery (for instance, hysterotomy or hysterectomy). The Act does apply both previability and postviability because, by common understanding and scientific terminology, a fetus is a living organism while within the womb, whether or not it is viable outside the womb. We do not understand this point to be contested by the parties.

Second, the Act's definition of partial-birth abortion requires the fetus to be delivered "until, in the case of a head-first presentation, the entire fetal head is outside the body of the mother, or, in the case of breech presentation, any part of the fetal trunk past the navel is outside the body of the mother." The Attorney General concedes, and we agree, that if an abortion procedure does not involve the delivery of a living fetus to one of these "anatomical landmarks" - where, depending on the presentation, either the fetal head or the fetal trunk past the navel is outside the body of the mother - the prohibitions of the Act do not apply.

It is so sad we have come to this. It is constitutional to rip the baby apart as long as it is done internally where no one can see such atrocity. That, of course, makes no difference to the deceased. Apparently the Act makes Congress feel better. Sorry for the cynicism. It is truly difficult to call this case a victory, but it is the most we have been able to muster for a long, long time in this horrific area of the law.

ONE

Third, to fall within the Act, a doctor must perform an "overt act, other than completion of delivery, that kills the partially delivered living fetus." For purposes of criminal liability, the overt act causing the fetus' death must be separate from delivery. And the overt act must occur after the delivery to an anatomical landmark. This is because the Act proscribes killing "the partially delivered" fetus, which, when read in context, refers to a fetus that has been delivered to an anatomical landmark.

Fourth, the Act contains scienter requirements concerning all the actions involved in the prohibited abortion. To begin with, the physician must have "deliberately and intentionally" delivered the fetus to one of the Act's anatomical landmarks. If a living fetus is delivered past the critical point by accident or inadvertence, the Act is inapplicable. In addition, the fetus must have been delivered "for the purpose of performing an overt act that the doctor knows will kill it." If either intent is absent, no crime has occurred. This follows from the general principle that where scienter is required no crime is committed absent the requisite state of mind.

> Scienter and mens rea are Latin terms that refer to a state of mind, a form of intent. So, I repeat. This victory isn't much, but we should rejoice over any victory at this point. A so-called "doctor" can beat a criminal charge under the Act if he persuades a jury it was a "mistake" to have delivered the baby past the critical point before ripping her limbs off and sucking her brains out. Once again, a tie (less than proof of intent beyond a reasonable doubt) goes to the doctor. Hard to believe anyone would ever be convicted under this Act!

B

Respondents contend the Act is unconstitutionally vague...As generally stated, the void-for-vagueness doctrine requires that a penal statute define the criminal offense with sufficient definiteness that ordinary people can understand what conduct is prohibited and in a manner that does not encourage arbitrary and discriminatory enforcement. The Act satisfies both requirements...

C

We next determine whether the Act imposes an undue burden ... The Act prohibits intact D & E; and, notwithstanding respondents' arguments, it does not prohibit the D & E procedure in which the fetus is removed in parts.

1

The Act prohibits a doctor from intentionally performing an intact D & E. The dual prohibitions of the Act, both of which are necessary for criminal liability, correspond with the steps generally undertaken during this type of procedure.

First, a doctor delivers the fetus until its head lodges in the cervix, which is usually past the anatomical landmark for a breech presentation. Second, the doctor proceeds to pierce the fetal skull with scissors or crush it with forceps. This step satisfies the overt-act requirement because it kills the fetus and is distinct from delivery. The Act's intent requirements, however, limit its reach to those physicians who carry out the intact D & E after intending to undertake both steps at the outset.

The Act excludes most D & Es in which the fetus is removed in pieces, not intact. If the doctor intends to remove the fetus in parts from the outset, the doctor will not have the requisite intent to incur criminal liability. A doctor performing a standard D & E procedure can often "take about 10–15 passes through the uterus to remove the entire fetus." Removing the fetus in this manner does not violate the Act because the doctor will not have delivered the living fetus to one of the anatomical landmarks or committed an additional overt act that kills the fetus after partial delivery…

Congress, it is apparent, responded to these concerns because the Act departs in material ways from the statute in *Stenberg*. It adopts the phrase "delivers a living fetus" instead of "delivering…a living unborn child, or a substantial portion thereof." The Act's language, unlike the statute in *Stenberg,* expresses the usual meaning of "deliver" when used in connection with "fetus," namely, extraction of an entire fetus rather than removal of fetal pieces…The Act thus displaces the interpretation of "delivering" dictated by the Nebraska statute's reference to a "substantial portion" of the fetus…Here, unlike in *Stenberg,* the language does not require a departure from the ordinary meaning. D & E does not involve the delivery of a fetus because it requires the removal of fetal parts that are ripped from the fetus as they are pulled through the cervix.

As stated, this Act does not ban "ripping fetal parts from the fetus" because that procedure (D&E) takes place before any degree of "delivery." This nation participates in an ongoing Holocaust of our own making.

The identification of specific anatomical landmarks to which the fetus must be partially delivered also differentiates the Act from the statute at issue in *Stenberg*…

By adding an overt-act requirement Congress sought further to meet the Court's objections to the state statute considered in *Stenberg*…

2

Contrary arguments by respondents are unavailing…

IV

Under the principles accepted as controlling here, the Act, as we have interpreted it, would be unconstitutional "if its purpose or effect is to place a substantial obstacle in the path of a woman seeking an abortion before the fetus attains viability." The abortions affected by the Act's regulations take place both previability and postviability; so the quoted language and the undue burden analysis it relies upon are applicable. The question is whether the Act, measured by its text in this facial attack, imposes a substantial obstacle to late-term, but previability, abortions. The Act does not on its face impose a substantial obstacle, and we reject this further facial challenge to its validity.

A

The Act's purposes are set forth in recitals preceding its operative provisions. A description of the prohibited abortion procedure demonstrates the rationale for the congressional enactment. The Act proscribes a method of abortion in which a fetus is killed just inches before completion of the birth process. Congress stated as follows: "Implicitly approving such a brutal and inhumane procedure by choosing not to prohibit it will further coarsen society to the humanity of not only newborns, but all vulnerable and innocent human life, making it increasingly difficult to protect such life." The Act expresses respect for the dignity of human life…

Although I rejoice in this outcome, it is so hard to refer to the motivation of Congress as being one of respect for the dignity of human life, especially when the law does not recognize a fetus as a "person." That we permit any form of such brutality to continue should embarrass us as a nation. This "Partial-Birth Abortion Ban Act" should more appropriately be named the "How-Much-Atrocity-Can-We-Americans-Stomach Act."

ONE

Where it has a rational basis to act, and it does not impose an undue burden, the State may use its regulatory power to bar certain procedures and substitute others, all in furtherance of its legitimate interests in regulating the medical profession in order to promote respect for life, including life of the unborn.

…Congress determined that the abortion methods it proscribed had a "disturbing similarity to the killing of a newborn infant" and thus it was concerned with "drawing a bright line that clearly distinguishes abortion and infanticide."…

Respect for human life finds an ultimate expression in the bond of love the mother has for her child. The Act recognizes this reality as well. Whether to have an abortion requires a difficult and painful moral decision. While we find no reliable data to measure the phenomenon, it seems unexceptionable to conclude some women come to regret their choice to abort the infant life they once created and sustained. Severe depression and loss of esteem can follow.

In a decision so fraught with emotional consequence some doctors may prefer not to disclose precise details of the means that will be used, confining themselves to the required statement of risks the procedure entails. From one standpoint this ought not to be surprising. Any number of patients facing imminent surgical procedures would prefer not to hear all details, lest the usual anxiety preceding invasive medical procedures become the more intense. This is likely the case with the abortion procedures here in issue. ("Most of the plaintiffs' experts acknowledged that they do not describe to their patients what the D & E and intact D & E procedures entail in clear and precise terms.")

It is, however, precisely this lack of information concerning the way in which the fetus will be killed that is of legitimate concern to the State. ("States are free to enact laws to provide a reasonable framework for a woman to make a decision that has such profound and lasting meaning.") The State has an interest in ensuring so grave a choice is well informed. It is self-evident that a mother who comes to regret her choice to abort must struggle with grief more anguished and sorrow more profound when she learns, only after the event, what she once did not know: that she allowed a doctor to pierce the skull and vacuum the fast-developing brain of her unborn child, a child assuming the human form.

It is a reasonable inference that a necessary effect of the regulation and the knowledge it conveys will be to encourage some women to carry the infant to full term, thus reducing the absolute number of late-term abortions. The medical profession, furthermore, may find different and less shocking methods to abort the fetus in the second trimester, thereby accommodating legislative demand. The State's interest in respect for life is advanced by the dialogue that better informs the political and legal systems, the medical profession, expectant mothers, and society as a whole of the consequences that follow from a decision to elect a late-term abortion.

It is objected that the standard D & E is in some respects as brutal, if not more, than the intact D & E, so that the legislation accomplishes little. What we have already said, however, shows ample justification for the regulation. Partial-birth abortion, as defined by the Act, differs from a standard D & E because the former occurs when the fetus is partially outside the mother to the point of one of the Act's anatomical landmarks. It was reasonable for Congress to think that partial-birth abortion, more than standard D & E, "undermines the public's perception of the appropriate role of a physician during the delivery process, and perverts a process during which life is brought into the world."…In sum, we reject the contention that the congressional purpose of the Act was "to place a substantial obstacle in the path of a woman seeking an abortion."

B

The Act's furtherance of legitimate government interests bears upon, but does not resolve, the next question: whether the Act has the effect of imposing an unconstitutional burden on the abortion right because it does not allow use of the barred procedure where "necessary, in appropriate medical judgment, for the preservation of the...**health** of the mother." The prohibition in the Act would be unconstitutional, under precedents we here assume to be controlling, if it "subjected women to significant health risks."...

Respondents presented evidence that intact D & E may be the safest method of abortion, for reasons similar to those adduced in *Stenberg*. Abortion doctors testified, for example, that intact D & E decreases the risk of cervical laceration or uterine perforation because it requires fewer passes into the uterus with surgical instruments and does not require the removal of bony fragments of the dismembered fetus, fragments that may be sharp. Respondents also presented evidence that intact D & E was safer both because it reduces the risks that fetal parts will remain in the uterus and because it takes less time to complete. Respondents, in addition, proffered evidence that intact D & E was safer for women with certain medical conditions or women with fetuses that had certain anomalies.

These contentions were contradicted by other doctors who testified in the District Courts and before Congress. They concluded that the alleged health advantages were based on speculation without scientific studies to support them. They considered D & E always to be a safe alternative...

The medical uncertainty over whether the Act's prohibition creates significant health risks provides a sufficient basis to conclude in this facial attack that the Act does not impose an undue burden.

The conclusion that the Act does not impose an undue burden is supported by other considerations. Alternatives are available to the prohibited procedure…In addition the Act's prohibition only applies to the delivery of "a living fetus." If the intact D & E procedure is truly necessary in some circumstances, it appears likely an injection that kills the fetus is an alternative under the Act that allows the doctor to perform the procedure…

The Act is not invalid on its face where there is uncertainty over whether the barred procedure is ever necessary to preserve a woman's health, given the availability of other abortion procedures that are considered to be safe alternatives.

V

…Respondents have not demonstrated that the Act…is void for vagueness or that it imposes an undue burden on a woman's right to abortion based on its overbreadth or lack of a health exception. For these reasons the judgments of the Courts of Appeals for the Eighth and Ninth Circuits are reversed.

CONCURRENCE: Thomas/Scalia…I join the Court's opinion because it accurately applies current jurisprudence…I write separately to reiterate my view that the Court's abortion jurisprudence, including…*Roe v. Wade,* has no basis in the Constitution…

> Justices Thomas and Scalia want to make it clear that they believe *Roe v. Wade* was wrongly decided. They do not believe the federal government has any business in what should be left to the states.

ONE

DISSENT: Ginsburg/Stevens/Souter/Breyer...Today's decision is alarming...

> I agree. It is alarming that we are discussing any of this as being "acceptable."

It tolerates, indeed applauds, federal intervention to ban nationwide a procedure found necessary and proper in certain cases by the American College of Obstetricians and Gynecologists. It blurs the line...between previability and postviability abortions. And, for the first time since *Roe,* the Court blesses a prohibition with no exception safeguarding a woman's health.

I dissent...Retreating from prior rulings that abortion restrictions cannot be imposed absent an exception safeguarding a woman's health, the Court upholds an Act that surely would not survive under the close scrutiny that previously attended state-decreed limitations on a woman's reproductive choices.

I
A

As *Casey* comprehended, at stake in cases challenging abortion restrictions is a woman's "control over her own destiny." "There was a time, not so long ago," when women were "regarded as the center of home and family life, with attendant special responsibilities that precluded full and independent legal status under the Constitution." Those views, this Court made clear in *Casey,* "are no longer consistent with our understanding of the family, the individual, or the Constitution." Women, it is now acknowledged, have the talent, capacity, and right "to participate equally in the economic and social life of the nation." Their ability to realize their full potential, the Court recognized, is intimately connected to "their ability to control their reproductive lives." Thus, legal challenges to undue restrictions on abortion procedures do not seek to vindicate some generalized notion of privacy; rather, they center on a woman's autonomy to determine her life's course, and thus to enjoy equal citizenship stature.

In keeping with this comprehension of the right to reproductive choice, the Court has consistently required that laws regulating abortion, at any stage of pregnancy and in all cases, safeguard a woman's health…

"A statute that altogether forbids intact D & E…consequently must contain a health exception."…

> These four liberal justices would clearly permit any procedure, no matter how heinous, as long as the physician believed the procedure to be in his own patient's interest. In other words, the fetus always loses.

C

…Intact D & E, plaintiffs' experts explained, provides safety benefits over D & E by dismemberment for several reasons: *First,* intact D & E minimizes the number of times a physician must insert instruments through the cervix and into the uterus, and thereby reduces the risk of trauma to, and perforation of, the cervix and uterus - the most serious complication associated with nonintact D & E. *Second,* removing the fetus intact, instead of dismembering it *in utero,* decreases the likelihood that fetal tissue will be retained in the uterus, a condition that can cause infection, hemorrhage, and infertility. *Third,* intact D & E diminishes the chances of exposing the patient's tissues to sharp bony fragments sometimes resulting from dismemberment of the fetus. *Fourth,* intact D & E takes less operating time

ONE

than D & E by dismemberment, and thus may reduce bleeding, the risk of infection, and complications relating to anesthesia...

> If the object is to prevent all conceivable harm to the mother, according to Ginsburg, why not just wait until the baby is born, then suffocate it before throwing it in the garbage? Given the foregoing justifications for partial-birth abortion, it's a fair question, is it not?

II
A

...As another reason for upholding the ban, the Court emphasizes that the Act does not proscribe the nonintact D & E procedure. But why not, one might ask. Nonintact D & E could equally be characterized as "brutal," involving as it does "tearing a fetus apart" and "ripping off" its limbs. "The notion that either of these two equally gruesome procedures...is more akin to infanticide than the other, or that the State furthers any legitimate interest by banning one but not the other, is simply irrational."

> Here is a rare instance where I agree with Justice Ginsburg. However, her solution is to allow both forms of atrocity to continue. That is where we part company.

Delivery of an intact, albeit nonviable, fetus warrants special condemnation, the Court maintains, because a fetus that is not dismembered resembles an infant. But so, too, does a fetus delivered intact after it is terminated by injection a day or two before the surgical evacuation or a fetus delivered through medical induction or cesarean. Yet, the availability of those procedures - along with D & E by dismemberment - the Court says, saves the ban on intact D & E from a declaration of unconstitutionality. Never mind that the procedures deemed acceptable might put a woman's health at greater risk.

141

Ultimately, the Court admits that "moral concerns" are at work, concerns that could yield prohibitions on any abortion…Notably, the concerns expressed are untethered to any ground genuinely serving the Government's interest in preserving life. By allowing such concerns to carry the day and case, overriding fundamental rights, the Court dishonors our precedent…

> I have little doubt that this woman would approve of infanticide.

B

…The Court's hostility to the right *Roe* and *Casey* secured is not concealed. Throughout, the opinion refers to obstetrician-gynecologists and surgeons who perform abortions not by the titles of their medical specialties, but by the pejorative label "abortion doctor." A fetus is described as an "unborn child," and as a "baby"; second-trimester, previability abortions are referred to as "late-term"; and the reasoned medical judgments of highly trained doctors are dismissed as "preferences" motivated by "mere convenience."…

> She just can't handle the truth. She prefers political correctness to reality.

IV

…Congress imposed a ban despite our clear prior holdings that the State cannot proscribe an abortion procedure when its use is necessary to protect a woman's health…In sum, the notion that the Partial–Birth Abortion Ban Act furthers any legitimate governmental interest is, quite simply, irrational…In candor, the Act, and the Court's defense of it, cannot be understood as anything other than an effort to chip away at a right declared again and again by this Court - and with increasing comprehension of its centrality to women's lives. When "a statute burdens constitutional rights and all that can be said on its behalf is that it is the vehicle that legislators have chosen for expressing their hostility to those rights, the burden is undue."

For the reasons stated, I dissent from the Court's disposition and would affirm the judgments before us for review.

SUMMARY: "One robe" saved us (even though marginally) from ourselves. The Supreme Court held there is a limit to legalized slaughter and the limit Congress set in the Partial-Birth Abortion Ban Act of 2003 is constitutionally valid.

COMMENT: I have used harsh terms in my commentary. And, yet, they are terms that speak to reality. I am a pro-life purist. That life, in my world, is a child of God from the moment of fertilization. And, therefore, I see little difference between the morning-after pill and partial-birth abortion – the child dies either way.

Let there be no mistake, however, that I understand the harsh realities of real life situations. I realize, first, that if I or my family ever has to face the abortion option, in spite of my beliefs, I may find myself, in certain circumstances, approving a decision that contradicts my principles. That doesn't mean the principles are wrong – it just means we are all human.

So, I would never attempt to judge the soul of anyone who has had an abortion or will have an abortion. That is most certainly not my job. But, this intact D&E procedure defines atrocity. Perhaps a mother who waits so long to abort that she puts herself at risk by not having an intact D&E should have made her decision much sooner and, having failed that, proceed to birth. There comes a point at which even this depraved society must establish a limit. This Court has done so. God help us!

PLEA: "One less robe" in the future will bring back intact D&E as an acceptable method of killing babies. If you vote for a president (with nomination power) who will likely nominate liberal candidates to the Supreme Court when seats become vacant or for senators (with confirmation power) who will likely confirm such nominees or you stay home or vote for a third party, a reversal of this case will be on your shoulders. **One less robe** will tear our souls apart, limb by limb. The next time you decide it is too inconvenient to vote, think again!

Chapter Ten

ONE ROBE LONG ON JUNE 26, 2008, COULD SAVE YOUR LIFE SOMEDAY!

On June 26, 2008, your Second Amendment right to bear arms to defend yourself in your home (if you live in the District of Columbia) was preserved because constitutional jurists out-numbered those that would take guns away from law-abiding citizens. Chief Justice Roberts and Associate Justices Scalia, Kennedy, Thomas and Alito voted in favor of your right to "keep and bear" arms; Associate Justices Stevens, Souter, Ginsburg and Breyer did not.

One robe was the difference in *District of Columbia v. Heller**!

Because this case involved a federal ban on guns, a law applicable only to D.C., it would take another case to determine whether state or city laws banning handguns entirely would also fail. On June 28, 2010, that case (*McDonald v. Chicago**) held that Second Amendment rights also apply to states and non-federal jurisdictions when laws in Chicago and Oak Park, similar to the ban in D.C., were struck down by the same 5-4 margin, but with a slightly different court. Justice Souter, who had retired after the *Heller* decision, was replaced when the Senate confirmed an Obama nominee, Sonia Sotomayor, by a vote of 68-31, before the *McDonald* decision. It was no surprise that President Obama's nominee would vote against your Second Amendment right. Please, people. Understand that the most important votes you will ever make are for presidents that nominate federal justices that understand their oath to uphold the Constitution and for senators that will confirm those nominations.

Had these cases gone the other way, I am convinced there would have been a strong and likely successful movement to amend the Constitution to then restore Second Amendment rights. Thankfully, at least for now, that is not necessary.

But, don't kid yourselves. If the make-up of the Court shifts by **one oath-breaking robe**, these cases will be reversed and, in the absence of a subsequent amendment, your right to defend yourself with "arms" will be shot down!

If you don't vote for constitutionally conservative senators and presidents that honor the Constitution (or if you stay home or vote for a third party), you may play a role in disarming law-abiding citizens. Wake up!

Let's take a look at the *Heller* decision. It is heavily edited due to its length. However, you may look at the long version on our website. See the Appendix for instructions.

I believe the Second Amendment is the most awkwardly worded provision in the Constitution. I also believe the majority got this one right. However, even I admit the dissenters make some points. Enjoy the power of knowledge!

DISTRICT OF COLUMBIA v. HELLER
SUPREME COURT OF THE UNITED STATES
554 US 570
June 26, 2008
[5 – 4]

OPINION: Scalia/ Roberts/ Kennedy/ Thomas/ Alito…We consider whether a District of Columbia prohibition on the possession of usable handguns in the home violates the Second Amendment to the Constitution…

II

We turn first to the meaning of the Second Amendment.

A

The Second Amendment provides: "A well regulated Militia, being necessary to the security of a free State, the right of the people to keep and bear Arms, shall not be infringed."...

The two sides in this case have set out very different interpretations of the Amendment. Petitioners and today's dissenting justices believe that it protects only the right to possess and carry a firearm in connection with militia service. Respondent argues that it protects an individual right to possess a firearm unconnected with service in a militia, and to use that arm for traditionally lawful purposes, such as self-defense within the home...

Operative Clause.

a. "Right of the People." The first salient feature of the operative clause is that it codifies a "right of the people." The unamended Constitution and the Bill of Rights use the phrase "right of the people" two other times, in the First Amendment's Assembly-and-Petition Clause and in the Fourth Amendment's Search-and-Seizure Clause. The Ninth Amendment uses very similar terminology ("The enumeration in the Constitution, of certain rights, shall not be construed to deny or disparage others retained by the people"). All three of these instances unambiguously refer to individual rights, not "collective" rights, or rights that may be exercised only through participation in some corporate body.

Three provisions of the Constitution refer to "the people" in a context other than "rights" - the famous preamble ("We the people"), §2 of Article I (providing that "the people" will choose members of the House), and the Tenth Amendment (providing that those powers not given the Federal Government remain with "the States" or "the people"). Those provisions arguably refer to "the people" acting

ONE

collectively - but they deal with the exercise or reservation of powers, not rights. Nowhere else in the Constitution does a "right" attributed to "the people" refer to anything other than an individual right.

What is more, in all six other provisions of the Constitution that mention "the people," the term unambiguously refers to all members of the political community, not an unspecified subset...This contrasts markedly with the phrase "the militia" in the prefatory clause. As we will describe below, the "militia" in colonial America consisted of a subset of "the people" - those who were male, able bodied, and within a certain age range. Reading the Second Amendment as protecting only the right to "keep and bear Arms" in an organized militia therefore fits poorly with the operative clause's description of the holder of that right as "the people."

> That does seem to make very good sense. To put it differently, I believe the Court is saying that if the "right" was intended to be limited to that subsection of "the people" who were in the militia, the amendment would not read: A well regulated Militia, being necessary to the security of a free State, the right of the people to keep and bear Arms, shall not be infringed. Instead, it would read: A well regulated Militia, being necessary to the security of a free State, the right of the people <u>in the militia</u> to keep and bear Arms, shall not be infringed. I'm not sure I would call it a "strong presumption," but it <u>is</u> a point favoring the Majority.

We start therefore with a strong presumption that the Second Amendment right is exercised individually and belongs to all Americans.

b. "Keep and bear Arms." We move now from the holder of the right - "the people" - to the substance of the right: "to keep and bear Arms."...

The 18th-century meaning is no different from the meaning today...

The term was applied, then as now, to weapons that were not specifically designed for military use and were not employed in a military capacity...

Some have made the argument, bordering on the frivolous, that only those arms in existence in the 18th century are protected by the Second Amendment. We do not interpret constitutional rights that way. Just as the First Amendment protects modern forms of communications (*Reno v. American Civil Liberties Union* (1997) - [internet obscenity]), and the Fourth Amendment applies to modern forms of search, (*Kyllo v. United States** (2001) - [thermal imaging]), the Second Amendment extends...to all instruments that constitute bearable arms, even those that were not in existence at the time of the founding.

We turn to the phrases "keep arms" and "bear arms."...The most natural reading of "keep arms" in the Second Amendment is to "have weapons."

The phrase "keep arms" was not prevalent in the written documents of the founding period that we have found, but there are a few examples, all of which favor viewing the right to "keep arms" as an individual right unconnected with militia service...

From our review of founding-era sources, we conclude that this natural meaning was also the meaning that "bear arms" had in the 18th century. In numerous instances, "bear arms" was unambiguously used to refer to the carrying of weapons outside of an organized militia. The most prominent examples are those most relevant to the Second Amendment: Nine state constitutional provisions written in the 18th century or the first two decades of the 19th, which

ONE

enshrined a right of citizens to "bear arms in defense of themselves and the state" or "bear arms in defense of himself and the state." It is clear from those formulations that "bear arms" did not refer only to carrying a weapon in an organized military unit. Justice James Wilson interpreted the Pennsylvania Constitution's arms-bearing right, for example, as a recognition of the natural right of defense "of one's person or house" - what he called the law of "self-preservation." See also T. Walker, Introduction to American Law (1837) ("Thus the right of self-defence is guaranteed by the Ohio constitution")...That was also the interpretation of those state constitutional provisions adopted by pre-Civil War state courts. These provisions demonstrate - again, in the most analogous linguistic context - that "bear arms" was not limited to the carrying of arms in a militia...

> It may well be true that the phrase "bear arms" was not limited to militia use.

> However, one might ask the tough question: "If nine state constitutions written in the late 1700s could clearly use the phrase "bear arms in defense of themselves and the state," why couldn't the Framers have done so, assuming that was their intent? One could argue that the evidence of the majority actually favors the dissenters on this point. What do you think?

In any event, the meaning of "bear arms" that petitioners and JUSTICE STEVENS propose...[is] a hybrid definition, whereby "bear arms" connotes the actual carrying of arms...but only in the service of an organized militia. No dictionary has ever adopted that definition, and we have been apprised of no source that indicates that it carried that meaning at the time of the founding. But it is easy to see why petitioners and the dissent are driven to the hybrid definition. Giving "bear Arms" its idiomatic meaning would cause the protected right to consist of the right to be a soldier or to wage war - an absurdity that no commentator has ever endorsed…

c. Meaning of the Operative Clause. Putting all of these textual elements together, we find that they guarantee the individual right to possess and carry weapons in case of confrontation. This meaning is strongly confirmed by the historical background of the Second Amendment. We look to this because it has always been widely understood that the Second Amendment, like the First and Fourth Amendments, codified a pre-existing right. The very text of the Second Amendment implicitly recognizes the pre-existence of the right and declares only that it "shall not be infringed." As we said in *United States v. Cruikshank** (1876), "this is not a right granted by the Constitution. Neither is it in any manner dependent upon that instrument for its existence. The Second Amendment declares that it shall not be infringed…"

…By the time of the founding, the right to have arms had become fundamental for English subjects. Blackstone, whose works… "constituted the preeminent authority on English law for the founding generation" cited the arms provision of the Bill of Rights as one of the fundamental rights of Englishmen. His description of it cannot possibly be thought to tie it to militia or military service. It was, he said, "the natural right of resistance and self-preservation" and "the right of having and using arms for self-preservation and defence." Other contemporary authorities concurred. Thus, the right secured in 1689 as a result of the Stuarts' abuses was by the time of the founding understood to be an individual right protecting against both public and private violence…

ONE

There seems to us no doubt, on the basis of both text and history, that the Second Amendment conferred an individual right to keep and bear arms. Of course the right was not unlimited, just as the First Amendment's right of free speech was not...Thus, we do not read the Second Amendment to protect the right of citizens to carry arms for <u>any</u> sort of confrontation, just as we do not read the First Amendment to protect the right of citizens to speak for <u>any</u> purpose. Before turning to limitations upon the individual right, however, we must determine whether the prefatory clause of the Second Amendment comports with our interpretation of the operative clause.

2. Prefatory Clause.

The prefatory clause reads: "A well regulated Militia, being necessary to the security of a free State…"

a. "Well-Regulated Militia." In *United States v. Miller** (1939), we explained that "the Militia comprised all males physically capable of acting in concert for the common defense." That definition comports with founding-era sources...

b. "Security of a Free State." The phrase "security of a free state" meant "security of a free polity," not security of each of the several States as the dissent below argued. Joseph Story wrote in his treatise on the Constitution that "the word 'state' is used in various senses and in its most enlarged sense, it means the people composing a particular nation or community." It is true that the term "State" elsewhere in the Constitution refers to individual States, but the phrase "security of a free state" and close variations seem to have been terms of art in 18th-century political discourse, meaning a "free country" or free polity. Moreover, the other instances of "state" in the Constitution are typically accompanied by modifiers making clear that the reference is to the several States - "each state," "several states," "any state," "that state," "particular states," "one state," "no state." And the presence of the term "foreign state" in Article I and Article III shows that the word "state" did not have a single meaning in the Constitution.

There are many reasons why the militia was thought to be "necessary to the security of a free state." First, of course, it is useful in repelling invasions and suppressing insurrections. Second, it renders large standing armies unnecessary - an argument that Alexander Hamilton made in favor of federal control over the militia. Third, when the able-bodied men of a nation are trained in arms and organized, they are better able to resist tyranny.

3. Relationship between Prefatory Clause and Operative Clause.

We reach the question, then: Does the preface fit with an operative clause that creates an individual right to keep and bear arms? It fits perfectly, once one knows the history that the founding generation knew and that we have described above. That history showed that the way tyrants had eliminated a militia consisting of all the able-bodied men was not by banning the militia but simply by taking away the people's arms, enabling a select militia or standing army to suppress political opponents. This is what had occurred in England that prompted codification of the right to have arms in the English Bill of Rights.

The debate with respect to the right to keep and bear arms, as with other guarantees in the Bill of Rights, was not over whether it was desirable (all agreed that it was) but over whether it needed to be codified in the Constitution. During the 1788 ratification debates, the fear that the federal government would disarm the people in order to impose rule through a standing army or select militia was

ONE

pervasive in Antifederalist rhetoric. John Smilie, for example, worried not only that Congress's "command of the militia" could be used to create a "select militia," or to have "no militia at all," but also, as a separate concern, that "when a select militia is formed; the people in general may be disarmed." Federalists responded that because Congress was given no power to abridge the ancient right of individuals to keep and bear arms, such a force could never oppress the people. It was understood across the political spectrum that the right helped to secure the ideal of a citizen militia, which might be necessary to oppose an oppressive military force if the constitutional order broke down.

It is therefore entirely sensible that the Second Amendment's prefatory clause announces the purpose for which the right was codified: to prevent elimination of the militia. The prefatory clause does not suggest that preserving the militia was the only reason Americans valued the ancient right; most undoubtedly thought it even more important for self-defense and hunting. But the threat that the new Federal Government would destroy the citizens' militia by taking away their arms was the reason that right - unlike some other English rights - was codified in a written Constitution. JUSTICE BREYER's assertion that individual self-defense is merely a "subsidiary interest" of the right to keep and bear arms is profoundly mistaken. He bases that assertion solely upon the prologue - but that can only show that self-defense had little to do with the right's codification; it was the central component of the right itself.

Besides ignoring the historical reality that the Second Amendment was not intended to lay down a "novel principle" but rather codified a right "inherited from our English ancestors," petitioners' interpretation does not even achieve the narrower purpose that prompted codification of the right. If, as they believe, the Second Amendment right is no more than the right to keep and use weapons as a member of an organized militia - if, that is, the organized militia is the sole institutional beneficiary of the Second Amendment's guarantee - it does not assure the existence of a "citizens' militia" as a safeguard against tyranny. For Congress retains plenary authority to organize the militia, which must include the authority to say who will belong to the organized force. That is why the first Militia Act's requirement that only whites enroll caused States to amend their militia laws to exclude free blacks. Thus, if petitioners are correct, the Second Amendment protects citizens' right to use a gun in an organization from which Congress has plenary authority to exclude them. It guarantees a select militia of the sort the Stuart kings found useful, but not the people's militia that was the concern of the founding generation...

> Sounds like a very valid point. To state (in the Amendment) that the "right" referred to "shall not be infringed" and to then <u>limit</u> that "right" to militia use when we know Congress has complete authority to "organize" or "not to organize" the militia, seems to be internally contradictory. In fact, although not emphasized, I think this might be the majority's best point. What do you think?

D

...As we will show, virtually all interpreters of the Second Amendment in the century after its enactment interpreted the amendment as we do.

1. Post-ratification Commentary.

Three important founding-era legal scholars interpreted the Second Amendment in published writings. All three understood it to protect an <u>individual right</u> unconnected with militia service...

ONE

2. Pre-Civil War Case Law.

The 19th-century cases that interpreted the Second Amendment universally support an individual right unconnected to militia service…

3. Post-Civil War Legislation.

In the aftermath of the Civil War, there was an outpouring of discussion of the Second Amendment in Congress and in public discourse, as people debated whether and how to secure constitutional rights for newly freed slaves. Since those discussions took place 75 years after the ratification of the Second Amendment, they do not provide as much insight into its original meaning as earlier sources. Yet those born and educated in the early 19th century faced a widespread effort to limit arms ownership by a large number of citizens; their understanding of the origins and continuing significance of the Amendment is instructive.

Blacks were routinely disarmed by Southern States after the Civil War. Those who opposed these injustices frequently stated that they infringed blacks' constitutional right to keep and bear arms. Needless to say, the claim was not that blacks were being prohibited from carrying arms in an organized state militia. A Report of the Commission of the Freedmen's Bureau in 1866 stated plainly: "The civil law of Kentucky prohibits the colored man from bearing arms…Their arms are taken from them by the civil authorities… Thus, the right of the people to keep and bear arms as provided in the Constitution is infringed." A joint congressional Report decried:

> "In some parts of [South Carolina], armed parties are, without proper authority, engaged in seizing all firearms found in the hands of the freemen. Such conduct is in clear and direct violation of their

personal rights as guaranteed by the Constitution of the United States, which declares that 'the right of the people to keep and bear arms shall not be infringed.' The freemen of South Carolina have shown by their peaceful and orderly conduct that they can safely be trusted with fire-arms, and they need them to kill game for subsistence, and to protect their crops from destruction by birds and animals."

The view expressed in these statements was widely reported and was apparently widely held. For example, an editorial in The Loyal Georgian (Augusta) on February 3, 1866, assured blacks that "all men, without distinction of color, have the right to keep and bear arms to defend their homes, families or themselves."

Congress enacted the Freedmen's Bureau Act on July 16, 1866. Section 14 stated:

> "The right…to have full and equal benefit of all laws and proceedings concerning personal liberty, personal security, and the acquisition, enjoyment, and disposition of estate, real and personal, including the constitutional right to bear arms, shall be secured to and enjoyed by all the citizens…without respect to race or color, or previous condition of slavery…"

The understanding that the Second Amendment gave freed blacks the right to keep and bear arms was reflected in congressional discussion of the bill, with even an opponent of it saying that the founding generation "were for every man bearing his arms about him and keeping them in his house, his castle, for his own defense."

…It was plainly the understanding in the post-Civil War Congress that the Second Amendment protected an individual right to use arms for self-defense.

4. Post-Civil War Commentators.

Every late-19th-century legal scholar that we have read interpreted the Second Amendment to secure an individual right unconnected with militia service...

We conclude that nothing in our precedents forecloses our adoption of the original understanding of the Second Amendment...

III

Like most rights, the right secured by the Second Amendment is not unlimited. From Blackstone through the 19th-century cases, commentators and courts routinely explained that the right was not a right to keep and carry any weapon whatsoever in any manner whatsoever and for whatever purpose...Nothing in our opinion should be taken to cast doubt on longstanding prohibitions on the possession of firearms by felons and the mentally ill, or laws forbidding the carrying of firearms in sensitive places such as schools and government buildings, or laws imposing conditions and qualifications on the commercial sale of arms...

IV

We turn finally to the law at issue here. As we have said, the law totally bans handgun possession in the home. It also requires that any lawful firearm in the home be disassembled or bound by a trigger lock at all times, rendering it inoperable.

As the quotations earlier in this opinion demonstrate, the inherent right of self-defense has been central to the Second Amendment right. The handgun ban amounts to a prohibition of an entire class of "arms" that is overwhelmingly chosen by American society for that lawful purpose. The prohibition extends, moreover, to the home, where the need for defense of self, family, and property is most acute. Under any of the standards of scrutiny that we have applied to enumerated constitutional rights, banning from the home "the most preferred firearm in the nation to 'keep' and use for protection of one's home and family," would fail constitutional muster.

…Whatever the reason, handguns are the most popular weapon chosen by Americans for self-defense in the home, and a complete prohibition of their use is invalid.

We must also address the District's requirement (as applied to respondent's handgun) that firearms in the home be rendered and kept inoperable at all times. This makes it impossible for citizens to use them for the core lawful purpose of self-defense and is hence unconstitutional…

We are aware of the problem of handgun violence in this country, and we take seriously the concerns raised by the many amici who believe that prohibition of handgun ownership is a solution. The Constitution leaves the District of Columbia a variety of tools for combating that problem, including some measures regulating handguns. But the enshrinement of constitutional rights necessarily takes certain policy choices off the table. These include the absolute prohibition of handguns held and used for self-defense in the home. Undoubtedly some think that the Second Amendment is outmoded in a society where our standing army is the pride of our nation, where well-trained police forces provide personal security, and where gun violence is a serious problem. That is perhaps debatable, but what is not debatable is that it is not the role of this Court to pronounce the Second Amendment extinct. We affirm the judgment of the Court of Appeals. It is so ordered.

Amici: plural derivative of amicus curiae, a Latin term meaning "friend of the court." In judicial terms, when a non-party to a case is granted the right to file a brief on behalf of an issue that involves their cause to aid the Court in rendering a decision, that is called an amicus brief. Several such friends (or interested non-parties), then, are referred to as amici.

ONE

DISSENT: Stevens/Souter/Ginsburg/Breyer…Guns are used to hunt, for self-defense, to commit crimes, for sporting activities, and to perform military duties. The Second Amendment plainly does not protect the right to use a gun to rob a bank; it is equally clear that it does encompass the right to use weapons for certain military purposes. Whether it also protects the right to possess and use guns for nonmilitary purposes like hunting and personal self-defense is the question presented by this case. The text of the Amendment, its history, and our decision in *United States v. Miller*, provide a clear answer to that question.

> Just as I criticized some of Justice Scalia's arguments as a bit of a stretch, it appears that Justice Stevens is equally capable of overreaching. Please, surely no one can couch "the text of the Amendment" as being "clear" on either side of this issue. And, it is at least arguable that neither its history nor *United States v. Miller* provides "clear" answers. If that were really true, shouldn't the vote be 9-0, one way or the other?

The Second Amendment was adopted to protect the right of the people of each of the several States to maintain a well-regulated militia. It was a response to concerns raised during the ratification of the Constitution that the power of Congress to disarm the state militias and create a national standing army posed an intolerable threat to the sovereignty of the several States. Neither the text of the Amendment nor the arguments advanced by its proponents evidenced the slightest interest in limiting any legislature's authority to regulate private civilian uses of firearms. Specifically, there is no indication that the Framers of the Amendment intended to enshrine the common-law right of self-defense in the Constitution.

> And, yet, doesn't that sound very odd? To think that it is possible there is no constitutional right to defend one's self with arms? No one suggests that government cannot constitutionally regulate private civilian use of firearms. The primary issue here is the banning of such use. I also find it absurd that a majority of the Supreme Court of the United States, with no specific provision to fall back on, found a right (somewhere in the Constitution) for a woman to choose to terminate a fetus, but Justice Stevens does not believe there is a right in the Second Amendment (implied) to self-defense. Doesn't quite fit, does it?

…Even if the textual and historical arguments on both sides of the issue were evenly balanced, respect for the well-settled views of all of our predecessors on this Court, and for the rule of law itself, would prevent most jurists from endorsing such a **dramatic upheaval** in the law. As Justice Cardozo observed years ago, the "labor of judges would be increased almost to the breaking point if every past decision could be reopened in every case, and one could not lay one's own course of bricks on the secure foundation of the courses laid by others who had gone before him."…

> There aren't many that would think this decision comes close to a **dramatic upheaval**. In fact, if the dissent had prevailed, such a description would have been appropriate!

I

…Three portions of [the Second Amendment] merit special focus: the introductory language defining the Amendment's purpose, the class of persons encompassed within its reach, and the unitary nature of the right that it protects.

"A well regulated Militia, being necessary to the security of a free State…"

ONE

The preamble to the Second Amendment...identifies the preservation of the militia as the Amendment's purpose; it explains that the militia is necessary to the security of a free State; and it recognizes that the militia must be "well regulated."...

"The right of the people"

The centerpiece of the Court's textual argument is its insistence that the words "the people" as used in the Second Amendment must have the same meaning, and protect the same class of individuals, as when they are used in the First and Fourth Amendments. According to the Court, in all three provisions - as well as the Constitution's preamble, section 2 of Article I, and the Tenth Amendment - "the term unambiguously refers to all members of the political community, not an unspecified subset." But the Court itself reads the Second Amendment to protect a "subset" significantly narrower than the class of persons protected by the First and Fourth Amendments; when it finally drills down on the substantive meaning of the Second Amendment, the Court limits the protected class to "law-abiding, responsible citizens." But the class of persons protected by the First and Fourth Amendments is not so limited; for even felons (and presumably irresponsible citizens as well) may invoke the protections of those constitutional provisions...

Please, Justice Stevens. You surely don't mean to suggest that literally everyone "may invoke the protections of the First Amendment," do you?

Because obscenity is not protected speech - defamation is not protected speech - convicted sex offenders cannot "assemble" just anywhere - and there are numerous additional exceptions for both the First and Fourth Amendments.

"To keep and bear Arms"

Although the Court's discussion of these words treats them as two "phrases" - as if they read "to keep" and "to bear" - they describe a unitary right: to possess arms if needed for military purposes and to use them in conjunction with military activities...

The unmodified use of "bear arms," by contrast, refers most naturally to a military purpose, as evidenced by its use in literally dozens of contemporary texts. The absence of any reference to civilian uses of weapons tailors the text of the Amendment to the purpose identified in its preamble. But when discussing these words, the Court simply ignores the preamble.

The Court argues that a "qualifying phrase that contradicts the word or phrase it modifies is unknown this side of the looking glass." But this fundamentally fails to grasp the point. The stand-alone phrase "bear arms" most naturally conveys a military meaning unless the addition of a qualifying phrase signals that a different meaning is intended. When, as in this case, there is no such qualifier, the most natural meaning is the military one...

> I'm not convinced that is true. Wouldn't the right to "bear arms" in self-defense of a Hatfield-McCoy neighborly dispute "fit" just as well? There is no military meaning in such a right.

When each word in the text is given full effect, the Amendment is most naturally read to secure to the people a right to use and possess arms in conjunction with service in a well-regulated militia. So far as appears, no more than that was contemplated by its drafters or is encompassed within its terms...

One

II

...The history of the adoption of the Amendment thus describes an overriding concern about the potential threat to state sovereignty that a federal standing army would pose, and a desire to protect the States' militias as the means by which to guard against that danger. But state militias could not effectively check the prospect of a federal standing army so long as Congress retained the power to disarm them, and so a guarantee against such disarmament was needed...

V

The Court concludes its opinion by declaring that it is not the proper role of this Court to change the meaning of rights "enshrined" in the Constitution. But the right the Court announces was not "enshrined" in the Second Amendment by the Framers; it is the product of today's law-changing decision. The majority's exegesis has utterly failed to establish that as a matter of text or history, "the right of law-abiding, responsible citizens to use arms in defense of hearth and home" is "elevated above all other interests" by the Second Amendment...

The Court properly disclaims any interest in evaluating the wisdom of the specific policy choice challenged in this case, but it fails to pay heed to a far more important policy choice - the choice made by the Framers themselves. The Court would have us believe that over 200 years ago, the Framers made a choice to limit the tools available to elected officials wishing to regulate civilian uses of weapons, and to authorize this Court to use the common-law process of case-by-case judicial lawmaking to define the contours of acceptable gun control policy. Absent compelling evidence that is nowhere to be found in the Court's opinion, I could not possibly conclude that the Framers made such a choice. For these reasons, I respectfully dissent.

> Bad form! I don't know of any Constitutional provision that has not been the subject of a case-by-case definition, otherwise known as judicial interpretation.

DISSENT: Breyer/Stevens/Souter/Ginsburg...

I

The majority's conclusion is wrong for two independent reasons. The first reason is that...the Second Amendment protects militia-related, not self-defense-related, interests...

The second independent reason is that the protection the Amendment provides is not absolute. The Amendment permits government to regulate the interests that it serves. Thus, irrespective of what those interests are - whether they do or do not include an independent interest in self-defense - the majority's view cannot be correct unless it can show that the District's regulation is unreasonable or inappropriate in Second Amendment terms. This the majority cannot do...

The District's regulation, which focuses upon the presence of handguns in high-crime urban areas, represents a permissible legislative response to a serious, indeed life-threatening, problem.

Thus I here assume that one objective (but, as the majority concedes, not the primary objective) of those who wrote the Second Amendment was to help assure citizens that they would have arms available for purposes of self-defense. Even so, a legislature could reasonably conclude that the law will advance goals of great public importance, namely, saving lives, preventing injury, and reducing crime. The law is tailored to the urban crime problem in that it is local in scope and thus affects only a geographic area both limited in size and entirely urban; the law concerns handguns, which

ONE

are specially linked to urban gun deaths and injuries, and which are the overwhelmingly favorite weapon of armed criminals; and at the same time, the law imposes a burden upon gun owners that seems proportionately no greater than restrictions in existence at the time the Second Amendment was adopted. In these circumstances, the District's law falls within the zone that the Second Amendment leaves open to regulation by legislatures.

II

...Although I adopt for present purposes the majority's position that the Second Amendment embodies a general concern about self-defense, I shall not assume that the Amendment contains a specific untouchable right to keep guns in the house to shoot burglars. The majority, which presents evidence in favor of the former proposition, does not, because it cannot, convincingly show that the Second Amendment seeks to maintain the latter in pristine, unregulated form.

I don't follow. How can you have a right to self-defense and a ban on the most (and, perhaps, only) effective method to defend at the same time? Regulation, I get, but a complete ban seems out of step with a right Justice Breyer assumes to exist.

To the contrary, colonial history itself offers important examples of the kinds of gun regulation that citizens would then have thought compatible with the "right to keep and bear arms," whether embodied in Federal or State Constitutions, or the background common law. And those examples include substantial regulation of firearms in urban areas, including regulations that imposed obstacles to the use of firearms for the protection of the home...

> Yes, but "substantial regulation" and "obstacles to the use of" do not amount to a "ban," do they?

III

I therefore begin by asking a process-based question: How is a court to determine whether a particular firearm regulation (here, the District's restriction on handguns) is consistent with the Second Amendment? What kind of constitutional standard should the court use? How high a protective hurdle does the Amendment erect?

The question matters. The majority is wrong when it says that the District's law is unconstitutional "under any of the standards of scrutiny that we have applied to enumerated constitutional rights." How could that be? It certainly would not be unconstitutional under, for example, a "rational basis" standard, which requires a court to uphold regulation so long as it bears a "rational relationship" to a "legitimate governmental purpose." The law at issue here, which in part seeks to prevent gun-related accidents, at least bears a "rational relationship" to that "legitimate" life-saving objective...

> Surely, you jest. Congress can ban a right provided in the Constitution if they have a rational basis for doing so? Then, why have a Constitution? Some criticize my teaching method as being too demanding - too much material to cover for laymen. But there really is no substitute for our intensity. For example, many of the same justices who argue that "saving lives" (even if that were true) justifies D.C.'s ban in spite of an assumed Second Amendment "right," have no problem with "costing" lives in other settings. To wit: (1) President Truman's take-over of our steel mills during the Korean War was held to be unconstitutional even though such a ruling would knowingly cost lives of our military personnel; (2) The right of a woman to choose abortion trumps the life of a fetus.

ONE

> Question: Even if a ban on handguns in D.C. would save lives, how do the dissenters square that with other constitutional rights that have been granted greater importance than life itself?

IV
A

No one doubts the constitutional importance of the statute's basic objective, saving lives. But there is considerable debate about whether the District's statute helps to achieve that objective. I begin by reviewing the statute's tendency to secure that objective from the perspective of (1) the legislature (namely, the Council of the District of Columbia) that enacted the statute in 1976, and (2) a court that seeks to evaluate the Council's decision today.

1

First, consider the facts as the legislature saw them when it adopted the District statute. As stated by the local council committee that recommended its adoption, the major substantive goal of the District's handgun restriction is "to reduce the potentiality for gun-related crimes and gun-related deaths from occurring within the District of Columbia." The committee concluded, on the basis of "extensive public hearings" and "lengthy research," that "the easy availability of firearms in the United States has been a major factor contributing to the drastic increase in gun-related violence and crime over the past 40 years." It reported to the Council "startling statistics" regarding gun-related crime, accidents, and deaths, focusing particularly on the relation between handguns and crime and the proliferation of handguns within the District.

The committee informed the Council that guns were "responsible for 69 deaths in this country each day," for a total of "approximately 25,000 gun-deaths…each year," along with an additional 200,000 gun-related injuries. Three thousand of these deaths, the report stated, were accidental. A quarter of the victims in those accidental deaths were children under the age of 14. And according to the committee, "for every intruder stopped by a homeowner with a firearm, there are 4 gun-related accidents within the home."

> How many stabbing deaths would it take, Justice Breyer, before you would ban knives? Golf club beatings - golf clubs? Bats? Poisonous household liquids? Contact sports? Diving? Automobiles? Freedom has to come in here somewhere, does it not?

…The District's special focus on handguns thus reflects the fact that the committee report found them to have a particularly strong link to undesirable activities in the District's exclusively urban environment. The District did not seek to prohibit possession of other sorts of weapons deemed more suitable for an "urban area." Indeed, an original draft of the bill, and the original committee recommendations, had sought to prohibit registration of shotguns as well as handguns, but the Council as a whole decided to narrow the prohibition…

3

…For these reasons, I conclude that the District's statute properly seeks to further the sort of life-preserving and public-safety interests that the Court has called "compelling."

> I am betting Justice Breyer would say he is entitled to body guards with handguns when traveling through D.C. But, of course, homeowners who live in crime-ridden neighborhoods are not. Seems a bit elitist to me.

ONE

B

2

The majority briefly suggests that the "right to keep and bear Arms" might encompass an interest in hunting. But in enacting the present provisions, the District sought "to take nothing away from sportsmen." And any inability of District residents to hunt near where they live has much to do with the jurisdiction's exclusively urban character and little to do with the District's firearm laws. For reasons similar to those I discussed in the preceding subsection - that the District's law does not prohibit possession of rifles or shotguns, and the presence of opportunities for sporting activities in nearby States - I reach a similar conclusion, namely, that the District's law burdens any sports-related or hunting-related objectives that the Amendment may protect little, or not at all.

3

The District's law does prevent a resident from keeping a loaded handgun in his home. And it consequently makes it more difficult for the householder to use the handgun for self-defense in the home against intruders, such as burglars. As the Court of Appeals noted, statistics suggest that handguns are the most popular weapon for self-defense. And there are some legitimate reasons why that would be the case: Amici suggest (with some empirical support) that handguns are easier to hold and control (particularly for persons with physical infirmities), easier to carry, easier to maneuver in enclosed spaces, and that a person using one will still have a hand free to dial 911. To that extent the law burdens to some degree an interest in self-defense that for present purposes I have assumed the Amendment seeks to further.

C

In weighing needs and burdens, we must take account of the possibility that there are reasonable, but less restrictive alternatives.

Are there other potential measures that might similarly promote the same goals while imposing lesser restrictions? Here I see none…

VI

For these reasons, I conclude that the District's measure is a proportionate, not a disproportionate, response to the compelling concerns that led the District to adopt it. And, for these reasons as well as the independently sufficient reasons set forth by JUSTICE STEVENS, I would find the District's measure consistent with the Second Amendment's demands. With respect, I dissent.

SUMMARY: With the *Heller* and *McDonald* decisions, by a **"one robe margin"** the Supreme Court preserved your right to own a handgun to defend you and your family in your home.

COMMENT: It remains to be seen how far the Court will permit government to "regulate" that right. Stay tuned! Stay engaged! Many cases in the near future will set those parameters. What do you bet they will likely be 5-4 decisions?

PLEA: With **"one less robe,"** *District of Columbia v. Heller* and *McDonald v. Chicago* would be reversed and gun confiscation would ensue. The only way to help insure that won't happen is to vote for a president (with nomination power) who will likely nominate Constitutional conservatives to the Supreme Court when seats become vacant and to vote for senators (with confirmation power) who will likely block the appointment of liberal nominees and confirm the appointment of conservative nominees. It's up to "You, the People."

Chapter Eleven

ONE ROBE SHORT ON MAY 23, 2011, FREED THE GUILTY!

Yes, on May 23, 2011, five members of your Supreme Court freed 46,000 convicted criminals in the California prison system. But, as startling as that may seem, it is not the real story Americans should take away from this constitutional disaster.

One of the first surprises my students learn when embarking upon a study of constitutional law is that the proper role of an appellate judge does not include "doing the right thing." I suppose that may surprise you, as well. I will explain.

Article VI requires all judges to be bound by the Constitution and to take an oath to support it. Pull it out and take a look - it is very short. If someone challenges the constitutionality of a state or federal statute, it is the judge's solemn responsibility to rule in accordance with the Constitution even if that interpretation goes against the judge's personal feelings about the wisdom of the law and, even if that interpretation, in his or her opinion, is counter to what is best for the nation. We can always change the Constitution, but until that is done the right way pursuant to the provisions of Article V, it is the supreme law of the land – it is what we call "the rule of law" – it is the only constitutional law that has the will of the people behind it.

It is the role of appellate judges, inclusive of Supreme Court justices, to "interpret" the law – not to make it up as they go in the manner they would like. Elected legislators are the ones that get to "make it up." Elected executive branch leaders get to enforce it. And, judges at all levels (sometimes elected and sometimes appointed) interpret it. That is, where not otherwise clear, it is the job of judges to determine what was intended by the language they are interpreting. When judges exceed their role by legislating the result, they violate their oath of office and disregard the rule of law. When that happens, tyranny gives way to anarchy.

Plata v. Brown* is about judicial abuse of power. Its ramifications for our future are nothing short of the likely dismantling of our republic, one case at a time. See you on the other side of this decision that fell **one robe short**. Sad, isn't it? Your vote could have made the difference if you had exercised it. By now, you know what I mean.

PLATA v. BROWN
SUPREME COURT OF THE UNITED STATES
131 S. Ct. 1910
May 23, 2011
[5 – 4]

OPINION: Kennedy/Ginsburg/Breyer/Sotomayor/Kagan…This case arises from serious constitutional violations in California's prison system. The violations have persisted for years. They remain uncorrected. The appeal comes to this Court from a three-judge District Court order directing California to remedy two ongoing violations of the Cruel and Unusual Punishments Clause …The violations are the subject of two class actions in two Federal District Courts. The first involves the class of prisoners with serious mental disorders. That case is *Coleman v. Brown*. The second involves prisoners with serious medical conditions. That case is *Plata v. Brown*. The order of the three-judge District Court is applicable to both cases.

We have two class action cases consolidated for this appeal. A class action is a lawsuit whereby one or a few representative plaintiffs take on a cause for a defined class of people who likely will never come before the court. It is designed to keep down costs and work a remedy for the masses who are both damaged and "in" the defined class. The focus of this case is an interpretation of a statute, mentioned below, in conjunction with the Eighth Amendment. In pertinent part, for this case, it reads: "Cruel and unusual punishments [shall not be] inflicted." Pull it out and take a look. These are words you have likely heard.

After years of litigation, it became apparent that a remedy for the constitutional violations would not be effective absent a reduction in the prison system population...

The appeal presents the question whether the remedial order issued by the three-judge court is consistent with requirements and procedures set forth in a congressional statute, the Prison Litigation Reform Act of 1995 (PLRA). The order leaves the choice of means to reduce overcrowding to the discretion of state officials. But absent compliance through new construction, out-of-state transfers, or other means - or modification of the order upon a further showing by the State - the State will be required to release some number of prisoners before their full sentences have been served. High recidivism rates must serve as a warning that mistaken or premature release of even one prisoner can cause injury and harm. The release of prisoners in large numbers - assuming the State finds no other way to comply with the order - is a matter of undoubted, grave concern.

At the time of trial, California's correctional facilities held some 156,000 persons. This is nearly double the number that California's prisons were designed to hold, and California has been ordered to reduce its prison population to 137.5% of design capacity. By the three-judge court's own estimate, the required population reduction could be as high as 46,000 persons...As will be noted, the reduction need not be accomplished in an indiscriminate manner or in these substantial numbers if satisfactory, alternate remedies or means for compliance are devised. The State may employ measures, including good-time credits and diversion of low-risk offenders and technical parole violators to community-based programs, that will mitigate the order's impact. The population reduction potentially required is nevertheless of unprecedented sweep and extent.

One

Yet so too is the continuing injury and harm resulting from these serious constitutional violations. For years the medical and mental health care provided by California's prisons has fallen short of minimum constitutional requirements and has failed to meet prisoners' basic health needs. Needless suffering and death have been the well-documented result. Over the whole course of years during which this litigation has been pending, no other remedies have been found to be sufficient. Efforts to remedy the violation have been frustrated by severe overcrowding in California's prison system. Short term gains in the provision of care have been eroded by the long-term effects of severe and pervasive overcrowding.

Overcrowding has overtaken the limited resources of prison staff; imposed demands well beyond the capacity of medical and mental health facilities; and created unsanitary and unsafe conditions that make progress in the provision of care difficult or impossible to achieve. The overcrowding is the primary cause of…the severe and unlawful mistreatment of prisoners through grossly inadequate provision of medical and mental health care.

This Court now holds that the PLRA does authorize the relief afforded in this case and that the court-mandated population limit is necessary to remedy the violation of prisoners' constitutional rights. The order of the three-judge court, subject to the right of the State to seek its modification in appropriate circumstances, must be affirmed.

I urge a proper perspective until you have read Justice Scalia's dissent. The majority is saying that the Prison Litigation Reform Act authorizes turning 46,000 convicted criminals loose to "remedy the violation of prisoners' constitutional rights"; yet, as you will see, no one prisoner's rights were found to have been violated.

I
A

The degree of overcrowding in California's prisons is exceptional… As many as 200 prisoners may live in a gymnasium, monitored by as few as two or three correctional officers. As many as 54 prisoners may share a single toilet…The consequences of overcrowding identified by the Governor include "increased, substantial risk for transmission of infectious illness" and a suicide rate "approaching an average of one per week."

Keep in mind that the Court is addressing concerns that affect over 156,000 prisoners spread throughout California. I do not defend any single deplorable condition; however, the occasional horror story does not move me in a population of 156,000. I realize the prison system has a constitutional duty to not subject prisoners to cruel and unusual punishment, but, please, we can find much worse stories affecting far more people in any unjailed population of 156,000 people. Furthermore, perhaps it's the lawyer in me, but the majority says "<u>as many as</u> 200 prisoners <u>may</u> live in a gym - <u>as many as</u> 54 prisoners <u>may</u> share a single toilet." "May" is not a finding of fact.

Furthermore, "if" such a deplorable condition does exist, it hardly justifies freeing 46,000 prisoners for the sake of a handful of true victims.

And, by the way, it would be safe to assume that <u>as many as</u> just one murder <u>may</u> be visited upon a law-abiding society with this release. Victims get very little consideration in the land of the free. In 2013 there were well over 38,000 suicides in this country. I'm thinking that one suicide per week in a total population of 156,000 prisoners isn't that far off from the average rate of suicide in the non-incarcerated population. Hmmm? Wouldn't you expect a higher rate among the universe of convicted criminals regardless of how they are treated?

ONE

Prisoners in California with serious mental illness do not receive minimal, adequate care. Because of a shortage of treatment beds, suicidal inmates may be held for prolonged periods in telephone-booth sized cages without toilets. A psychiatric expert reported observing an inmate who had been held in such a cage for nearly 24 hours, standing in a pool of his own urine, unresponsive and nearly catatonic. Prison officials explained they had "no place to put him."

…Prisoners suffering from physical illness also receive severely deficient care. California's prisons were designed to meet the medical needs of a population at 100% of design capacity and so have only half the clinical space needed to treat the current population. A correctional officer testified that, in one prison, up to 50 sick inmates may be held together in a 12- by 20-foot cage for up to five hours awaiting treatment…A prisoner with severe abdominal pain died after a 5-week delay in referral to a specialist; a prisoner with "constant and extreme" chest pain died after an 8-hour delay in evaluation by a doctor; and a prisoner died of testicular cancer after a "failure of MDs to work up for cancer in a young man with 17 months of testicular pain."…

B

…The Coleman District Court found "overwhelming evidence of the systematic failure to deliver necessary care to mentally ill inmates" in California prisons. The prisons were "seriously and chronically understaffed" and had "no effective method for ensuring…the competence of their staff." The prisons had failed to implement necessary suicide-prevention procedures, "due in large measure to the severe understaffing." Mentally ill inmates "languished for months, or even years, without access to necessary care."…

C

The second action, *Plata v. Brown*, involves the class of state prisoners with serious medical conditions. After this action commenced in 2001, the State conceded that deficiencies in prison medical care violated prisoners' Eighth Amendment rights. The State stipulated to a remedial injunction. The State failed to comply with that injunction, and in 2005 the court appointed a Receiver to oversee remedial efforts. The court found that "the California prison medical care system is broken beyond repair," resulting in an "unconscionable degree of suffering and death." The court found: "It is an uncontested fact that, on average, an inmate in one of California's prisons needlessly dies every six to seven days due to constitutional deficiencies in the California prisons' medical delivery system."…

D

The *Coleman* and *Plata* plaintiffs, believing that a remedy for unconstitutional medical and mental health care could not be achieved without reducing overcrowding, moved their respective District Courts to convene a three-judge court empowered under the PLRA to order reductions in the prison population…

The three-judge court…ordered California to reduce its prison population to 137.5% of the prisons' design capacity within two years. Assuming the State does not increase capacity through new construction, the order requires a population reduction of 38,000 to 46,000 persons. Because it appears all but certain that the State cannot complete sufficient construction to comply fully with the order, the prison population will have to be reduced to at least some extent. The court did not order the State to achieve this reduction in any particular manner. Instead, the court ordered the State to formulate a plan for compliance and submit its plan for approval by the court…

ONE

II

As a consequence of their own actions, prisoners may be deprived of rights that are fundamental to liberty. Yet the law and the Constitution demand recognition of certain other rights. Prisoners retain the essence of human dignity inherent in all persons.

Respect for that dignity animates the Eighth Amendment prohibition against cruel and unusual punishment...

To incarcerate, society takes from prisoners the means to provide for their own needs. Prisoners are dependent on the State for food, clothing, and necessary medical care...Just as a prisoner may starve if not fed, he or she may suffer or die if not provided adequate medical care. A prison that deprives prisoners of basic sustenance, including adequate medical care, is incompatible with the concept of human dignity and has no place in civilized society.

If government fails to fulfill this obligation, the courts have a responsibility to remedy the resulting Eighth Amendment violation. Courts...must not shrink from their obligation to "enforce the constitutional rights of all 'persons,' including prisoners." Courts may not allow constitutional violations to continue simply because a remedy would involve intrusion into the realm of prison administration...

> Alarm bells should be going off! I get the feeling that this majority believes it is the function of the judiciary to solve the problems of the executive and legislative branches. Why shouldn't they just take over the education system, police departments, the IRS, etc.?

By its terms, the PLRA restricts the circumstances in which a court may enter an order "that has the purpose or effect of reducing or limiting the prison population." The order in this case does not necessarily require the State to release any prisoners. The State may comply by raising the design capacity of its prisons or by transferring prisoners to county facilities or facilities in other States. Because the order limits the prison population as a percentage of design capacity, it nonetheless has the "effect of reducing or limiting the prison population."

…The three-judge court must…find by clear and convincing evidence that "crowding is the primary cause of the violation of a Federal right" and that "no other relief will remedy the violation of the Federal right." As with any award of prospective relief under the PLRA, the relief "shall extend no further than necessary to correct the violation of the Federal right of a particular plaintiff or plaintiffs." The three-judge court must therefore find that the relief is "narrowly drawn, extends no further than necessary…and is the least intrusive means necessary to correct the violation of the Federal right." In making this determination, the three-judge court must give "substantial weight to any adverse impact on public safety or the operation of a criminal justice system caused by the relief."

The PLRA requires that any order "shall extend no further than necessary to correct the violation of the Federal right of <u>a particular plaintiff or plaintiffs</u>." Even if the two or three representatives of the two classes really do have facts that justify being exposed to real "cruel and unusual" punishment, the statute is clear. The judiciary cannot enter an order releasing 46,000 prisoners based upon a handful of proven claims. Or, perhaps, I should say **"should not,"** for it appears they "can" do whatever they want to do.

Applying these standards, the three-judge court found a population limit appropriate, necessary, and authorized in this case…

B

Once a three-judge court has been convened, the court must find additional requirements satisfied before it may impose a population limit. The first of these requirements is that "crowding is the primary cause of the violation of a Federal right."

1

The three-judge court found the primary cause requirement satisfied by the evidence at trial...

The record documents the severe impact of burgeoning demand on the provision of care. At the time of trial, vacancy rates for medical and mental health staff ranged as high as 20% for surgeons, 25% for physicians, 39% for nurse practitioners, and 54.1% for psychiatrists. These percentages are based on the number of positions budgeted by the State...

> I wholeheartedly agree that government is broken, but not just for prisoners. It is broken for VA hospital patients, Medicare patients, Obamacare insureds, targeted taxpayers, etc.

C

...California's Legislature has not been willing or able to allocate the resources necessary to meet this crisis absent a reduction in overcrowding. There is no reason to believe it will begin to do so now, when the State of California is facing an unprecedented budgetary shortfall. As noted above, the legislature recently failed to allocate funds for planned new construction. Without a reduction in overcrowding, there will be no efficacious remedy for the unconstitutional care of the sick and mentally ill in California's prisons.

D
1

The three-judge court acknowledged that its order "is likely to affect inmates without medical conditions or serious mental illness." This is because reducing California's prison population will require reducing the number of prisoners outside the class through steps such as parole reform, sentencing reform, use of good-time credits, or other means to be determined by the State.

Reducing overcrowding will also have positive effects beyond facilitating timely and adequate access to medical care, including reducing the incidence of prison violence and ameliorating unsafe living conditions. According to the State, these collateral consequences are evidence that the order sweeps more broadly than necessary…

The PLRA states that a remedy shall extend no further than necessary to remedy the violation of the rights of a "particular plaintiff or plaintiffs." This means only that the scope of the order must be determined with reference to the constitutional violations established by the specific plaintiffs before the court.

> The majority is going to turn 46,000 prisoners loose in spite of the clear wording of the statute to the contrary just because the immediate class representatives have a beef. These justices know they are exceeding their role; they do it anyway because they wish to impose their made up rule of law on a disengaged people.

This case is unlike cases where courts have impermissibly reached out to control the treatment of persons or institutions beyond the scope of the violation. Even prisoners with no present physical or mental illness may become afflicted, and all prisoners in California are at risk so long as the State continues to provide inadequate care…

One

Prisoners who are not sick or mentally ill do not yet have a claim that they have been subjected to care that violates the Eighth Amendment, but in no sense are they remote bystanders in California's medical care system. They are that system's next potential victims.

A release order limited to prisoners within the plaintiff classes would, if anything, unduly limit the ability of State officials to determine which prisoners should be released...

> You wouldn't believe it if I <u>told</u> you. That is why my method of teaching is to <u>show</u> you. This majority is actually saying it would be too much of a burden on the State to release only those prisoners whose Eighth Amendment rights have been violated (cruel and unusual punishment victims). No, they are free to release anyone - even those who have not had their Eighth Amendment rights violated - even those who have never had any medical or mental problems at all!

2

In reaching its decision, the three-judge court gave "substantial weight" to any potential adverse impact on public safety from its order...Ultimately, the court concluded that it would be possible to reduce the prison population "in a manner that preserves public safety and the operation of the criminal justice system."...

> Yet another fiction endorsed by five members of the Supreme Court. They accept the notion that releasing 46,000 convicted criminals will "preserve public safety and the operation of the criminal justice system." I am at a loss for words.

III
A

The three-judge court concluded that the population of California's prisons should be capped at 137.5% of design capacity. This conclusion is supported by the record…

B

…The judgment of the three-judge court is affirmed. It is so ordered.

DISSENT: Scalia/Thomas…Today the Court affirms what is perhaps the most radical injunction issued by a court in our nation's history: an order requiring California to release the staggering number of 46,000 convicted criminals.

…One would think that, before allowing the decree of a federal district court to release 46,000 convicted felons, this Court would bend every effort to read the law in such a way as to avoid that outrageous result. Today, quite to the contrary, the Court disregards stringently drawn provisions of the governing statute, and traditional constitutional limitations upon the power of a federal judge, in order to uphold the absurd.

The proceedings that led to this result were a judicial travesty. I dissent because the institutional reform the District Court has undertaken violates the terms of the governing statute, ignores bedrock limitations on the power of Article III judges, and takes federal courts wildly beyond their institutional capacity.

I
A

The Prison Litigation Reform Act (PLRA) states that "prospective relief in any civil action with respect to prison conditions shall extend no further than necessary to correct the violation of the Federal right of a particular plaintiff or plaintiffs"; that such relief must be "narrowly drawn, and extend no further than necessary to correct the violation of the Federal right"; and that it must be "the least intrusive means necessary to correct the violation of the Federal right." In deciding whether these multiple limitations have been complied with, it is necessary to identify with precision what is the "violation of the Federal right of a particular plaintiff or plaintiffs" that has been alleged. What has been alleged here, and what the injunction issued by the Court is tailored...to remedy is the running of a prison system with inadequate medical facilities. [Such an inadequate system] may result in the denial of needed medical treatment to "a particular prisoner or prisoners," thereby violating (according to our cases) his or their Eighth Amendment rights. But the mere existence of the inadequate system does not subject to cruel and unusual punishment the entire prison population in need of medical care, including those who receive it.

The Court acknowledges that the plaintiffs "do not base their case on deficiencies in care provided on any one occasion"; rather, "plaintiffs rely on system-wide deficiencies in the provision of medical and mental health care that, taken as a whole, subject sick and mentally ill prisoners in California to 'substantial risk of serious harm' and cause the delivery of care in the prisons to fall below the evolving standards of decency that mark the progress of a maturing society." But our judge-empowering "evolving standards of decency" jurisprudence (with which, by the way, I heartily disagree), does not prescribe (or at least has not until today prescribed) rules for the "decent" running of schools, prisons, and other government institutions. It forbids "indecent" treatment of individuals - in the context of this case, the denial of medical care to those who need it. And the persons who have a constitutional claim for denial of medical care are those who are denied medical care - not all who face a "substantial risk" (whatever that is) of being denied medical care...

The plaintiffs do not appear to claim - and it would be absurd to suggest - that every single one of those prisoners has personally experienced "torture or a lingering death" as a consequence of that bad medical system. Indeed, it is inconceivable that anything more than a small proportion of prisoners in the plaintiff classes have personally received sufficiently atrocious treatment that their Eighth Amendment right was violated - which, as the Court recognizes, is why the plaintiffs do not premise their claim on "deficiencies in care provided on any one occasion." Rather, the plaintiffs' claim is that they are all part of a medical system so defective that some number of prisoners will inevitably be injured by incompetent medical care, and that this number is sufficiently high so as to render the system, as a whole, unconstitutional.

But what procedural principle justifies certifying a class of plaintiffs so they may assert a claim of systemic unconstitutionality? I can think of two possibilities, both of which are untenable. The first is that although some or most plaintiffs in the class do not individually have viable Eighth Amendment claims, the class as a whole has collectively suffered an Eighth Amendment violation. That theory is contrary to the bedrock rule that the sole purpose of class-wide adjudication is to aggregate claims that are **individually viable**...

The second possibility is that every member of the plaintiff class has suffered an Eighth Amendment violation merely by virtue of being a patient in a poorly-run prison system, and the purpose of the class is merely to aggregate all those individually viable claims. This theory has the virtue of being consistent with procedural principles, but at the cost of a gross substantive departure from our case law. Under this theory, each and every prisoner who happens to be a patient in a system that has systemic weaknesses - such as "hiring any doctor who had a license, a pulse and a pair of shoes" - has suffered cruel

ONE

or unusual punishment, even if that person cannot make an individualized showing of mistreatment. Such a theory of the Eighth Amendment is preposterous. And we have said as much in the past: "If...a healthy inmate who had suffered no deprivation of needed medical treatment were able to claim violation of his constitutional right to medical care...simply on the ground that the prison medical facilities were inadequate, the essential distinction between judge and executive would have disappeared: it would have become the function of the courts to assure adequate medical care in prisons."

...The notion that the plaintiff class can allege an Eighth Amendment violation based on "system-wide deficiencies" is assuredly wrong. It follows that the remedy decreed here is also contrary to law, since the theory of systemic unconstitutionality is central to the plaintiffs' case. The PLRA requires plaintiffs to establish that the system-wide injunction entered by the District Court was "narrowly drawn" and "extends no further than necessary" to correct "the violation of the Federal right of a particular plaintiff or plaintiffs." If (as is the case) the only viable constitutional claims consist of individual instances of mistreatment, then a remedy reforming the system as a whole goes far beyond what the statute allows.

> The arrogance of this majority is breathtaking. They have taken on power constitutionally reserved to the legislative and executive branches. What is next? Will these five start modeling schools in their own image? Highway departments? The EPA? I hope you see how important this decision is to our freedom.

It is also worth noting the peculiarity that the vast majority of inmates most generously rewarded by the release order - the 46,000 whose incarceration will be ended - do not form part of any aggrieved class even under the Court's expansive notion of constitutional violation.

Most of them will not be prisoners with medical conditions or severe mental illness; and many will undoubtedly be fine physical specimens who have developed intimidating muscles pumping iron in the prison gym.

B

Even if I accepted the implausible premise that the plaintiffs have established a system-wide violation of the Eighth Amendment, I would dissent from the Court's endorsement of a decrowding order. That order is an example of what has become known as a "structural injunction."…Structural injunctions depart from that historical practice, turning judges into long-term administrators of complex social institutions such as schools, prisons, and police departments. Indeed, they require judges to play a role essentially indistinguishable from the role ordinarily played by executive officials. Today's decision not only affirms the structural injunction but vastly expands its use, by holding that an entire system is unconstitutional because it may produce constitutional violations.

The drawbacks of structural injunctions have been described at great length elsewhere…This case illustrates one of their most pernicious aspects: that they force judges to engage in a form of factfinding-as-policymaking that is outside the traditional judicial role…

When a judge manages a structural injunction, however, he will inevitably be required to make very broad empirical predictions necessarily based in large part upon policy views - the sort of predictions regularly made by legislators and executive officials, but inappropriate for the Third Branch…

C

My general concerns associated with judges' running social institutions are magnified when they run prison systems, and doubly magnified when they force prison officials to release convicted criminals…

These principles apply doubly to a prisoner-release order. As the author of today's opinion explained earlier this Term, granting a writ of habeas corpus "disturbs the State's significant interest in repose for concluded litigation, denies society the right to punish some admitted offenders, and intrudes on state sovereignty to a degree matched by few exercises of federal judicial authority."… Recognizing that habeas relief must be granted sparingly, we have reversed the Ninth Circuit's erroneous grant of habeas relief to individual California prisoners four times this Term alone…And yet here, the Court affirms an order granting the functional equivalent of 46,000 writs of habeas corpus, based on its paean to courts' "substantial flexibility when making these judgments." It seems that the Court's respect for state sovereignty has vanished in the case where it most matters.

Habeas corpus: a writ requiring a person under arrest to be brought before a judge or into court, especially to secure the person's release unless lawful grounds are shown for his detention.

Paean: enthusiastic praise.

...
III

…In my view, a court may not order a prisoner's release unless it determines that the prisoner is suffering from a violation of his constitutional rights, and that his release, and no other relief, will remedy that violation. Thus, if the court determines that a particular prisoner is being denied constitutionally required medical treatment, and the release of that prisoner (and no other remedy) would enable him to obtain medical treatment,

then the court can order his release; but a court may not order the release of prisoners who have suffered no violations of their constitutional rights, merely to make it less likely that that will happen to them in the future.

This view follows from the PLRA's text that I discussed at the outset. "Narrowly drawn" means that the relief applies only to the "particular prisoner or prisoners" whose constitutional rights are violated; "extends no further than necessary" means that prisoners whose rights are not violated will not obtain relief; and "least intrusive means necessary to correct the violation of the Federal right" means that no other relief is available…

The District Court's order that California release 46,000 prisoners extends "further than necessary to correct the violation of the Federal right of a particular plaintiff or plaintiffs" who have been denied needed medical care. It is accordingly forbidden by the PLRA - besides defying all sound conception of the proper role of judges.

DISSENT: Alito/Roberts…The decree in this case is a perfect example of what the Prison Litigation Reform Act of 1995 was enacted to prevent.

The Constitution does not give federal judges the authority to run state penal systems. Decisions regarding state prisons have profound public safety and financial implications, and the States are generally free to make these decisions as they choose.

The Eighth Amendment imposes an important - but limited - restraint on state authority in this field. The Eighth Amendment prohibits prison officials from depriving inmates of "the minimal civilized measure of life's necessities." Federal courts have the responsibility to ensure that this constitutional standard is met, but undesirable prison conditions that do not violate the Constitution are beyond the federal courts' reach...

Two cases were before the three-judge court, and neither targeted the general problem of overcrowding...Both of the cases were brought not on behalf of all inmates subjected to overcrowding, but rather in the interests of much more limited classes of prisoners, namely, those needing mental health treatment and those with other serious medical needs. But these cases were used as a springboard to implement a criminal justice program far different from that chosen by the state legislature. Instead of crafting a remedy to attack the specific constitutional violations that were found - which related solely to prisoners in the two plaintiff classes - the lower court issued a decree that will at best provide only modest help to those prisoners but that is very likely to have a major and deleterious effect on public safety...

The three-judge court would have us believe that the early release of 46,000 inmates will not imperil - and will actually improve - public safety. Common sense and experience counsel greater caution.

I would reverse the decision below...I fear that today's decision, like prior prisoner release orders, will lead to a grim roster of victims. I hope that I am wrong. In a few years, we will see.

SUMMARY & COMMENT: With permission from the *St. Louis Post-Dispatch*, I produce, below, an article I wrote about this case when I was on their payroll:

> "California Prisons"
>
> The only thing cruel and unusual about the Supreme Court's decision is its ruling.

St. Louis Post-Dispatch
Tad Armstrong
Thursday, June 2, 2011

Last week's Supreme Court decision in *Plata v. Brown* affirmed a lower court injunction that will practically require the release of approximately 26% of California's current prison population (40,000) by May 23, 2013. I say "practically" because, although the decision requires a reduction from the state's current volume of nearly 200% of facility design capacity to a maximum of 137.5% (and, therefore, could be achieved by an increase in prison construction with no reduction in the guest list), it is no surprise that California, like many states, is broke. New prisons are not on the horizon.

When government cannot accomplish its basic function of ensuring public safety due to the cost of its patronizing interest in excessive control of its citizens through the adoption of non-essential programs (otherwise known as the nanny state), anarchy is the inevitable victor. Innocents will die, homes will be robbed and women will be raped in the aftermath of this prisoner release due, in part, to California's past entitlement handouts. Folks, government at all levels is flat out of money. Why is that so difficult to understand?

But, big government issues aside, the *Plata* majority decision, authored by Justice Kennedy, is a gross misinterpretation of the congressional Prison Litigation Reform Act of 1995 (PLRA).

The Eighth Amendment to the United States Constitution prohibits the infliction of cruel and unusual punishment. When society removes the ability of a person to provide his own food, clothing, shelter and health care by incarcerating him, clearly there are certain minimal obligations the constitution imposes upon those charged with administering his punishment. No justice would disagree that some of the examples of past horrors in the California system, as outlined in this decision, represent clear Eighth Amendment violations. But, this decision does not address the release of any of those victims.

This case was brought by two classes of California prisoners - those with serious mental disorders and those with serious medical conditions. The PLRA states that judicial relief with respect to prison conditions shall extend "no further than necessary to correct the violation of a Federal right of a particular plaintiff or plaintiffs"; that the relief must be "narrowly drawn and extend no further than necessary to correct the violation"; and that it must be "the least intrusive means necessary to correct the violation."

Justice Scalia, in dissent, has a novel idea. How about interpreting the terms of the PLRA, above, in accordance with what they say? He states: "In my view, a court may not order a prisoner's release unless it determines that the prisoner is suffering from a violation of his constitutional rights, and that his release, and no other relief, will remedy that violation. Thus, if the court determines that a particular prisoner is being denied constitutionally required medical treatment, and the release of that prisoner (and no other remedy) would enable him to obtain medical treatment, then the court can order his release; but a court may not order the release of prisoners who have suffered no violations of their constitutional rights, merely to make it less likely that that will happen to them in the future."

It is conceivable that none of the 40,000 to be released will ever have been subjected to any cruel or unusual punishment (even as defined by the liberal majority) and the vast majority of them will never have suffered a serious mental disorder or medical condition while incarcerated. Yet, the majority justifies the release of prisoners whose rights will never have been violated on the premise that a reduction in overcrowding will decrease the odds of Eighth Amendment violations occurring in the future. On that theory, closing all prisons would better achieve their goal.

The majority supports its warm-and-fuzzy-feel-good outcome, in part, by the testimony of a correctional officer who said that, in one prison, "up to" 50 sick inmates "may" be held together in a 12- by 20-foot cage for "up to" five hours awaiting treatment. This testimony is meaningless and ambiguous at best, but the majority apparently believes it important enough to mention in support of this massive release of prisoners. The officer appears to be describing a typical emergency room in a major urban community hospital on a Friday night. Such is hardly the fodder of cruel and unusual punishment.

My conservative heart bleeds for the prosecutors, witnesses, taxpayers and victims of at least 40,000 proven crimes in California, not to mention their countless extended families. These "classes" rarely get any mention in a case like this because there is no constitutional right to justice for "victims" of crime. Perhaps there should be.

One

PLEA: By now, you should be getting the clear message. If we fail to elect presidents that will nominate constitutional conservatives to the High Court and fail to elect senators of the same breed, we will run the grave risk of a power shift in the wrong direction. I am hoping that is as clear as a Liberty Bell to you.

Chapter Twelve

ONE ROBE SHORT ON JUNE 26, 2013, ALTERED THE TRADITIONAL INSTITUTION OF MARRIAGE!

On June 26, 2013, the traditional family - the Biblical family - was severely undermined in the United States of America because constitutional jurists were outnumbered by **one robe**.

The ruling in *United States v. Windsor* will continue to harm the traditional family fabric of this nation unless and until one more constitutional jurist replaces a progressive, agenda-driven, policy-making jurist on the High Court. As we go to press, the five justices who disregarded their oath of office in this case remain on the Court. Justice Kennedy (who authored the opinion) and Justices Ginsburg, Breyer, Sotomayor and Kagan (who went along with it) outnumbered the four who did not: Chief Justice Roberts and Justices Scalia, Thomas and Alito.

Our Constitution gives the presidents we elect the power to nominate the jurists that make up the group of nine on the Supreme Court. We, in our various states, also elect the senators who vote to confirm or reject those nominations.

Christians! I'm talkin' to you. Justices Sotomayor and Kagan were nominated by President Obama during his first term and were then confirmed (68-31 and 63-37, respectively) by a Democratic-controlled Senate. A "President McCain" would not have appointed liberals to fill seats on the Court and the conservative balance would have shifted by at least one more vote, altering the following case from 5-4 against to 5-4 in favor of preserving marriage as an institution between one man and one woman. If you voted for President Obama (or you did not vote or voted for a third party which is tantamount to voting for President Obama), then you - yes, you - own the decision that altered the institution of marriage in America.

ONE

To fully understand what a difference **one robe** and **one vote** - your vote - can make, please read this case carefully. You simply have to gain this knowledge and share it with your family and neighbors. I will help with commentary throughout. This is a case where we fell **one robe short** of victory – **one robe short** of preserving our Judeo-Christian heritage.

UNITED STATES V. WINDSOR

SUREME COURT OF THE UNITED STATES
June 26, 2013
[5 – 4]

OPINION: Kennedy/Ginsburg/Breyer/Sotomayor/Kagan...[New York residents Edith Windsor and Thea Spyer were married in a lawful ceremony in Canada in 2007 and then returned to their home in New York City.] When Spyer died in 2009, she left her entire estate to Windsor. Windsor sought to claim the estate tax exemption for surviving spouses. She was barred from doing so, however, by a federal law, the Defense of Marriage Act (DOMA). [That Act] excludes a same-sex partner from the definition of "spouse" as that term is used in federal statutes. Windsor paid the taxes, [then] filed suit to challenge the constitutionality of this provision. The United States District Court and the Court of Appeals ruled that this portion of the statute is unconstitutional and ordered the United States to pay Windsor a refund. This Court granted certiorari and now affirms the judgment in Windsor's favor.

Certiorari: the act of granting permission to hear an appeal.

> A short summary should get you off on the right foot. The tax code provides for an exemption from estate tax on property left by a spouse to a surviving spouse. Having been lawfully married in Canada, Windsor sought this exemption in the U.S. as a surviving spouse. The Defense of Marriage Act (DOMA), however, excludes a same-sex partner from the definition of "spouse" for federal estate tax purposes. She challenged the constitutionality of DOMA's definition in the federal District Court and won. She then won in the Court of Appeals and wins, again, here in the Supreme Court - the end of the road for traditional marriage at the federal level, at least for the time being. Let's explore this disaster.

I

In 1996, as some States were beginning to consider the concept of same-sex marriage and before any State had acted to permit it, Congress enacted the Defense of Marriage Act. DOMA… [defines] "marriage" and "spouse"…as follows:

> "In determining the meaning of any [federal law], the word 'marriage' means only a legal union between one man and one woman as husband and wife, and the word 'spouse' refers only to a person of the opposite sex who is a husband or a wife."

The definitional provision does not by its terms forbid States from enacting laws permitting same-sex marriages or civil unions or providing state benefits to residents in that status. The enactment's comprehensive definition of marriage…, however, does control over 1,000 federal laws in which marital or spousal status is addressed as a matter of federal law.

[The State of New York recognizes their Canadian marriage to be a valid one.]

ONE

Because DOMA denies federal recognition to same-sex spouses, Windsor did not qualify for the marital exemption from the federal estate tax, which excludes from taxation "any interest in property which passes or has passed from the decedent to his surviving spouse." Windsor paid $363,053 in estate taxes and sought a refund...She contended that DOMA violates the guarantee of equal protection, as applied to the Federal Government through the Fifth Amendment.

While the tax refund suit was pending, the Attorney General of the United States notified the Speaker of the House of Representatives that the Department of Justice [per the president's directive] would no longer defend the constitutionality of DOMA's [definition of marriage.]

> This notification is called a §530D letter. Apparently, it is sent to Congress when the administration refuses to defend a law it deems to be unconstitutional.

...This case is unusual...because the §530D letter was not preceded by an adverse judgment...

> In other words, normally a §530D letter would be sent after first losing a constitutional challenge in a trial or appellate court and then deciding not to appeal that ruling. President Obama's administration decided to send this §530D letter before the initial District Court ruling striking down the law was even reached.

In response to the notice from the Attorney General, the Bipartisan Legal Advisory Group (BLAG) of the House of Representatives voted to intervene in the litigation to defend the constitutionality of...DOMA [and was permitted to do so.]...

Effectively, all that means is that instead of the United States Government (the administration) defending the constitutionality of DOMA, the Supreme Court granted permission to the Bipartisan Legal Advisory Group of the House of Representatives to take on that role.

II

> Here, the Court discusses standing, a concept not relevant to our discussion and, therefore, not provided.

III

...[Until recently,] many citizens had not even considered the possibility that two persons of the same sex might aspire to occupy the same status and dignity as that of a man and woman in lawful marriage. For marriage between a man and a woman no doubt had been thought of by most people as essential to the very definition of that term and to its role and function throughout the history of civilization. That belief, for many who long have held it, became even more urgent, more cherished when challenged. For others, however, came the beginnings of a new perspective, a new insight. Accordingly,... the limitation of lawful marriage to heterosexual couples, which for centuries had been deemed both necessary and fundamental, came to be seen in New York and certain other States as an unjust exclusion.

Slowly at first and then in rapid course, the laws of New York came to acknowledge the urgency of this issue for same-sex couples who wanted to affirm their commitment to one another before their children, their family, their friends, and their community. And so New York recognized same-sex marriages performed elsewhere; and then it later amended its own marriage laws to permit same-sex marriage. [As of this writing,] New York [plus 11 other States and the District of Columbia] decided that same-sex couples should have the right to marry and so live with pride in themselves and their union and in a status of equality with all other married persons. After a statewide deliberative process that enabled its citizens to discuss and weigh arguments for and against same-sex marriage, New York acted to enlarge the definition of marriage to correct what its citizens and elected representatives perceived to be an injustice that they had not earlier known or understood.

Against this background of lawful same-sex marriage in some States, the design, purpose, and effect of DOMA should be considered as the beginning point in deciding whether it is valid under the Constitution. By history and tradition the definition and regulation of marriage…has been treated as being within the authority and realm of the separate States. Yet it is further established that Congress, in enacting discrete statutes, can make determinations that bear on marital rights and privileges...

DOMA…enacts a directive applicable to over 1,000 federal statutes and the whole realm of federal regulations. And its operation is directed to a class of persons that the laws of New York, and of 11 other States, have sought to protect...

State laws defining and regulating marriage, of course, must respect the constitutional rights of persons (*Loving v. Virginia* (1967)); but, subject to those guarantees, "regulation of domestic relations" is "an area that has long been regarded as a virtually exclusive province of the States."

> The ruling in *Loving v. Virginia* struck down Virginia's law that had prohibited interracial marriage.

The recognition of civil marriages is central to state domestic relations law applicable to its residents and citizens...The definition of marriage is the foundation of the State's broader authority to regulate the subject of domestic relations with respect to the "protection of offspring, property interests, and the enforcement of marital responsibilities. The states, at the time of the adoption of the Constitution, possessed full power over the subject of marriage and divorce...and the Constitution delegated no authority to the Government of the United States on the subject of marriage and divorce."...

Consistent with this allocation of authority, the Federal Government, through our history, has deferred to state-law policy decisions with respect to domestic relations...

The significance of state responsibilities for the definition and regulation of marriage dates to the nation's beginning; for "when the Constitution was adopted the common understanding was that the domestic relations of husband and wife and parent and child were matters reserved to the States." Marriage laws vary in some respects from State to State. For example, the required minimum age is 16 in Vermont, but only 13 in New Hampshire. Likewise the permissible degree of consanguinity can vary (most States permit first cousins to marry, but a handful - such as Iowa and Washington - prohibit the practice)...

Against this background DOMA rejects the long-established precept that the incidents, benefits, and obligations of marriage are uniform for all married couples within each State, though they may vary, subject to constitutional guarantees, from one State to the next. Despite these considerations, it is unnecessary to decide whether this federal intrusion on state power is a violation of the Constitution because it disrupts the federal balance. The State's power in defining the marital relation is of central relevance in this case quite apart from principles of federalism. Here the State's decision to give this class of persons the right to marry conferred upon them a dignity and status of immense import. When the State used its historic and essential authority to define the marital relation in this way, its role and its power in making the decision enhanced the recognition, dignity, and protection of the class in their own community. DOMA, because of its reach and extent, departs from this history and tradition of reliance on state law to define marriage...

Federalism: a system of government whereby the same geographic area is controlled by two separate governments. In our nation, that means the Feds govern the nation within its sphere and each state governs itself within its sphere. The tension between state rights and nationalism was designed to promote a healthy check on the power of each.

I wonder? What do you think this same Court will do when they are asked to rely on a state's law that excludes same-sex relationships from the legal status of marriage?

The States' interest in defining and regulating the marital relation, subject to constitutional guarantees, stems from the understanding that marriage is more than a routine classification for purposes of certain statutory benefits. Private, consensual sexual intimacy between two adult persons of the same sex may not be punished by the State, and it can form "but one element in a personal bond that is more enduring." *Lawrence v. Texas* (2003).

The ruling in *Lawrence v. Texas* struck down sodomy laws that [had criminalized] same-sex activity...

> The ruling in *Lawrence v. Texas* struck down sodomy laws that criminalized same-sex sex. Laws similar in nature had been considered constitutional for well-over 200 years; indeed, they had been considered to set the moral standard for the world for thousands of years! If that statement angers you, I'm not sure why. It is simply a fact.

By its recognition of the validity of same-sex marriages performed in other jurisdictions and then by authorizing same-sex unions and same-sex marriages, New York sought to give further protection and dignity to that bond. For same-sex couples who wished to be married, the State acted to give their lawful conduct a lawful status. This status is a far-reaching legal acknowledgment of the intimate relationship between two people, a relationship deemed by the State worthy of dignity in the community equal with all other marriages. It reflects both the community's considered perspective on the historical roots of the institution of marriage and its **evolving understanding** of the meaning of equality.

> Liberal justices have embraced the phrase "evolving understanding" or "evolving standards" in the past few decades. The problem with the terminology is that it has become a judicial philosophy of some jurists that they are somehow empowered with authority to make law by deciding for themselves, as opposed to our elected legislators, just exactly what has "evolved" and when it has sufficiently "evolved" to make it the law of the land without your consent.

IV

DOMA seeks to injure the very class New York seeks to protect. By doing so it violates basic due process and equal protection principles applicable to the Federal Government. The Constitution's guarantee of equality "must at the very least mean that a bare congressional desire to harm a politically unpopular group cannot" justify disparate treatment of that group. In determining whether a law is [motivated] by an improper...purpose, "discriminations of an unusual character" especially require careful consideration. DOMA cannot survive under these principles. The responsibility of the States for the regulation of domestic relations is an important indicator of the substantial societal impact the State's classifications have in the daily lives and customs of its people. DOMA's unusual deviation from the usual tradition of recognizing and accepting state definitions of marriage here operates to deprive same-sex couples of the benefits and responsibilities that come with the federal recognition of their marriages...

The history of DOMA's enactment and its own text demonstrate that interference with the equal dignity of same-sex marriages, a dignity conferred by the States in the exercise of their sovereign power, was more than an incidental effect of the federal statute. It was its essence. The House Report announced its conclusion that "it is both appropriate and necessary for Congress to do what it can to defend the institution of traditional heterosexual marriage...[It] is appropriately entitled the 'Defense of Marriage Act.' The effort to redefine 'marriage' to extend to homosexual couples is a truly radical proposal that would fundamentally alter the institution of marriage." The House concluded that DOMA expresses "both moral disapproval of homosexuality, and a moral conviction that heterosexuality better comports with traditional (especially Judeo-Christian) morality." The stated purpose of the law was to promote an "interest in protecting the traditional moral teachings reflected in heterosexual-only marriage laws."...

DOMA...places same-sex couples in an unstable position of being in a second-tier marriage. The differentiation demeans the couple, whose moral and sexual choices the Constitution protects and whose relationship the State has sought to dignify. And it humiliates tens of thousands of children now being raised by same-sex couples…

> Humiliation is the direct result of defying God's law. Christians, I feel your frustration. You will feel much better when you read the dissenting opinions in this case even though they leave us **one robe short**.

What has been explained to this point should more than suffice to establish that the principal purpose and the necessary effect of this law are to demean those persons who are in a lawful same-sex marriage. This requires the Court to hold, as it now does, that DOMA is unconstitutional as a deprivation of the liberty of the person protected by the Fifth Amendment of the Constitution…

DOMA instructs all federal officials, and indeed all persons with whom same-sex couples interact, including their own children, that their marriage is less worthy than the marriages of others. The federal statute is invalid, for no legitimate purpose overcomes the purpose and effect to disparage and to injure those whom the State, by its marriage laws, sought to protect in personhood and dignity. By seeking to displace this protection and treating those persons as living in marriages less respected than others, the federal statute is in violation of the Fifth Amendment. This opinion and its holding are confined to those lawful marriages.

> Justice Scalia, in dissent, believes this statement will be short-lived. Nevertheless, the majority is saying that the Act's definition of marriage is unconstitutional only in cases where the underlying state law favors same-sex marriage.
>
> Also, the decided implication is that this majority would not strike down a state law prohibiting same-sex marriage. Scalia isn't buying it.

ONE

The judgment of the Court of Appeals for the Second Circuit is affirmed. It is so ordered.

DISSENT: Roberts...The Court does not have before it, and the logic of its opinion does not decide, the distinct question whether the States, in the exercise of their "historic and essential authority to define the marital relation," may continue to utilize the traditional definition of marriage.

> So, at least for now, this ruling does not affect a state's right to define marriage as it sees fit, even if that definition should exclude same-sex participation.

...We may in the future have to resolve challenges to state marriage definitions affecting same-sex couples. That issue, however, is not before us in this case...I write only to highlight the limits of the majority's holding and reasoning today, lest its opinion be taken to resolve...a question that all agree, and the Court explicitly acknowledges, is not at issue.

DISSENT: Scalia/Thomas/Roberts...This case is about...the power of our people to govern themselves, and the power of this Court to pronounce the law. Today's opinion aggrandizes the latter, with the predictable consequence of diminishing the former...We have no power under the Constitution to invalidate this democratically adopted legislation. The Court's errors on both points spring forth from the same diseased root: an exalted conception of the role of this institution in America.

> Again, the discussion of the concept of "standing" is not provided as it is irrelevant to the issues of concern to us.

A

There are many remarkable things about the majority's...holding. The first is how rootless and shifting its justifications are. For example, the opinion starts with seven full pages about the traditional power of States to define domestic relations - initially fooling many readers, I am sure, into thinking that this is a federalism opinion. But we are eventually told that "it is unnecessary to decide whether this federal intrusion on state power is a violation of the Constitution" and that "the State's power in defining the marital relation is of central relevance in this case quite apart from principles of federalism" because "the State's decision to give this class of persons the right to marry conferred upon them a dignity and status of immense import." But no one questions the power of the States to define marriage (with the concomitant conferral of dignity and status), so what is the point of devoting seven pages to describing how long and well established that power is? Even after the opinion has formally disclaimed reliance upon principles of federalism, mentions of "the usual tradition of recognizing and accepting state definitions of marriage" continue. What to make of this? The opinion never explains. My guess is that the majority, while reluctant to suggest that defining the meaning of "marriage" in federal statutes is unsupported by any of the Federal Government's enumerated powers, nonetheless needs some rhetorical basis to support its pretense that today's prohibition of laws excluding same-sex marriage is confined to the Federal Government (leaving the second, state-law shoe to be dropped later, maybe next Term). But I am only guessing.

> "I am only guessing" is sarcasm for "wait until you see what these five have in store for America down the line."

Equally perplexing are the opinion's references to "the Constitution's guarantee of equality." Near the end of the opinion, we are told that although the "equal protection guarantee of the Fourteenth

ONE

Amendment makes the Fifth Amendment due process right all the more specific and all the better understood and preserved"—what can that mean?— "the Fifth Amendment itself withdraws from Government the power to degrade or demean in the way this law does." The only possible interpretation of this statement is that the Equal Protection Clause...is not the basis for today's holding...

The majority opinion...says that DOMA is unconstitutional as "a deprivation of the liberty of the person protected by the Fifth Amendment of the Constitution"; that it violates "basic due process" principles; and that it inflicts an "injury and indignity" of a kind that denies "an essential part of the liberty protected by the Fifth Amendment." The majority never utters the dreaded words "substantive due process," perhaps sensing the disrepute into which that doctrine has fallen, but that is what those statements mean. Yet the opinion does not argue that same-sex marriage is "deeply rooted in this nation's history and tradition," a claim that would of course be quite absurd. So would the further suggestion (also necessary, under our substantive-due-process precedents) that a world in which DOMA exists is one bereft of "ordered liberty." Some might conclude that this loaf could have used a while longer in the oven. But that would be wrong; it is already overcooked. The most expert care in preparation cannot redeem a bad recipe. The sum of all the Court's nonspecific hand-waving is that this law is invalid (maybe on equal-protection grounds, maybe on substantive-due-process grounds, and perhaps with some amorphous federalism component playing a role) because it is motivated by a "bare...desire to harm" couples in same-sex marriages. It is this proposition with which I will therefore engage...

Justice Alito will explain the concept of "substantive due process" in his dissent, below.

B

The Constitution does not forbid the government to enforce traditional moral and sexual norms...It is enough to say that the Constitution neither requires nor forbids our society to approve of same-sex marriage, much as it neither requires nor forbids us to approve of no-fault divorce, polygamy, or the consumption of alcohol.

However, even setting aside traditional moral disapproval of same-sex marriage (or indeed same-sex sex), there are many perfectly valid - indeed, downright boring - justifying rationales for this legislation. Their existence ought to be the end of this case. For they give the lie to the Court's conclusion that only those with hateful hearts could have voted "aye" on this Act. And more importantly, they serve to make the contents of the legislators' hearts quite irrelevant: "It is a familiar principle of constitutional law that this Court will not strike down an otherwise constitutional statute on the basis of an alleged illicit legislative motive." Or at least it was a familiar principle. By holding to the contrary, the majority has declared open season on any law that (in the opinion of the law's opponents and any panel of like-minded federal judges) can be characterized as mean-spirited.

The majority concludes that the only motive for this Act was the "bare...desire to harm a politically unpopular group." Bear in mind that the object of this condemnation is...our respected coordinate branches, the Congress and Presidency of the United States. Laying such a charge against them should require the most extraordinary evidence, and I would have thought that every attempt would be made to indulge a [less offensive] explanation for the statute. The majority does the opposite - affirmatively concealing from the reader the arguments that exist in justification. It makes only a passing mention of the "arguments put forward" by the Act's defenders, and

ONE

does not even trouble to paraphrase or describe them. I imagine that this is because it is harder to maintain the illusion of the Act's supporters as unhinged members of a wild-eyed lynch mob when one first describes their views as they see them.

To choose just one of these defenders' arguments, DOMA avoids difficult choice-of-law issues that will now arise absent a uniform federal definition of marriage. Imagine a pair of women who marry in Albany and then move to Alabama, which does not "recognize as valid any marriage of parties of the same sex." When the couple files their next federal tax return, may it be a joint one? Which State's law controls, for federal-law purposes: their State of celebration (which recognizes the marriage) or their State of domicile (which does not)? (Does the answer depend on whether they were just visiting in Albany?) Are these questions to be answered as a matter of federal common law, or perhaps by borrowing a State's choice-of-law rules? If so, which State's? And what about States where the status of an out-of-state same-sex marriage is an unsettled question under local law? DOMA avoided all of this uncertainty by specifying which marriages would be recognized for federal purposes. That is a classic purpose for a definitional provision.

Further, DOMA preserves the intended effects of prior legislation against then-unforeseen changes in circumstance. When Congress provided (for example) that a special estate-tax exemption would exist for spouses, this exemption reached only opposite-sex spouses - those being the only sort that were recognized in any State at the time of DOMA's passage. When it became clear that changes in state law might one day alter that balance, DOMA's definitional section was enacted to ensure that state-level experimentation did not automatically alter the basic operation of federal law, unless and until Congress made the further judgment to do so on its own. That is not animus - just stabilizing prudence. Congress has hardly demonstrated itself unwilling to make such further, revising judgments upon due deliberation.

The Court mentions none of this. Instead, it accuses the Congress that enacted this law and the president who signed it of something much worse than, for example, having acted in excess of enumerated federal powers - or even having drawn distinctions that prove to be irrational. Those legal errors may be made in good faith, errors though they are. But the majority says that the supporters of this Act acted with malice - with the "purpose to disparage and to injure" same-sex couples. It says that the motivation for DOMA was to "demean"; to "impose inequality"; to "impose...a stigma"; to deny people "equal dignity"; to brand gay people as "unworthy"; and to "humiliate" their children.

I am sure these accusations are quite untrue. To be sure (as the majority points out), the legislation is called the Defense of Marriage Act. But to defend traditional marriage is not to condemn, demean, or humiliate those who would prefer other arrangements, any more than to defend the Constitution of the United States is to condemn, demean, or humiliate other constitutions. **To hurl such accusations so casually demeans this institution.** In the majority's judgment, any resistance to its holding is beyond the pale of reasoned disagreement. To question its high-handed invalidation of a presumptively valid statute is to act (the majority is sure) with the purpose to "disparage," "injure," "degrade," "demean," and "humiliate" our fellow human beings, our fellow citizens, who are homosexual. All that, simply for supporting an Act that did no more than codify an aspect of marriage that had been unquestioned in our society for most of

ONE

its existence - indeed, had been unquestioned in virtually all societies for virtually all of human history. **It is one thing for a society to elect change; it is another for a court of law to impose change by adjudging those who oppose it...enemies of the human race.**

> Five of nine justices of the Supreme Court label our motivation to preserve traditional marriage as born out of hate - a position that has been thought virtuous for almost all of human history and most certainly founded upon Judeo-Christian principles. Does judicial arrogance come to mind?

The penultimate sentence of the majority's opinion is a naked declaration that "this opinion and its holding are confined" to those couples "joined in same-sex marriages made lawful by the State." I have heard such "bald, unreasoned disclaimers" before. When the Court declared a constitutional right to homosexual sodomy, we were assured that the case had nothing, nothing at all to do with "whether the government must give formal recognition to any relationship that homosexual persons seek to enter." Now we are told that DOMA is invalid because it "demeans the couple, whose moral and sexual choices the Constitution protects" - with an accompanying citation of *Lawrence v. Texas*. It takes real cheek for today's majority to assure us, as it is going out the door, that a constitutional requirement to give formal recognition to same-sex marriage is not at issue here - when what has preceded that assurance is a lecture on how superior the majority's moral judgment in favor of same-sex marriage is to the Congress's hateful moral judgment against it. I promise you this: The only thing that will "confine" the Court's holding is its sense of what it can get away with.

I do not mean to suggest disagreement with THE CHIEF JUSTICE's view that lower federal courts and state courts can distinguish today's case when the issue before them is state denial of marital status to same-sex couples - or even that this Court could theoretically do so. Lord, an opinion with such scatter-shot rationales as this one…can be distinguished in many ways. And deserves to be. State and lower federal courts should take the Court at its word and distinguish away.

> Distinguish: to show dissimilarities between a prior case and the facts of the present case.

In my opinion, however, the view that this Court will take of state prohibition of same-sex marriage is indicated beyond mistaking by today's opinion. As I have said, the real rationale of today's opinion, whatever disappearing trail of its legalistic argle-bargle one chooses to follow, is that DOMA is motivated by "bare…desire to harm" couples in same-sex marriages. How easy it is, indeed how inevitable, to reach the same conclusion with regard to state laws denying same-sex couples marital status...

> Argle-bargle: disagreement.

In sum, that Court which finds it so horrific that Congress irrationally and hatefully robbed same-sex couples of the "personhood and dignity" which state legislatures conferred upon them, will of a certitude be similarly appalled by state legislatures' irrational and hateful failure to acknowledge that "personhood and dignity" in the first place. As far as this Court is concerned, no one should be fooled; it is just a matter of listening and waiting for the other shoe.

By formally declaring anyone opposed to same-sex marriage an enemy of human decency, the majority arms well every challenger to a

ONE

state law restricting marriage to its traditional definition. Henceforth those challengers will lead with this Court's declaration that there is "no legitimate purpose" served by such a law, and will claim that the traditional definition has "the purpose and effect to disparage and to injure" the "personhood and dignity" of same-sex couples. The majority's limiting assurance will be meaningless in the face of language like that, as the majority well knows. That is why the language is there. The result will be a judicial distortion of our society's debate over marriage - a debate that can seem in need of our clumsy "help" only to a member of this institution.

As to that debate: Few public controversies touch an institution so central to the lives of so many, and few inspire such attendant passion by good people on all sides. Few public controversies will ever demonstrate so vividly the beauty of what our Framers gave us, a gift the Court pawns today to buy its stolen moment in the spotlight: a system of government that permits us to rule ourselves. Since DOMA's passage, citizens on all sides of the question have seen victories and they have seen defeats. There have been plebiscites, legislation, persuasion, and loud voices - in other words, democracy. Victories in one place for some (North Carolina amended their constitution to provide that "marriage between one man and one woman is the only domestic legal union that shall be valid or recognized in this State" - approved by a popular vote of 61% to 39% on May 8, 2012) are offset by victories in other places for others (Maryland voted to establish "that Maryland's civil marriage laws allow gay and lesbian couples to obtain a civil marriage license" - approved by a popular vote of 52% to 48% on November 6, 2012). Even in a single State, the question has come out differently on different occasions. Compare Maine (permitting "the State of Maine to issue marriage licenses to same-sex couples" - approved by a popular vote 53% to 47% on November 6, 2012) with Maine (rejecting "the new law that lets same-sex couples marry" - approved by a popular vote 53% to 47%, on November 3, 2009).

In the majority's telling, this story is black-and-white: Hate your neighbor or come along with us. The truth is more complicated. It is hard to admit that one's political opponents are not monsters, especially in a struggle like this one, and the challenge in the end proves more than today's Court can handle. Too bad. A reminder that disagreement over something so fundamental as marriage can still be politically legitimate would have been a fit task for what in earlier times was called the judicial temperament. We might have covered ourselves with honor today, by promising all sides of this debate that it was theirs to settle and that we would respect their resolution. We might have let the People decide.

> "Theirs to settle" in the sense that deciding this question is no business of judges.

But that the majority will not do. Some will rejoice in today's decision, and some will despair at it; that is the nature of a controversy that matters so much to so many. **But the Court has cheated both sides, robbing the winners of an honest victory, and the losers of the peace that comes from a fair defeat. We owed both of them better. I dissent.**

DISSENT: Alito/Thomas...Our nation is engaged in a heated debate about...the nature of the institution of marriage. Respondent Edith Windsor, supported by the United States, asks this Court to intervene in that debate, and although she couches her argument in different terms, what she seeks is a holding that enshrines in the Constitution a particular understanding of marriage under which the sex of the

ONE

partners makes no difference. The Constitution, however, does not dictate that choice. It leaves the choice to the people, acting through their elected representatives at both the federal and state levels. I would therefore hold that Congress did not violate Windsor's constitutional rights by enacting...the Defense of Marriage Act (DOMA), which defines the meaning of marriage under federal statutes that either confer upon married persons certain federal benefits or impose upon them certain federal obligations.

I

> Again, the discussion of "standing" is not provided.

II

...Same-sex marriage presents a highly emotional and important question of public policy - but not a difficult question of constitutional law. The Constitution does not guarantee the right to enter into a same-sex marriage. Indeed, no provision of the Constitution speaks to the issue.

The Court has sometimes found the Due Process Clauses to have a substantive component that guarantees liberties beyond the absence of physical restraint. And the Court's holding that "DOMA is unconstitutional as a deprivation of the liberty of the person protected by the Fifth Amendment of the Constitution" suggests that substantive due process may partially underlie the Court's decision today. But it is well established that any "substantive" component to the Due Process Clause protects only "those fundamental rights and liberties which are, objectively, 'deeply rooted in this nation's history and tradition'"...as well as "implicit in the concept of ordered liberty, such that neither liberty nor justice would exist if they were sacrificed."

> The reason "substantive due process" is disapproved as a jurist's tool is that it gives judges too much power. Too much power to "find" a right that otherwise does not exist in the Constitution. But, when used, they still must find that the alleged right at hand is "deeply rooted in this nation's history and tradition" and that it is "implicit in the concept of ordered liberty." At least that was so before this decision.

It is beyond dispute that the right to same-sex marriage is not deeply rooted in this nation's history and tradition. In this country, no State permitted same-sex marriage until the Massachusetts Supreme Judicial Court held in 2003 that limiting marriage to opposite-sex couples violated the State Constitution. Nor is the right to same-sex marriage deeply rooted in the traditions of other nations. No country allowed same-sex couples to marry until the Netherlands did so in 2000.

What Windsor and the United States seek, therefore, is not the protection of a deeply rooted right but the recognition of a very new right, and they seek this innovation not from a legislative body elected by the people, but from unelected judges. Faced with such a request, judges have cause for both caution and humility.

The family is an ancient and universal human institution. Family structure reflects the characteristics of a civilization, and changes in family structure and in the popular understanding of marriage and the family can have profound effects. Past changes in the understanding of marriage - for example, the gradual ascendance of the idea that romantic love is a prerequisite to marriage - have had far-reaching consequences. But the process by which such consequences come about is complex, involving the interaction of numerous factors, and tends to occur over an extended period of time.

ONE

We can expect something similar to take place if same-sex marriage becomes widely accepted. The long-term consequences of this change are not now known and are unlikely to be ascertainable for some time to come. There are those who think that allowing same-sex marriage will seriously undermine the institution of marriage.

At present, no one - including social scientists, philosophers, and historians - can predict with any certainty what the long-term ramifications of widespread acceptance of same-sex marriage will be.

> I would expect such a statement from a sociologist, with one caveat. At a minimum, very "long-term" widespread acceptance will lead to extinction. Additionally, a Bible scholar can predict with certainty what ramifications will befall our society.

And judges are certainly not equipped to make such an assessment. The Members of this Court have the authority and the responsibility to interpret and apply the Constitution. Thus, if the Constitution contained a provision guaranteeing the right to marry a person of the same sex, it would be our duty to enforce that right. But the Constitution simply does not speak to the issue of same-sex marriage. In our system of government, ultimate sovereignty rests with the people, and the people have the right to control their own destiny. Any change on a question so fundamental should be made by the people through their elected officials…

III

…To the extent that the Court takes the position that the question of same-sex marriage should be resolved primarily at the state level, I wholeheartedly agree. I hope that the Court will ultimately permit the people of each State to decide this question for themselves. Unless the Court is willing to allow this to occur,

the whiffs of federalism in the today's opinion of the Court will soon be scattered to the wind... I respectfully dissent.

SUMMARY: By a **one robe margin** the Supreme Court denied your elected representatives in Congress the right to pass legislation that defines marriage as being exclusively between one man and one woman. This decision destroys the fabric of our society that is based upon Judeo-Christian values and has served us well for over 200 years. Where states have adopted same-sex marriage, this decision says that all federal laws that apply to a hetero-sexual married couple, must also apply to a same-sex married couple. It does not rule upon whether a state may deny same-sex marriage - in fact, it strongly implies that it may.

COMMENT: I believe most gay and lesbian folks respect the views of those of us who believe their lifestyle is a sin. Most do not hate a different point of view and we certainly do not hate them. Christians aren't any "better" than anyone else, but to ask us to embrace beliefs that are counter to our faith is to ask us to deny our God and thousands of years of human history. We believe same-sex marriage will ultimately destroy the very values our nation was built upon. If we cannot agree to disagree in a free society, something is seriously wrong with our nation. And, if you are honest, you will readily conclude that most of the true hate being fomented on this topic is emanating from the gay/lesbian extremists.

I could easily be good friends with a gay neighbor and I realize the possibility of someone in my immediate family taking on that lifestyle, but I will never deny my God. Why would a gay neighbor expect me to do so, except out of hate? And, I would love my family no less. Loving people can agree to disagree.

One

In spite of clear indications in support of the right of voters within a state to determine their own definition of marriage, **with the current balance on the Court**, the likelihood is very strong that, one day, the Supreme Court will strike down all state laws that deny same-sex marriage, regardless of the will of the people.

In fact, as I was writing this chapter, on Monday, October 6, 2014, the Supreme Court rejected appeals from five jurisdictions on this very issue of states' rights. Courts of Appeal in Indiana, Utah, Oklahoma, Virginia and Wisconsin all struck down the will of the voters in these respective states to ban same-sex marriage. Until further action, it appears the will of the people of these states doesn't count.

It takes four of nine justices to hear an appeal. It is possible that the votes necessary to hear an appeal on this issue will be forthcoming if and when a Court of Appeal rules in favor of a state's ban on same-sex marriage, but the odds of a conservative outcome with this court do not appear favorable. It didn't take long for Justice Scalia's forebodings to come about. Read the *Windsor* case again. The majority emphasized over and over again that the definition of marriage belongs to the voters of each state. In little over one year since *Windsor* was decided, the High Court could not even muster four votes to hear appeals from these traditional minded states who lost what the majority in *Windsor* implied they had the right to control.

I wholeheartedly agree with Justice Scalia's criticism of the *Windsor* majority: "We might have covered ourselves with honor today, by promising all sides of this debate that it was theirs to settle and that we would respect their resolution. We might have let the People decide…[T]he Court has cheated both sides, robbing the winners of an honest victory, and the losers of the peace that comes from a fair defeat. We owed both of them better."

In other words, not unlike the decision in *Roe v. Wade** on abortion, the definition of marriage should have been left to the majority of the citizens of each state, not to the overreach of five unelected Supreme Court justices.

As it turns out, this issue is moving along rather quickly. As I was proofing this chapter on November 6, 2014, the 6th Circuit Court of Appeal ruled that the states of Michigan, Kentucky, Ohio and Tennessee (all of whom had voted to define marriage as a male-female institution), were within their constitutional rights to do so. In other words, this most recent ruling conflicts with the ruling on October 6th, referred to above. And, the Supreme Court has since agreed to take on this appeal and heard oral arguments in that appeal recently. A decision is expected in June of 2015. I have high hopes, but I'm not holding my breath.

PLEA: With **one more robe**, *United States v. Windsor* can be reversed. The only way to help insure that will happen is to vote for a president (with nomination power) who will likely nominate Constitutional conservatives to the Supreme Court when seats become vacant and to vote for senators (with confirmation power) who will likely block the appointment of liberal nominees and confirm the appointment of conservative nominees. If you do not participate with your **one vote**, you will become part of the reason why this decision will continue to harm America. Either own this decision or help change it with your vote. There is no middle ground.

[NOTE: I left the foregoing timeline intact to reveal how fast this issue has moved along. Because, as we now know, the Supreme Court's ruling in *Obergefell v. Hodges** on June 26, 2015, took away the right of each State to define marriage as it has been defined for over 2,000 years! Without question, this outcome represents the

ONE

single greatest dereliction of the Article VI duty of each of these five justices to support the Constitution. These five are responsible for the worst attack upon our republic since our founding. They need to be named. They are Anthony Kennedy, Ruth Ginsburg, Stephen Breyer, Sonia Sotomayor and Elena Kagan. They need to be impeached. It won't happen. The fault lies with me. The fault lies with Everyman who has selfishly enjoyed the benefits of freedoms won by others while complacently letting them slowly slip away, relegated to the pages of history books. The *Obergefell* case is not about same-sex marriage. It is about an arrogance of power designed to transform America from the vision of Madison, Jefferson and "We, the People" to the vision of Pelosi, Reid, Durbin, Marx, Obama and Clinton without the consent of the governed.]

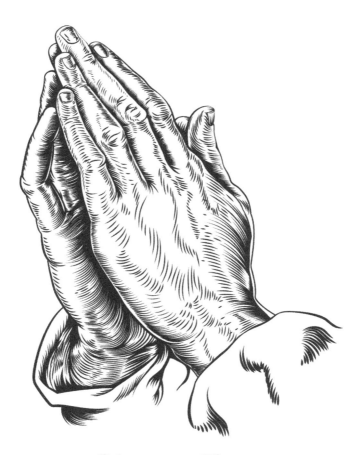

Chapter Thirteen

ONE ROBE LONG ON MAY 5, 2014, PRESERVED PRAYER IN GREECE!

Most of you will likely rejoice in the outcome of this case that preserved prayer to open monthly government meetings in Greece, New York – preserved, that is, by **one robe**.

I can predict the outcome of cases before the Supreme Court that involve constitutional questions with 90% accuracy, but this one surprised me. And, much to your surprise, this conservative Christian is ambivalent about its outcome. I believe in prayer. I believe no one should leave their faith at home, especially those who work in government and, yet, I have concerns that this outcome will come back to haunt Christians.

I am just wondering how the folks of Greece, New York, will feel when their community becomes less Christian and more Muslim. And, I have always wondered why Christianity seems to lean on the support of government for its survival. Are we that weak? No one has ever been able to show me where Jesus Christ sought the support of Rome. Guess who survived?

So, while this case is a victory in the short run, just keep in mind that government entities who wish to have prayer as an official part of their meetings cannot turn down prayers to Allah, Buddha, whatever "god" witches pray to or even a "prayer" to some type of atheist symbol. I have no problem with the idea that government cannot prefer Christianity. I am just wondering whether this victory might be of the Pyrrhic variety.

> Pyrrhic victory: a victory that inflicts such a devastating toll on the victor that it is tantamount to defeat.

My concerns aside, if you like this outcome, please understand that **one robe** added to the Court of the Kagan philosophy (see the dissent) will reverse this decision in *Greece v. Galloway**.

GREECE v. GALLOWAY
SUPREME COURT OF THE UNITED STATES
No. 12-696
May 5, 2014
[5 – 4]

OPINION: Kennedy/Roberts/Scalia/Thomas/Alito...The Court must decide whether the town of Greece, New York, imposes an impermissible establishment of religion by opening its monthly board meetings with a prayer. It must be concluded, consistent with the Court's opinion in *Marsh* v. *Chambers**, that no violation of the Constitution has been shown.

In other words, the procedure to open monthly board meetings with prayer in Greece, New York, was upheld by a 5-4 margin. Prayer wins!

I

Greece, a town with a population of 94,000, is in upstate New York. For some years, it began its monthly town board meetings with a moment of silence. In 1999, the newly elected town supervisor, John Auberger, decided to replicate the prayer practice he had found meaningful while serving in the county legislature. Following the roll call and recitation of the Pledge of Allegiance, Auberger would invite a local clergyman to the front of the room to deliver an invocation. After the prayer, Auberger would thank the minister for serving as the board's "chaplain for the month" and present him with a commemorative plaque. The prayer was intended to place town board members in a solemn and deliberative frame of mind, invoke divine guidance in town affairs, and follow a tradition practiced by Congress and dozens of state legislatures.

The town followed an informal method for selecting prayer givers, all of whom were unpaid volunteers. A town employee would call the congregations listed in a local directory until she found a minister available for that month's meeting. The town eventually compiled a list of willing "board chaplains" who had accepted invitations and agreed to return in the future. The town at no point excluded or denied an opportunity to a would-be prayer giver. Its leaders maintained that a minister or layperson of any persuasion, including an atheist, could give the invocation. But nearly all of the congregations in town were Christian; and from 1999 to 2007, all of the participating ministers were too.

Greece neither reviewed the prayers in advance of the meetings nor provided guidance as to their tone or content, in the belief that exercising any degree of control over the prayers would infringe both the free exercise and speech rights of the ministers. The town instead left the guest clergy free to compose their own devotions. The resulting prayers often sounded both civic and religious themes. Typical were invocations that asked the divinity to abide at the meeting and bestow blessings on the community:

> "Lord we ask you to send your spirit of servanthood upon all of us gathered here this evening to do your work for the benefit of all in our community. We ask you to bless our elected and appointed officials so they may deliberate with wisdom and act with courage. Bless the members of our community who come here to speak before the board so they may state their cause with honesty and humility...Lord we ask you to bless us all, that everything we do here tonight will move you to welcome us one day into your kingdom as good and faithful servants. We ask this in the name of our brother Jesus. Amen."

ONE

Some of the ministers spoke in a distinctly Christian idiom; and a minority invoked religious holidays, scripture, or doctrine, as in the following prayer:

> "Lord, God of all creation, we give you thanks and praise for your presence and action in the world. We look with anticipation to the celebration of Holy Week and Easter. It is in the solemn events of next week that we find the very heart and center of our Christian faith. We acknowledge the saving sacrifice of Jesus Christ on the cross. We draw strength, vitality, and confidence from his resurrection at Easter…We pray for peace in the world, an end to terrorism, violence, conflict, and war. We pray for stability, democracy, and good government in those countries in which our armed forces are now serving, especially in Iraq and Afghanistan…Praise and glory be yours, O Lord, now and forever more. Amen."

Respondents Susan Galloway and Linda Stephens attended town board meetings to speak about issues of local concern, and they objected that the prayers violated their religious or philosophical views. At one meeting, Galloway admonished board members that she found the prayers "offensive," "intolerable," and an affront to a "diverse community." After respondents complained that Christian themes pervaded the prayers, to the exclusion of citizens who did not share those beliefs, the town invited a Jewish layman and the chairman of the local Baha'i temple to deliver prayers. A Wiccan priestess who had read press reports about the prayer controversy requested, and was granted, an opportunity to give the invocation.

Galloway and Stephens brought suit in the United States District Court for the Western District of New York. They alleged that the town violated the First Amendment's Establishment Clause by preferring Christians over other prayer givers and by sponsoring sectarian prayers, such as those given "in Jesus' name." <u>They did not seek an end to the prayer practice, but rather requested an injunction that would limit the town to "inclusive and ecumenical" prayers that referred only to a "generic God" and would not associate the government with any one faith or belief.</u>

The District Court…upheld the prayer practice as consistent with the First Amendment. It found no impermissible preference for Christianity, noting that the town had opened the prayer program to all creeds and excluded none. Although most of the prayer givers were Christian, this fact reflected only the predominantly Christian identity of the town's congregations, rather than an official policy or practice of discriminating against minority faiths. The District Court found no authority for the proposition that the First Amendment required Greece to invite clergy from congregations beyond its borders in order to achieve a minimum level of religious diversity.

The District Court also rejected the theory that legislative prayer must be nonsectarian. The court began its inquiry with the opinion in *Marsh* v. *Chambers* which permitted prayer in state legislatures by a chaplain paid from the public purse, so long as the prayer opportunity was not "exploited to proselytize or advance any one, or to disparage any other, faith or belief." With respect to the prayer in Greece, the District Court concluded that references to Jesus, and the occasional request that the audience stand for the prayer, did not amount to impermissible proselytizing. It located in *Marsh* no additional requirement that the prayers be purged of sectarian content. In this regard the court quoted recent invocations offered in the U. S. House of Representatives "in the name of our Lord Jesus Christ" and situated prayer in this context as part a long tradition. Finally, the trial court noted this Court's statement in *Allegheny* v. *ACLU** that the

One

prayers in *Marsh* did not offend the Establishment Clause "because the particular chaplain had 'removed all references to Christ.'" But the District Court did not read that statement to mandate that legislative prayer be nonsectarian, at least in circumstances where the town permitted clergy from a variety of faiths to give invocations. By welcoming many viewpoints, the District Court concluded, the town would be unlikely to give the impression that it was affiliating itself with any one religion.

The Court of Appeals for the Second Circuit reversed. It held that some aspects of the prayer program, viewed in their totality by a reasonable observer, conveyed the message that Greece was endorsing Christianity. The town's failure to promote the prayer opportunity to the public, or to invite ministers from congregations outside the town limits, all but "ensured a Christian viewpoint." Although the court found no inherent problem in the sectarian content of the prayers, it concluded that the "steady drumbeat" of Christian prayer, unbroken by invocations from other faith traditions, tended to affiliate the town with Christianity. Finally, the court found it relevant that guest clergy sometimes spoke on behalf of all present at the meeting, as by saying "let us pray," or by asking audience members to stand and bow their heads: "The invitation . . . to participate in the prayer. . . placed audience members who are nonreligious or adherents of non-Christian religion in the awkward position of either participating in prayers invoking beliefs they did not share or appearing to show disrespect for the invocation." That board members bowed their heads or made the sign of the cross further conveyed the message that the town endorsed Christianity. The Court of Appeals emphasized that it was the "interaction of the facts present in this case," rather than any single element, that rendered the prayer unconstitutional.

Having granted certiorari to decide whether the town's prayer practice violates the Establishment Clause, the Court now reverses the judgment of the Court of Appeals.

> Therefore, five members of the Supreme Court sided with the Town of Greece and its prayer policy. Justice Kennedy is about to tell us why.

II

In *Marsh* v. *Chambers* the Court found no First Amendment violation in the Nebraska Legislature's practice of opening its sessions with a prayer delivered by a chaplain paid from state funds. The decision concluded that legislative prayer, while religious in nature, has long been understood as compatible with the Establishment Clause. As practiced by Congress since the framing of the Constitution, legislative prayer lends gravity to public business, reminds lawmakers to transcend petty differences in pursuit of a higher purpose, and expresses a common aspiration to a just and peaceful society. The Court has considered this symbolic expression to be a "tolerable acknowledgement of beliefs widely held," *Marsh,* rather than a first, treacherous step towards establishment of a state church.

Marsh is sometimes described as "carving out an exception" to the Court's Establishment Clause jurisprudence, because it sustained legislative prayer without subjecting the practice to "any of the formal 'tests' that have traditionally structured" this inquiry. The Court in *Marsh* found those tests unnecessary because history supported the conclusion that legislative invocations are compatible with the Establishment Clause. The First Congress made it an early item of business to appoint and pay official chaplains, and both the House and Senate have maintained the office virtually uninterrupted since that time. When *Marsh* was decided, in 1983, legislative prayer had

ONE

persisted in the Nebraska Legislature for more than a century, and the majority of the other States also had the same, consistent practice. Although no information has been cited by the parties to indicate how many local legislative bodies open their meetings with prayer, this practice too has historical precedent...In light of the unambiguous and unbroken history of more than 200 years, there can be no doubt that the practice of opening legislative sessions with a prayer has become part of the fabric of our society.

Yet *Marsh* must not be understood as permitting a practice that would amount to a constitutional violation if not for its historical foundation. The case teaches instead that the Establishment Clause must be interpreted "by reference to historical practices and understandings." That the First Congress provided for the appointment of chaplains only days after approving language for the First Amendment demonstrates that the Framers considered legislative prayer a benign acknowledgment of religion's role in society. In the 1850's, the judiciary committees in both the House and Senate reevaluated the practice of official chaplaincies after receiving petitions to abolish the office. The committees concluded that the office posed no threat of an establishment because lawmakers were not compelled to attend the daily prayer; no faith was excluded by law, nor any favored; and the cost of the chaplain's salary imposed a vanishingly small burden on taxpayers. *Marsh* stands for the proposition that it is not necessary to define the precise boundary of the Establishment Clause where history shows that the specific practice is permitted. Any test the Court adopts must acknowledge a practice that was accepted by the Framers and has withstood the critical scrutiny of time and political change. *Allegheny*; see also *Abington* v. *Schempp** ("The line we must draw between the permissible and the impermissible is one which accords with history and faithfully reflects the understanding of the Founding Fathers"). A test that would sweep away what has so long been settled would create new controversy and begin anew the very divisions along religious lines that the Establishment Clause seeks to prevent. *Van Orden v. Perry**.

The Court's inquiry, then, must be to determine whether the prayer practice in the town of Greece fits within the tradition long followed in Congress and the state legislatures. Respondents assert that the town's prayer exercise falls outside that tradition and transgresses the Establishment Clause for two independent but mutually reinforcing reasons. First, they argue that *Marsh* did not approve prayers containing sectarian language or themes, such as the prayers offered in Greece that referred to the "death, resurrection, and ascension of the Savior Jesus Christ" and the "saving sacrifice of Jesus Christ on the cross." Second, they argue that the setting and conduct of the town board meetings create social pressures that force nonadherents to remain in the room or even feign participation in order to avoid offending the representatives who sponsor the prayer and will vote on matters citizens bring before the board. The sectarian content of the prayers compounds the subtle coercive pressures, they argue, because the nonbeliever who might tolerate ecumenical prayer is forced to do the same for prayer that might be inimical to his or her beliefs.

A

Respondents maintain that prayer must be nonsectarian, or not identifiable with any one religion; and they fault the town for permitting guest chaplains to deliver prayers that "use overtly Christian terms" or "invoke specifics of Christian theology." A prayer is fitting for the public sphere, in their view, only if it contains the "most general, nonsectarian reference to God" and eschews mention of doctrines associated with any one faith. They argue that prayer which contemplates "the workings of the Holy Spirit, the events of Pentecost, and the belief that God 'has raised up the Lord Jesus' and 'will raise us, in our turn, and put us by His side'" would be impermissible, as would any prayer that reflects dogma particular to a single faith tradition.

An insistence on nonsectarian or ecumenical prayer as a single, fixed standard is not consistent with the tradition of legislative prayer outlined in the Court's cases. The Court found the prayers in *Marsh* consistent with the First Amendment not because they espoused only a generic theism but because our history and tradition have shown that prayer in this limited context could "coexist with the principles of disestablishment and religious freedom." The Congress that drafted the First Amendment would have been accustomed to invocations containing explicitly religious themes of the sort respondents find objectionable. One of the Senate's first chaplains, the Rev. William White, gave prayers in a series that included the Lord's Prayer, the Collect for Ash Wednesday, prayers for peace and grace, a general thanksgiving, St. Chrysostom's Prayer, and a prayer seeking "the grace of our Lord Jesus Christ, &c."...The decidedly Christian nature of these prayers must not be dismissed as the relic of a time when our nation was less pluralistic than it is today. Congress continues to permit its appointed and visiting chaplains to express themselves in a religious idiom. It acknowledges our growing diversity not by proscribing sectarian content but by welcoming ministers of many creeds...

The contention that legislative prayer must be generic or nonsectarian derives from dictum in *Allegheny* that was disputed when written and has been repudiated by later cases.

> Dicta: expressions in a court's opinion that go beyond the facts before the court and therefore are individual views of the author of the opinion and not binding in subsequent cases as precedent. Dicta is the plural of dictum.

There the Court held that a creche placed on the steps of a county courthouse to celebrate the Christmas season violated the Establishment Clause because it had "the effect of endorsing a patently Christian message." Four dissenting justices disputed that endorsement could be the proper test, as it likely would condemn a host of traditional practices that recognize the role religion plays in our society, among them legislative prayer and the "forthrightly religious" Thanksgiving proclamations issued by nearly every president since Washington. The Court sought to counter this criticism by recasting *Marsh* to permit only prayer that contained no overtly Christian references:

> "However history may affect the constitutionality of nonsectarian references to religion by the government, history cannot legitimate practices that demonstrate the government's allegiance to a particular sect or creed...The legislative prayers involved in *Marsh* did not violate this principle because the particular chaplain had 'removed all references to Christ.'"

This proposition is irreconcilable with the facts of *Marsh* and with its holding and reasoning. *Marsh* nowhere suggested that the constitutionality of legislative prayer turns on the neutrality of its content. The opinion noted that Nebraska's chaplain, the Rev. Robert E. Palmer, modulated the "explicitly Christian" nature of his prayer and "removed all references to Christ" after a Jewish lawmaker complained. With this footnote, the Court did no more than observe the practical demands placed on a minister who holds a permanent, appointed position in a legislature and chooses to write his or her prayers to appeal to more members, or at least to give less offense to those who object. *Marsh* did not suggest that Nebraska's prayer practice would have failed had the chaplain not acceded to the legislator's request. Nor did the Court imply the rule that prayer violates the Establishment Clause any time it is given in the name of a figure deified by only one faith or creed…To the contrary, the Court instructed that the "content of the prayer is not of concern to judges," provided "there is no indication that the prayer opportunity has been exploited to proselytize or advance any one, or to disparage any other, faith or belief."

To hold that invocations must be nonsectarian would force the legislatures that sponsor prayers and the courts that are asked to decide these cases to act as supervisors and censors of religious speech, a rule that would involve government in religious matters to a far greater degree than is the case under the town's current practice of neither editing or approving prayers in advance nor criticizing their content after the fact. Our Government is prohibited from prescribing prayers to be recited in our public institutions in order to promote a preferred system of belief or code of moral behavior. *Engel* v. *Vitale**. It would be but a few steps removed from that prohibition for legislatures to require chaplains to redact the religious content from their message in order to make it acceptable for the public sphere. Government may not mandate a civic religion that stifles any but the most generic reference to the sacred any more than it may prescribe a religious orthodoxy. See *Lee* v. *Weisman** ("The suggestion that government may establish an official or civic religion as a means of avoiding the establishment of a religion with more specific creeds strikes us as a contradiction that cannot be accepted"); *Schempp* (Goldberg, J., concurring) (arguing that "untutored devotion to the concept of neutrality" must not lead to "a brooding and pervasive devotion to the secular").

Respondents argue, in effect, that legislative prayer may be addressed only to a generic God. The law and the Court could not draw this line for each specific prayer or seek to require ministers to set aside their nuanced and deeply personal beliefs for vague and artificial ones. There is doubt, in any event, that consensus might be reached as to what qualifies as generic or nonsectarian. Honorifics like "Lord of Lords" or "King of Kings" might strike a Christian audience as ecumenical, yet these titles may have no place in the vocabulary of other faith traditions. The difficulty, indeed the futility, of sifting sectarian from nonsectarian speech is illustrated by a letter that a lawyer for the respondents sent the town in the early stages of this litigation. The letter opined that references to "Father, God, Lord God, and the Almighty" would be acceptable in public prayer, but that references to "Jesus Christ, the Holy Spirit, and the Holy Trinity" would not. Perhaps the writer believed the former grouping would be acceptable to monotheists. Yet even seemingly general references to God or the Father might alienate nonbelievers or polytheists. Because it is unlikely that prayer will be inclusive beyond dispute, it would be unwise to adopt what respondents think is the next-best option: permitting those religious words, and only those words, that are acceptable to the majority, even if they will exclude some. The First Amendment is not a majority rule, and government may not seek to define permissible categories of religious speech. Once it invites prayer into the public sphere, government must permit a prayer giver to address his or her own God or gods as conscience dictates, unfettered by what an administrator or judge considers to be nonsectarian.

In rejecting the suggestion that legislative prayer must be nonsectarian, the Court does not imply that no constraints remain on its content. The relevant constraint derives from its place at the opening of legislative sessions, where it is meant to lend gravity to the occasion

ONE

and reflect values long part of the nation's heritage. Prayer that is solemn and respectful in tone, that invites lawmakers to reflect upon shared ideals and common ends before they embark on the fractious business of governing, serves that legitimate function. If the course and practice over time shows that the invocations denigrate nonbelievers or religious minorities, threaten damnation, or preach conversion, many present may consider the prayer to fall short of the desire to elevate the purpose of the occasion and to unite lawmakers in their common effort. That circumstance would present a different case than the one presently before the Court.

The tradition reflected in *Marsh* permits chaplains to ask their own God for blessings of peace, justice, and freedom that find appreciation among people of all faiths. That a prayer is given in the name of Jesus, Allah, or Jehovah, or that it makes passing reference to religious doctrines, does not remove it from that tradition. These religious themes provide particular means to universal ends. Prayer that reflects beliefs specific to only some creeds can still serve to solemnize the occasion, so long as the practice over time is not "exploited to proselytize or advance any one, or to disparage any other, faith or belief." *Marsh*.

It is thus possible to discern in the prayers offered to Congress a commonality of theme and tone. While these prayers vary in their degree of religiosity, they often seek peace for the nation, wisdom for its lawmakers, and justice for its people, values that count as universal and that are embodied not only in religious traditions, but in our founding documents and laws. The first prayer delivered to the Continental Congress by the Rev. Jacob Duche on Sept. 7, 1774, provides an example:

> "Be Thou present O God of Wisdom and direct the counsel of this Honorable Assembly; enable them to

settle all things on the best and surest foundations; that the scene of blood may be speedily closed; that Order, Harmony, and Peace be effectually restored, and the Truth and Justice, Religion and Piety, prevail and flourish among the people.

"Preserve the health of their bodies, and the vigor of their minds, shower down on them, and the millions they here represent, such temporal Blessings as Thou seest expedient for them in this world, and crown them with everlasting Glory in the world to come. All this we ask in the name and through the merits of Jesus Christ, Thy Son and our Saviour, Amen." W. Federer, America's God and Country (2000).

From the earliest days of the nation, these invocations have been addressed to assemblies comprising many different creeds. These ceremonial prayers strive for the idea that people of many faiths may be united in a community of tolerance and devotion. Even those who disagree as to religious doctrine may find common ground in the desire to show respect for the divine in all aspects of their lives and being. Our tradition assumes that adult citizens, firm in their own beliefs, can tolerate and perhaps appreciate a ceremonial prayer delivered by a person of a different faith. Letter from John Adams to Abigail Adams (Sept. 16, 1774).

The prayers delivered in the town of Greece do not fall outside the tradition this Court has recognized. A number of the prayers did invoke the name of Jesus, the Heavenly Father, or the Holy Spirit, but they also invoked universal themes, as by celebrating the changing of the seasons or calling for a "spirit of cooperation" among town leaders. Among numerous examples of such prayer in the record is the invocation given by the Rev. Richard Barbour at the September 2006 board meeting:

ONE

> "Gracious God, you have richly blessed our nation and this community. Help us to remember your generosity and give thanks for your goodness. Bless the elected leaders of the Greece Town Board as they conduct the business of our town this evening. Give them wisdom, courage, discernment and a single-minded desire to serve the common good. We ask your blessing on all public servants, and especially on our police force, firefighters, and emergency medical personnel...Respectful of every religious tradition, I offer this prayer in the name of God's only son Jesus Christ, the Lord, Amen."

Respondents point to other invocations that disparaged those who did not accept the town's prayer practice. One guest minister characterized objectors as a "minority" who are "ignorant of the history of our country," while another lamented that other towns did not have "God-fearing" leaders. Although these two remarks strayed from the rationale set out in *Marsh*, they do not despoil a practice that on the whole reflects and embraces our tradition. Absent a pattern of prayers that over time denigrate, proselytize, or betray an impermissible government purpose, a challenge based solely on the content of a prayer will not likely establish a constitutional violation. *Marsh*, indeed, requires an inquiry into the prayer opportunity as a whole, rather than into the contents of a single prayer.

Finally, the Court disagrees with the view taken by the Court of Appeals that the town of Greece contravened the Establishment Clause by inviting a predominantly Christian set of ministers to lead the prayer. The town made reasonable efforts to identify all of the congregations located within its borders and represented that it would welcome a prayer by any minister or layman who wished to give one. That nearly all of the congregations in town turned out to be Christian does not reflect an aversion or bias on the part of town leaders against minority faiths. So long as the town maintains a policy of nondiscrimination, the Constitution does not require it to search beyond its borders for non-Christian prayer givers in an effort to achieve religious balancing. The quest to promote "a 'diversity' of religious views" would require the town "to make wholly inappropriate judgments about the number of religions it should sponsor and the relative frequency with which it should sponsor each," a form of government entanglement with religion that is far more troublesome than the current approach.

B

Respondents further seek to distinguish the town's prayer practice from the tradition upheld in *Marsh* on the ground that it coerces participation by nonadherents. They and some *amici* contend that prayer conducted in the intimate setting of a town board meeting differs in fundamental ways from the invocations delivered in Congress and state legislatures, where the public remains segregated from legislative activity and may not address the body except by occasional invitation. Citizens attend town meetings, on the other hand, to accept awards; speak on matters of local importance; and petition the board for action that may affect their economic interests, such as the granting of permits, business licenses, and zoning variances. Respondents argue that the public may feel subtle pressure to participate in prayers that violate their beliefs in order to please the board members from whom they are about to seek a favorable ruling. In their view the fact that board members in small towns know many of their constituents by name only increases the pressure to conform.

Amici: plural derivative of amicus curiae, a Latin term meaning "friend of the court."

One

> In judicial terms, when a non-party to a case is granted the right to file a brief on behalf of an issue that involves their cause to aid the Court in rendering a decision, that is called an amicus brief. Several such friends (or interested non-parties), then, are referred to as amici.

It is an elemental First Amendment principle that government may not coerce its citizens "to support or participate in any religion or its exercise."…On the record in this case the Court is not persuaded that the town of Greece, through the act of offering a brief, solemn, and respectful prayer to open its monthly meetings, compelled its citizens to engage in a religious observance. The inquiry remains a fact-sensitive one that considers both the setting in which the prayer arises and the audience to whom it is directed.

The prayer opportunity in this case must be evaluated against the backdrop of historical practice. As a practice that has long endured, legislative prayer has become part of our heritage and tradition, part of our expressive idiom, similar to the Pledge of Allegiance, inaugural prayer, or the recitation of "God save the United States and this honorable Court" at the opening of this Court's sessions.

> This is a good example of dicta - something said that is not directly involved with a determination of the outcome. Justice Kennedy implies that the Pledge, inaugural prayer and the Court's opening statement would be just as constitutional as the prayer was in the *Marsh* case. I believe that is correct in principle. I just wanted to give you a crystal clear example of dicta, for the constitutionality of the Pledge, inaugural prayer, or the Court's opening statement have never been decided by the Supreme Court and are not directly relevant to the facts here.

It is presumed that the reasonable observer is acquainted with this tradition and understands that its purposes are to lend gravity to public proceedings and to acknowledge the place religion holds in the lives of many private citizens, not to afford government an opportunity to proselytize or force truant constituents into the pews. That many appreciate these acknowledgments of the divine in our public institutions does not suggest that those who disagree are compelled to join the expression or approve its content.

The principal audience for these invocations is not, indeed, the public but lawmakers themselves, who may find that a moment of prayer or quiet reflection sets the mind to a higher purpose and thereby eases the task of governing…To be sure, many members of the public find these prayers meaningful and wish to join them. But their purpose is largely to accommodate the spiritual needs of lawmakers and connect them to a tradition dating to the time of the Framers. For members of town boards and commissions, who often serve part-time and as volunteers, ceremonial prayer may also reflect the values they hold as private citizens. The prayer is an opportunity for them to show who and what they are without denying the right to dissent by those who disagree.

The analysis would be different if town board members directed the public to participate in the prayers, singled out dissidents for opprobrium, or indicated that their decisions might be influenced by a person's acquiescence in the prayer opportunity. No such thing occurred in the town of Greece…

In their declarations in the trial court, respondents stated that the prayers gave them offense and made them feel excluded and disrespected. Offense, however, does not equate to coercion. <u>Adults often encounter speech they find disagreeable; and an Establishment</u>

ONE

<u>Clause violation is not made out any time a person experiences a sense of affront from the expression of contrary religious views in a legislative forum, especially where, as here, any member of the public is welcome in turn to offer an invocation reflecting his or her own convictions</u>...If circumstances arise in which the pattern and practice of ceremonial, legislative prayer is alleged to be a means to coerce or intimidate others, the objection can be addressed in the regular course. But the showing has not been made here, where the prayers neither chastised dissenters nor attempted lengthy disquisition on religious dogma. Courts remain free to review the pattern of prayers over time to determine whether they comport with the tradition of solemn, respectful prayer approved in *Marsh,* or whether coercion is a real and substantial likelihood. But in the general course legislative bodies do not engage in impermissible coercion merely by exposing constituents to prayer they would rather not hear and in which they need not participate.

> Take a look at Chapter Six and compare the comments the Court makes about the *Lee v. Weisman* case, below.

This case can be distinguished from the conclusions and holding of *Lee* v. *Weisman.* There the Court found that, in the context of a graduation where school authorities maintained close supervision over the conduct of the students and the substance of the ceremony, a religious invocation was coercive as to an objecting student. Four justices dissented in *Lee,* but the circumstances the Court confronted there are not present in this case and do not control its outcome. Nothing in the record suggests that members of the public are dissuaded from leaving the meeting room during the prayer, arriving late, or even, as happened here, making a later protest. In this case, as in *Marsh,* board members and constituents are "free to enter and leave with little comment and for any number of reasons." Should nonbelievers choose to exit the room during a prayer they find distasteful, their absence will not stand out as disrespectful or even noteworthy. And should they remain, their quiet acquiescence will not, in light of our traditions, be interpreted as an agreement with the words or ideas expressed. Neither choice represents an unconstitutional imposition as to mature adults, who "presumably" are "not readily susceptible to religious indoctrination or peer pressure." *Marsh.*

In the town of Greece, the prayer is delivered during the ceremonial portion of the town's meeting. Board members are not engaged in policymaking at this time, but in more general functions, such as swearing in new police officers, inducting high school athletes into the town hall of fame, and presenting proclamations to volunteers, civic groups, and senior citizens. It is a moment for town leaders to recognize the achievements of their constituents and the aspects of community life that are worth celebrating. By inviting ministers to serve as chaplain for the month, and welcoming them to the front of the room alongside civic leaders, the town is acknowledging the central place that religion, and religious institutions, hold in the lives of those present. Indeed, some congregations are not simply spiritual homes for town residents but also the provider of social services for citizens regardless of their beliefs. [Examples: thanking a pastor for his "community involvement"; thanking a deacon "for the job that you have done on behalf of our community."] The inclusion of a brief, ceremonial prayer as part of a larger exercise in civic recognition suggests that its purpose and effect are to acknowledge religious leaders and the institutions they represent rather than to exclude or coerce nonbelievers.

Ceremonial prayer is but a recognition that, since this nation was founded and until the present day, many Americans deem that their own existence must be understood by precepts far beyond the authority of government to alter or define and that willing participation in civic affairs can be consistent with a brief acknowledgment of their belief in a higher power, always with due respect for those who adhere to other beliefs. The prayer in this case has a permissible ceremonial purpose. It is not an unconstitutional establishment of religion.

The town of Greece does not violate the First Amendment by opening its meetings with prayer that comports with our tradition and does not coerce participation by nonadherents. The judgment of the U. S. Court of Appeals for the Second Circuit is reversed.

CONCURRENCE: Alito/Scalia...I write separately to respond to the principal dissent, which really consists of two very different but intertwined opinions. One is quite narrow; the other is sweeping. I will address both.

I

First, however, since the principal dissent accuses the Court of being blind to the facts of this case, I recount facts that I find particularly salient…

For some time, the town's practice does not appear to have elicited any criticism, but when complaints were received, the town made it clear that it would permit any interested residents, including nonbelievers, to provide an invocation, and the town has never refused a request to offer an invocation. The most recent list in the record of persons available to provide an invocation includes representatives of many non-Christian faiths…

II

I turn now to the narrow aspect of the principal dissent, and what we find here is that the principal dissent's objection, in the end, is really quite niggling. According to the principal dissent, the town could have avoided any constitutional problem in either of two ways.

A

...Not only is there no historical support for the proposition that only generic prayer is allowed, but as our country has become more diverse, composing a prayer that is acceptable to all members of the community who hold religious beliefs has become harder and harder. It was one thing to compose a prayer that is acceptable to both Christians and Jews; it is much harder to compose a prayer that is also acceptable to followers of Eastern religions that are now well represented in this country. Many local clergy may find the project daunting, if not impossible, and some may feel that they cannot in good faith deliver such a vague prayer...

V

...I am troubled by the message that some readers may take from the principal dissent's rhetoric and its highly imaginative hypotheticals. For example, the principal dissent conjures up the image of a litigant awaiting trial who is asked by the presiding judge to rise for a Christian prayer, of an official at a polling place who conveys the expectation that citizens wishing to vote make the sign of the cross before casting their ballots, and of an immigrant seeking naturalization who is asked to bow her head and recite a Christian prayer. Although I do not suggest that the implication is intentional, I am concerned that at least some readers will take these hypotheticals as a warning that this is where today's decision leads - to a country in which religious minorities are denied the equal benefits of citizenship.

Nothing could be further from the truth. All that the Court does today is to allow a town to follow a practice that we have previously held is permissible for Congress and state legislatures. In seeming to suggest otherwise, the principal dissent goes far astray.

CONCURRENCE: Thomas/Scalia...[Not Provided.]

ONE

DISSENT: Breyer...[Not Provided.]

DISSENT: Kagan/Ginsburg/Breyer/Sotomayor ... For centuries now, people have come to this country from every corner of the world to share in the blessing of religious freedom. Our Constitution promises that they may worship in their own way, without fear of penalty or danger, and that in itself is a momentous offering. Yet our Constitution makes a commitment still more remarkable - that however those individuals worship, they will count as full and equal American citizens. A Christian, a Jew, a Muslim (and so forth) - each stands in the same relationship with her country, with her state and local communities, and with every level and body of government. So that when each person performs the duties or seeks the benefits of citizenship, she does so not as an adherent to one or another religion, but simply as an American.

Justice Kagan is emphatically out of touch. Most Christians I know will tell you their first duty is to their God. They love their country, but they seek to live their lives as Christ would have them live, not as government would have them live. They do not leave that primary obligation at the door when entering City Hall, the ballpark, a courthouse or a grocery store. That is not to say that people of all faiths cannot live in peace with one another in a pluralistic society. However, Christians wouldn't expect anyone of whatever religion to live two lives – one of faith when not interacting with government and one of no faith when crossing government's path. Such was never intended as a premise of the "separation of church/state philosophy." Justice Kagan could well be tipping her hand. She just may be one of those who would like to see "free exercise" narrowed to "free worship in church buildings." I will be watching as future opinions are handed down.

I respectfully dissent from the Court's opinion because I think the Town of Greece's prayer practices violate that norm of religious equality - the breathtakingly generous constitutional idea that our public institutions belong no less to the Buddhist or Hindu than to the Methodist or Episcopalian. I do not contend that principle translates here into a bright separationist line. To the contrary, I agree with the Court's decision in *Marsh* v. *Chambers* upholding the Nebraska Legislature's tradition of beginning each session with a chaplain's prayer. And I believe that pluralism and inclusion in a town hall can satisfy the constitutional requirement of neutrality; such a forum need not become a religion-free zone. But still, the Town of Greece should lose this case. The practice at issue here differs from the one sustained in *Marsh* because Greece's town meetings involve participation by <u>ordinary</u> citizens, and the invocations given - directly to those citizens - were predominantly sectarian in content. Still more, Greece's Board did nothing to recognize religious diversity: In arranging for clergy members to open each meeting, the Town never sought (except briefly when this suit was filed) to involve, accommodate, or in any way reach out to adherents of non-Christian religions. So month in and month out for over a decade, prayers steeped in only one faith, addressed toward members of the public, commenced meetings to discuss local affairs and distribute government benefits. In my view, that practice does not square with the First Amendment's promise that every citizen, irrespective of her religion, owns an equal share in her government.

I might be a little hard on Justice Kagan. You may see the reference to "ordinary" citizens differently. I see it as judicial arrogance. It seems like she is saying Nebraska legislators wouldn't be as offended or coerced or affected by government prayer as "ordinary" citizens of a small town like Greece, New York, because the political class is so much more educated and less likely to be misled.

ONE

I

To begin to see what has gone wrong in the Town of Greece, consider several hypothetical scenarios in which sectarian prayer - taken straight from this case's record - infuses governmental activities. None involves, as this case does, a proceeding that could be characterized as a legislative session, but they are useful to elaborate some general principles. In each instance, assume (as was true in Greece) that the invocation is given pursuant to government policy and is representative of the prayers generally offered in the designated setting:

> The following hypotheticals of Justice Kagan have nothing to do with the majority holding.

- You are a party in a case going to trial; let's say you have filed suit against the government for violating one of your legal rights. The judge bangs his gavel to call the court to order, asks a minister to come to the front of the room, and instructs the 10 or so individuals present to rise for an opening prayer. The clergyman faces those in attendance and says: "Lord, God of all creation,...We acknowledge the saving sacrifice of Jesus Christ on the cross. We draw strength... from his resurrection at Easter. Jesus Christ, who took away the sins of the world, destroyed our death, through his dying and in his rising, he has restored our life. Blessed are you, who has raised up the Lord Jesus, you who will raise us, in our turn, and put us by His side...Amen." The judge then asks your lawyer to begin the trial.

- It's election day, and you head over to your local polling place to vote. As you and others wait to give your names and receive your ballots, an election official asks everyone there to join him in prayer. He says: "We pray this day for the guidance of the Holy Spirit as we vote...Let's just say the Our Father together. 'Our Father, who art in Heaven, hallowed be thy name; thy Kingdom come, thy will be done, on earth as it is in Heaven...'" And after he concludes, he makes the sign of the cross, and appears to wait expectantly for you and the other prospective voters to do so too.

- You are an immigrant attending a naturalization ceremony to finally become a citizen. The presiding official tells you and your fellow applicants that before administering the oath of allegiance, he would like a minister to pray for you and with you. The pastor steps to the front of the room, asks everyone to bow their heads, and recites: "Father, son, and Holy Spirit - it is with a due sense of reverence and awe that we come before you today seeking your blessing...You are...a wise God, oh Lord,...as evidenced even in the plan of redemption that is fulfilled in Jesus Christ. We ask that you would give freely and abundantly wisdom to one and to all...in the name of the Lord and Savior Jesus Christ, who lives with you and the Holy Spirit, one God for ever and ever. Amen."

I would hold that the government officials responsible for the above practices - that is, for prayer repeatedly invoking a single religion's beliefs in these settings - crossed a constitutional line. I have every confidence the Court would agree. And even Greece's attorney conceded that something like the first hypothetical (he was not asked about the others) would violate the First Amendment. Why?

The reason, of course, has nothing to do with Christianity as such. This opinion is full of Christian prayers, because those were the only invocations offered in the Town of Greece. But if my hypotheticals involved the prayer of some other religion, the outcome would be exactly the same. Suppose, for example, that government officials in a predominantly Jewish community asked a rabbi to begin all public functions with a chanting of the Sh'ma and V'ahavta. ("Hear O Israel! The Lord our God, the Lord is One. . . . Bind these words as a sign upon your hand; let them be a symbol before your eyes; inscribe them on the doorposts of your house, and on your gates.") Or assume officials in a mostly Muslim town requested a muezzin to commence such functions, over and over again, with a recitation of the Adhan. ("God is greatest, God is greatest. I bear witness that there is no deity but God. I bear witness that Muhammed is the Messenger of God.") In any instance, the question would be why such government-sponsored prayer of a single religion goes beyond the constitutional pale.

One glaring problem is that the government in all these hypotheticals has aligned itself with, and placed its imprimatur on, a particular religious creed. "The clearest command of the Establishment Clause," this Court has held, "is that one religious denomination cannot be officially preferred over another." *Larson* v. *Valente**. Justices have often differed about a further issue: whether and how the Clause applies to governmental policies favoring religion (of all kinds) over non-religion. Compare *McCreary County* v. *ACLU** ("The First Amendment mandates governmental neutrality between…religion and nonreligion"), with, *e.g.* (SCALIA, J., dissenting) ("The Court's oft repeated assertion that the government cannot favor religious practice generally is false"). But no one has disagreed with this much:

"Our constitutional tradition, from the Declaration of Independence and the first inaugural address of Washington . . . down to the present day, has . . . ruled out of order government-sponsored endorsement of religion . . . where the endorsement is sectarian, in the sense of specifying details upon which men and women who believe in a benevolent, omnipotent Creator and Ruler of the world are known to differ (for example, the divinity of Christ)." *Lee* v. *Weisman* (SCALIA, J., dissenting).

...By authorizing and overseeing prayers associated with a single religion - to the exclusion of all others - the government officials in my hypothetical cases (whether federal, state, or local does not matter) have violated that foundational principle. They have embarked on a course of religious favoritism anathema to the First Amendment.

> That is simply not true. The Town of Greece did not exclude all other religions.

And making matters still worse: They have done so in a place where individuals come to interact with, and participate in, the institutions and processes of their government. A person goes to court, to the polls, to a naturalization ceremony - and a government official or his hand-picked minister asks her, as the first order of official business, to stand and pray with others in a way conflicting with her own religious beliefs. Perhaps she feels sufficient pressure to go along - to rise, bow her head, and join in whatever others are saying: After all, she wants, very badly, what the judge or poll worker or immigration official has to offer. Or perhaps she is made of stronger mettle, and she opts not to participate in what she does not believe - indeed, what would, for her, be something like blasphemy. She then must make known her dissent from the common religious view, and place herself apart from other citizens, as well as from the officials responsible for the invocations. And so a civic function of some kind brings religious differences to the fore: That public proceeding becomes (whether intentionally or not) an instrument for dividing her from adherents to the community's majority religion, and for altering the very nature of her relationship with her government.

> How about some objectivity? Do we Christians love the outcome of this case because we are in the same position as the citizens of Greece - i.e., in the majority? Is it more difficult for us to understand the "plight" of a minority faith? It doesn't seem to be so coercive to ask for respect for the prayers of the majority most of the time, especially when we are in the majority. When the town of Greece is substantially more populated by Muslims someday, as it no doubt will be, I wonder how its Christian citizens will react to far more frequent prayers to Allah at the beginning of its meetings? I then wonder if religious warfare is what the Framers had in mind amidst shifting demographics? Anyway, I suggest you ponder these things before reaching a conclusion.
>
> And, keep in mind, Christians can hold a prayer vigil on the sidewalk outside City Hall any time they wish.

That is not the country we are, because that is not what our Constitution permits. Here, when a citizen stands before her government, whether to perform a service or request a benefit, her religious beliefs do not enter into the picture. See Thomas Jefferson, Virginia Act for Establishing Religious Freedom (Oct. 31, 1785) ("Opinions in matters of religion . . . shall in no wise diminish, enlarge, or affect our civil capacities.") The government she faces favors no particular religion, either by word or by deed. And that government, in its various processes and proceedings, imposes no religious tests on its citizens, sorts none of them by faith, and permits no exclusion based on belief. When a person goes to court, a polling place, or an immigration proceeding - I could go on: to a zoning agency, a parole board hearing, or the DMV - government officials do not engage in sectarian worship, nor do they ask her to do likewise. They all participate in the business of government not as Christians, Jews, Muslims (and more), but only as Americans - none of them different from any other for that civic purpose. Why not, then, at a town meeting?

II

...If the Town Board had let its chaplains know that they should speak in nonsectarian terms, common to diverse religious groups, then no one would have valid grounds for complaint. See *Joyner v. Forsyth County* (CA4 2011) (Such prayers show that "those of different creeds are in the end kindred spirits, united by a respect paid higher providence and by a belief in the importance of religious faith".) Priests and ministers, rabbis and imams give such invocations all the time; there is no great mystery to the project. (And providing that guidance would hardly have caused the Board to run afoul of the idea that "the First Amendment is not a majority rule," as the Court (headspinningly) suggests; what does that is the Board's *refusal* to reach out to members of minority religious groups.) Or if the Board preferred, it might have invited clergy of many faiths to serve as chaplains, as the majority notes that Congress does. When one month a clergy member refers to Jesus, and the next to Allah or Jehovah - as the majority hopefully though counterfactually suggests happened here - the government does not identify itself with one religion or align itself with that faith's citizens, and the effect of even sectarian prayer is transformed. So Greece had multiple ways of incorporating prayer into its town meetings - reflecting all the ways that prayer (as most of us know from daily life) can forge common bonds, rather than divide.

> I find it alarming that neither side in this case discusses the real world. The dissent would apparently be happy with a system that includes greater pluralism.
>
> Then, they argue, government would not be seen to "identify itself with one religion or align itself with that faith's citizens."
>
> Perhaps that is so in the long term; however, most citizens rarely attend City Hall meetings. For the vast majority of the citizens Justice Kagan is so worried about, their experience will be singular. Their "perceived alignment" will be an alignment with whatever voice gets the microphone on that rare day that any one citizen observes City Hall. No one discusses this. I'm surprised.

But Greece could not do what it did: infuse a participatory government body with one (and only one) faith, so that month in and month out, the citizens appearing before it become partly defined by their creed - as those who share, and those who do not, the community's majority religious belief. In this country, when citizens go before the government, <u>they go not as Christians</u> or Muslims or Jews (or what have you), but just as Americans (or here, as Grecians). That is what it means to be an equal citizen, irrespective of religion. And that is what the Town of Greece precluded by so identifying itself with a single faith.

III

How, then, does the majority go so far astray, allowing the Town of Greece to turn its assemblies for citizens into a forum for Christian prayer? The answer does not lie in first principles: I have no doubt that every member of this Court believes as firmly as I that our institutions of government belong equally to all, regardless of faith. Rather, the error reflects two kinds of blindness. First, the majority misapprehends the facts of this case, as distinct from those characterizing traditional legislative prayer. And second, the majority misjudges the essential meaning of the religious worship in Greece's town hall, along with its capacity to exclude and divide…

IV

In 1790, George Washington traveled to Newport, Rhode Island, a longtime bastion of religious liberty and the home of the first community of American Jews. Among the citizens he met there was Moses Seixas, one of that congregation's lay officials. The ensuing exchange between the two conveys, as well as anything I know, the promise this country makes to members of every religion.

Seixas wrote first, welcoming Washington to Newport. He spoke of "a deep sense of gratitude" for the new American Government - "a Government, which to bigotry gives no sanction, to persecution no assistance - but generously affording to All liberty of conscience, and immunities of Citizenship: deeming every one, of whatever nation, tongue, or language, equal parts of the great governmental Machine." The first phrase there is the more poetic: a government that to "bigotry gives no sanction, to persecution no assistance." But the second is actually the more startling and transformative: a government that, beyond not aiding persecution, grants "immunities of citizenship" to the Christian and the Jew alike, and makes them "equal parts" of the whole country.

Washington responded the very next day. Like any successful politician, he appreciated a great line when he saw one - and knew to borrow it too. And so he repeated, word for word, Seixas's phrase about neither sanctioning bigotry nor assisting persecution. But he no less embraced the point Seixas had made about equality of citizenship. "It is now no more," Washington said, "that toleration is spoken of,

ONE

as if it was by the indulgence of one class of people" to another, lesser one. For "all possess alike ... immunities of citizenship." That is America's promise in the First Amendment: full and equal membership in the polity for members of every religious group, assuming only that they, like anyone "who lives under the Government's protection, should demean themselves as good citizens."

For me, that remarkable guarantee means at least this much: When the citizens of this country approach their government, they do so only as Americans, not as members of one faith or another. And that means that even in a partly legislative body, they should not confront government-sponsored worship that divides them along religious lines. I believe, for all the reasons I have given, that the Town of Greece betrayed that promise. I therefore respectfully dissent from the Court's decision.

What Justice Kagan cannot understand is that Christians never approach their government or their lives without their faith. I cannot imagine anyone of whatever faith doing so, including atheists. In other words, atheists who complain about government sponsored prayer don't leave their unbelief at the town hall door. I cannot imagine ever approaching my city, county, state or nation only as an American to the exclusion of the very thing that defines me, my Christianity. I am at a loss as to how one could possibly do that without winning the Oscar for Best Leading Actor in a Hypocritical Role.

SUMMARY: Prayer to begin town hall meetings won the day as long as the opportunity is open to all faiths, cults and non-faith.

COMMENT: My thoughts on Supreme Court decisions about prayer are documented in Chapter Eight of my book, It's OK to Say "God,"[16] where, in addition to *Lee v. Weisman* (the topic of Chapter Six of this book), I discuss *Engel v. Vitale**, *Marsh v. Chambers*, and *Wallace v. Jaffree** in detail.

PLEA: Presidents and senators decide who determines these very serious questions. Vote. It's important.

---

16   Armstrong, Tad. *It's OK To Say "God."* WestBow Press, 2011. Print.

Chapter Fourteen

ONE ROBE SHORT ON JUNE 26, 2014, EMPOWERED THE EXECUTIVE BRANCH WHILE YOU WERE SLEEPING!

This is not a 5-4 decision. In fact, it is a unanimous decision. I am violating my rule for this one case. You see, the vote tally is based upon ultimate outcome, not upon rationale for the outcome. Since all nine justices agreed that President Obama violated the Constitution in this case, all nine also agreed that the remedy is to overturn several National Labor Relations Board decisions that his invalid appointments affected. You will see what I mean soon.

However, for our purposes, the ruling was effectively 5-4 the wrong way. Five of the justices interpreted several constitutional provisions very liberally. Four of the justices emphatically believed the majority stretched the Constitution beyond its limits. So, while we have a unanimous outcome (President Obama's appointments were unconstitutional in this case), we are left with faulty reasoning that won the day along a 5-4 margin; hence, **one robe short** in a very real sense.

The District of Columbia Circuit Court of Appeals, in ruling against President Obama, said the following: "The power of a written constitution lies in its words. It is those words that were adopted by the people. When those words speak clearly, it is not up to us to depart from their meaning in favor of our own concept of efficiency, convenience, or facilitation of the functions of government...We hold that the president may only make recess appointments to fill vacancies that arise during the recess." The District of Columbia Circuit Court of Appeals got it completely right. If you would like to read that opinion - the opinion being appealed from in this case - you can find it on our website. I would encourage you to do so. You can find it as *Canning v. NLRB**. See the appendix for the exact location.

What are the facts and how did the Supreme Court handle this case on appeal? The Court of Appeals was affirmed, but the reasoning of the majority was miles apart from the conservatives. Let's take the *National Labor Relations Board v. Canning** journey.

ONE

WARNING: The majority opinion may not make much sense to you. It is very confusing. But, stick with it and I believe you will be rewarded with understanding when you reach Justice Scalia's Concurrence, below.

NATIONAL LABOR RELATIONS BOARD
v.
CANNING
SUPREME COURT OF THE UNITED STATES
No. 12-1281
June 26, 2014
[9 – 0]

OPINION: Breyer/ Kennedy/ Ginsburg/ Sotomayor/ Kagan... Ordinarily the president must obtain "the Advice and Consent of the Senate" before appointing an "Officer of the United States." U. S. Const., Art. II, §2, cl. 2. But the Recess Appointments Clause creates an exception. It gives the president alone the power "to fill up all Vacancies that may happen during the Recess of the Senate, by granting Commissions which shall expire at the End of their next Session." Art. II, §2, cl. 3. We here consider three questions about the application of this Clause.

The first concerns the scope of the words "recess of the Senate." Does that phrase refer only to an inter-session recess (*i.e.*, a break between formal sessions of Congress), or does it also include an intra-session recess, such as a summer recess in the midst of a session? We conclude that the Clause applies to both kinds of recess.

> As you will see, that is not the likely conclusion that would have been reached by the Framers.

The second question concerns the scope of the words "vacancies that may happen." Does that phrase refer only to vacancies that first come into existence during a recess, or does it also include vacancies that arise prior to a recess but continue to exist during the recess? We conclude that the Clause applies to both kinds of vacancy.

> I repeat, that is not the likely conclusion that would have been reached by the Framers.

The third question concerns calculation of the length of a "recess." The president made the appointments here at issue on January 4, 2012. At that time the Senate was in recess pursuant to a December 17, 2011, resolution providing for a series of brief recesses punctuated by *"pro forma* sessions," with "no business …transacted," every Tuesday and Friday through January 20, 2012. In calculating the length of a recess are we to ignore the *pro forma* sessions, thereby treating the series of brief recesses as a single, month-long recess? We conclude that we cannot ignore these *pro forma* sessions.

Our answer to the third question means that, when the appointments before us took place, the Senate was in the midst of a 3-day recess. Three days is too short a time to bring a recess within the scope of the Clause. Thus we conclude that the president lacked the power to make the recess appointments here at issue.

> Get comfortable and watch the liberal majority dismantle the work of the Framers of our Constitution. You are going to have to work with me on this one. If you stick with it to the end, I am confident the smoke will clear. It's important. Please hang in there.

I

The case before us arises out of a labor dispute…

ONE

> Because the nature of that dispute is entirely irrelevant to the issues in this case, it is not provided, except to say that the five-member National Labor Relations Board (NLRB) decided the issues against Noel Canning, a Pepsi distributor.

[Canning] subsequently asked the Court of Appeals for the District of Columbia Circuit to set the Board's order aside. It claimed that three of the five Board members had been invalidly appointed [by President Obama], leaving the Board without the three lawfully appointed members necessary for it to act...

The three members in question were Sharon Block, Richard Griffin, and Terence Flynn. In 2011 the president had nominated each of them to the Board. As of January 2012, Flynn's nomination had been pending in the Senate awaiting confirmation for approximately a year. The nominations of each of the other two had been pending for a few weeks. On January 4, 2012, the president, invoking the Recess Appointments Clause, appointed all three to the Board.

> Flynn, a Republican, subsequently resigned in disgrace over some unrelated scandal. I believe "tradition" has it that presidents nominate a given number of the five-member board from each party. In a subsequent deal in the Senate, President Obama withdrew Block and Griffin from consideration. I don't know all of the inside scoop on these appointments. However, one has to wonder why a president would resort to a tricky recess appointment when his party controls the Senate for confirmation purposes. At any rate, intransigence was part of the plan of the Framers. These nominees must have been poor choices or politics was being played. But, the basic idea is that somebody will get voted out for playing politics or "somebody" might want to appoint people with better qualifications so they could get confirmed without resorting to shenanigans. I'm not all that disturbed about intransigence. It is a valuable "check and balance" of uncontrolled power.

[Canning] argued that the Recess Appointments Clause did not authorize those appointments. It pointed out that on December 17, 2011, the Senate, by unanimous consent, had adopted a resolution providing that it would take a series of brief recesses beginning the following day. Pursuant to that resolution, the Senate held *pro forma* sessions every Tuesday and Friday until it returned for ordinary business on January 23, 2012. The president's January 4 appointments were made between the January 3 and January 6 *pro forma* sessions. In [Canning's] view, each *pro forma* session terminated the immediately preceding recess. Accordingly, the appointments were made during a 3-day adjournment, which is not long enough to trigger the Recess Appointments Clause.

The Court of Appeals agreed that the appointments fell outside the scope of the Clause. But the court set forth different reasons. It held that the Clause's words "the recess of the Senate" do not include recesses that occur *within* a formal session of Congress, *i.e.,* intra-session recesses. Rather those words apply only to recesses *between* those formal sessions, *i.e.,* inter-session recesses. Since the second session of the 112th Congress began on January 3, 2012, the day before the president's appointments, those appointments occurred during an intra-session recess, and the appointments consequently fell outside the scope of the Clause.

The Court of Appeals added that, in any event, the phrase "vacancies that may happen during the recess" applies only to vacancies that come into existence during a recess. The vacancies that Members Block, Griffin, and Flynn were appointed to fill had arisen before the beginning of the recess during which they were appointed. For this reason too the president's appointments were invalid. And, because the Board lacked a quorum of validly appointed members when it issued its order, the order was invalid.

We granted the Solicitor General's petition for certiorari. We asked the parties to address not only the Court of Appeals' interpretation of the Clause but also [Canning's] initial argument, namely, "whether the president's recess-appointment power may be exercised when the Senate is convening every three days in *pro forma* sessions."

We shall answer all three questions presented. We recognize that the president has nominated others to fill the positions once occupied by Members Block, Griffin, and Flynn, and that the Senate has confirmed these successors. But, as the parties recognize, the fact that the Board now unquestionably has a quorum does not moot the controversy about the validity of the previously entered Board order. And there are pending before us petitions from decisions in other cases involving challenges to the appointment of Board Member Craig Becker. The president appointed Member Becker during an intra-session recess that was not punctuated by *pro forma* sessions, and the vacancy Becker filled had come into existence prior to the recess. Other cases involving similar challenges are also pending in the Courts of Appeals. Thus, we believe it is important to answer all three questions that this case presents.

II

The Constitution giveth (the president has power to nominate Board members), then taketh away (the nominations must be confirmed with the advice and consent of the Senate), then giveth back (the president can make such appointments without Senate confirmation for vacancies "that may happen during the recess").

When the president wants to nominate people of an ideology that he reasonably predicts the Senate will not confirm (here, even when his own party was in the majority), can he overcome that nasty confirmation requirement via recess appointments? Was the Senate "in recess" when these appointments were made? Did the vacancies "happen" during a recess?

> **This is the very first time these issues have reached the Supreme Court!** Stay tuned!

> Please allow me to introduce you to **The Appointments Clause** (Article II, §2, cl. 2): "[...The President] shall nominate, and by and with the **Advice and Consent of the Senate**, shall appoint... all other Officers of the United States..." And here is **The Recess Appointments Clause** (Article II, §2, cl. 3): "The President shall have Power to fill up all Vacancies <u>**that may happen**</u> during <u>**the Recess of the Senate**</u>, by granting Commissions which shall expire at the End of their next Session."

Before turning to the specific questions presented, we shall mention two background considerations that we find relevant to all three. First, *the Recess Appointments Clause sets forth a subsidiary, not a primary, method for appointing officers of the United States.* The immediately preceding Clause - Article II, Section 2, Clause 2 - provides the primary method of appointment. It says that the president "shall nominate, *and by and with the Advice and Consent of the Senate,* shall appoint Ambassadors, other public Ministers and Consuls, Judges of the supreme Court, and all other Officers of the United States."

> Even the majority agrees that the preferred or primary way to fill certain federal vacancies is through nomination by the president <u>and</u> confirmation by the Senate. The recess appointment avenue is a subsidiary method.

The Federalist Papers make clear that the Founders intended this method of appointment, requiring Senate approval, to be the norm

ONE

(at least for principal officers). Alexander Hamilton wrote that the Constitution vests the power of *nomination* in the president alone because "one man of discernment is better fitted to analise and estimate the peculiar qualities adapted to particular offices, than a body of men of equal, or perhaps even of superior discernment." **At the same time, the need to secure Senate approval provides "an excellent check upon a spirit of favoritism in the president, and would tend greatly to preventing the appointment of unfit characters from State prejudice, from family connection, from personal attachment, or from a view to popularity."** Hamilton further explained that the "ordinary power of appointment is confided to the president and Senate *jointly,* and can therefore only be exercised during the session of the Senate; but as it would have been improper to oblige this body to be continually in session for the appointment of officers; and as vacancies might happen *in their recess,* which it might be necessary for the public service to fill without delay, the succeeding clause is evidently intended to authorise the president *singly* to make temporary appointments."

> That is, the Framers had the foresight to provide for an alternative method "under certain circumstances" whereby the president could fill vacancies on his own, without Senate confirmation. There was a reason for that – a limited reason.

Thus the Recess Appointments Clause reflects the tension between, on the one hand, the president's continuous need for "the assistance of subordinates" and, on the other, the Senate's practice, particularly during the Republic's early years, of meeting for a single brief session each year... We seek to interpret the Clause as granting the president the power to make appointments during a recess but not offering the president the authority routinely to avoid the need for Senate confirmation.

Second, *in interpreting the Clause, we put significant weight upon historical practice...*

There is a great deal of history to consider here. Presidents have made recess appointments since the beginning of the Republic.

> Ok. That doesn't tell us anything. There are legitimate recess appointments and not so legitimate recess appointments. We aren't in Court fighting over appointments clearly of the former variety.

Their frequency suggests that the Senate and president have recognized that recess appointments can be both necessary and appropriate in certain circumstances. **We have not previously interpreted the Clause, and, when doing so for the first time in more than 200 years, we must hesitate to upset the compromises and working arrangements that the elected branches of Government themselves have reached.**

III

The first question concerns the scope of the phrase *"the recess* of the Senate." Art. II, §2, cl. 3. The Constitution provides for congressional elections every two years. And the 2-year life of each elected Congress typically consists of two formal 1-year sessions, each separated from the next by an **"inter-session recess" [i.e., "between sessions"].** The Senate or the House of Representatives announces an inter-session recess by approving a resolution stating that it will "adjourn *sine die,"* i.e., without specifying a date to return (in which case Congress will reconvene when the next formal session is scheduled to begin).

The Senate and the House also take breaks in the midst of a session. The Senate or the House announces any such **"intra-session recess" [i.e., "within sessions"]** by adopting a resolution stating that it will "adjourn" to a fixed date, a few days or weeks or even months later. **All agree that the phrase "the recess of the Senate" covers inter-session recesses. The question is whether it includes intra-session recesses as well.**

> Can't you just feel it coming on? It's called "judicial legislation."

In our view, the phrase "the recess" includes an intra-session recess of substantial length. Its words taken literally can refer to both types of recess. Founding-era dictionaries define the word "recess," much as we do today, simply as "a period of cessation from usual work." The Founders themselves used the word to refer to intra-session, as well as to inter-session, breaks. (letter from George Washington to John Jay using "the recess" to refer to an intra-session break of the Constitutional Convention); (speech of Luther Martin with a similar usage); T. Jefferson (describing a "recess by adjournment" which did *not* end a session).

We recognize that the word "the" in "the recess" might suggest that the phrase refers to the single break separating formal sessions of Congress. That is because the word "the" frequently (but not always) indicates "a particular thing." But the word can also refer "to a term used generically or universally."...

The constitutional text is...ambiguous. And we believe the Clause's purpose demands the broader interpretation. The Clause gives the president authority to make appointments during "the recess of the Senate" so that the president can ensure the continued functioning of the Federal Government when the Senate is away. The Senate is equally away during both an inter-session and an intra-session recess, and its capacity to participate in the appointments process has nothing to do with the words it uses to signal its departure.

History also offers strong support for the broad interpretation. We concede that pre-Civil War history is not helpful. But it shows only that Congress generally took long breaks between sessions, while taking no significant intra-session breaks at all (five times it took a break of a week or so at Christmas). Obviously, if there are no significant intra-session recesses, there will be no intra-session recess appointments. In 1867 and 1868, Congress for the first time took substantial, non-holiday intra-session breaks, and President Andrew Johnson made dozens of recess appointments. The Federal Court of Claims upheld one of those specific appointments, writing "we have *no doubt* that a vacancy occurring while the Senate was thus temporarily adjourned" during the "first session of the Fortieth Congress" was "legally filled by appointment of the president alone." Attorney General Evarts also issued three opinions concerning the constitutionality of President Johnson's appointments, and it apparently did not occur to him that the distinction between intra-session and inter-session recesses was significant. Similarly, though the 40th Congress impeached President Johnson on charges relating to his appointment power, he was not accused of violating the Constitution by making intra-session recess appointments.

In all, between the founding and the Great Depression, Congress took substantial intra-session breaks (other than holiday breaks) in four years: 1867, 1868, 1921, and 1929. And in each of those years the president made intra-session recess appointments.

Since 1929, and particularly since the end of World War II, Congress has shortened its inter-session breaks as it has taken longer and more frequent intra-session breaks; presidents have correspondingly made more intra-session recess appointments. Indeed, if we include military appointments, presidents have made thousands of intra-session recess appointments. President Franklin Roosevelt, for

ONE

example, commissioned Dwight Eisenhower as a permanent Major General during an intra-session recess; President Truman made Dean Acheson Under Secretary of State; and President George H. W. Bush reappointed Alan Greenspan as Chairman of the Federal Reserve Board. JUSTICE SCALIA does not dispute any of these facts...

The upshot is that restricting the Clause to inter-session recesses would frustrate its purpose. It would make the president's recess-appointment power dependent on a formalistic distinction of Senate procedure. Moreover, the president has consistently and frequently interpreted the word "recess" to apply to intra-session recesses, and has acted on that interpretation. The Senate as a body has done nothing to deny the validity of this practice for at least three-quarters of a century. And three-quarters of a century of settled practice is long enough to entitle a practice to "great weight in a proper interpretation" of the constitutional provision.

> So, since the Executive branch has done it and the Legislative branch hasn't complained, the Judicial branch should look the other way? All branches have a duty to follow the Constitution, but the Judiciary has an additional obligation - to save it.

We are aware of, but we are not persuaded by, three important arguments to the contrary. First, some argue that the Founders would likely have intended the Clause to apply only to inter-session recesses, for they hardly knew any other. Indeed, from the founding until the Civil War inter-session recesses were the only kind of significant recesses that Congress took. The problem with this argument, however, is that it does not fully describe the relevant founding intent. The question is not: Did the Founders at the time think about intra-session recesses? Perhaps they did not. The question is: Did the Founders intend to restrict the scope of the Clause to the form of congressional recess then prevalent, or did they intend a broader scope permitting the Clause to apply, where appropriate, to somewhat changed circumstances? The Founders knew they were writing a document designed to apply to ever-changing circumstances over centuries…We therefore think the Framers likely did intend the Clause to apply to a new circumstance that so clearly falls within its essential purposes, where doing so is consistent with the Clause's language.

Second, some argue that the intra-session interpretation permits the president to make "illogically" long recess appointments. A recess appointment made between Congress' annual sessions would permit the appointee to serve for about a year, *i.e.,* until the "end" of the "next" Senate "session." Art. II, §2, cl. 3. But an intra-session appointment made at the beginning or in the middle of a formal session could permit the appointee to serve for 1½ or almost 2 years (until the end of the following formal session).

We agree that the intra-session interpretation permits somewhat longer recess appointments, but we do not agree that this consequence is "illogical." A president who makes a recess appointment will often also seek to make a regular appointment, nominating the appointee and securing ordinary Senate confirmation. And the Clause ensures that the President and Senate always have at least a full session to go through the nomination and confirmation process. That process may take several months (from 1987 to 2005 the nomination and confirmation process took an average of 236 days for non-cabinet agency heads). A recess appointment that lasts somewhat longer than a year will ensure the president the continued assistance of subordinates that the Clause permits him to obtain while he and the Senate select a regular appointee. An appointment should last until

ONE

the Senate has "an opportunity to act on the subject" and the Clause embodies a determination that a full session is needed to select and vet a replacement.

Third, the Court of Appeals believed that application of the Clause to intra-session recesses would introduce "vagueness" into a Clause that was otherwise clear. One can find problems of uncertainty, however, either way. In 1867, for example, President Andrew Johnson called a special session of Congress, which took place during a lengthy intra-session recess. Consider the period of time that fell just after the conclusion of that special session. Did that period remain an intra-session recess, or did it become an inter-session recess? Historians disagree about the answer.

Or suppose that Congress adjourns *sine die,* but it does so conditionally, so that the leadership can call the members back into session when "the public interest shall warrant it." If the Senate Majority Leader were to reconvene the Senate, how would we characterize the preceding recess? Is it still inter-session? On the narrower interpretation the label matters; on the broader it does not.

The greater interpretive problem is determining how long a recess must be in order to fall within the Clause. Is a break of a week, or a day, or an hour too short to count as a "recess"? The Clause itself does not say. And JUSTICE SCALIA claims that this silence itself shows that the Framers intended the Clause to apply only to an inter-session recess.

We disagree. For one thing, the most likely reason the Framers did not place a textual floor underneath the word "recess" is that they did not foresee the *need* for one. They might have expected that the Senate would meet for a single session lasting at most half a year. And they might not have anticipated that intra-session recesses would become lengthier and more significant than inter-session ones. The Framers' lack of clairvoyance on that point is not dispositive. Unlike JUSTICE SCALIA, we think it most consistent with our constitutional structure to presume that the Framers would have allowed intra-session recess appointments where there was a long history of such practice.

Moreover, the lack of a textual floor raises a problem that plagues *both* interpretations—JUSTICE SCALIA's and ours. Today a brief inter-session recess is just as possible as a brief intra-session recess. And though JUSTICE SCALIA says that the "notion that the Constitution empowers the president to make unilateral appointments every time the Senate takes a half-hour lunch break is *so absurd as to be self-refuting,*" he must immediately concede (in a footnote) that the president "can make recess appointments during any break *between* sessions, *no matter how short.*"

Even the Solicitor General, arguing for a broader interpretation, acknowledges that there is a lower limit applicable to both kinds of recess. He argues that the lower limit should be three days by analogy to the Adjournments Clause of the Constitution. That Clause says: "Neither House, during the Session of Congress, shall, without the Consent of the other, adjourn for more than three days." Art. I, §5, cl. 4.

We agree with the Solicitor General that a 3-day recess would be too short. (Under Senate practice, "Sunday is generally not considered a day," and so is not counted for purposes of the Adjournments Clause.) The Adjournments Clause reflects the fact that a 3-day break is not a significant interruption of legislative business…A Senate recess that is so short that it does not require the consent of the House is not long enough to trigger the president's recess-appointment power.

That is not to say that the president may make recess appointments during any recess that is "more than three days." Art. I, §5, cl. 4. The Recess Appointments Clause seeks to permit the Executive Branch to function smoothly when Congress is unavailable. And though Congress has taken short breaks for almost 200 years, and there have been many thousands of recess appointments in that time, we have not found a single example of a recess appointment made during an intra-session recess that was shorter than 10 days...

> President Obama set the 200+ year record --- three days!

There are a few historical examples of recess appointments made during inter-session recesses shorter than 10 days...We therefore conclude, in light of historical practice, that a recess of more than 3 days but less than 10 days is presumptively too short to fall within the Clause. We add the word "presumptively" to leave open the possibility that some very unusual circumstance - a national catastrophe, for instance, that renders the Senate unavailable but calls for an urgent response - could demand the exercise of the recess-appointment power during a shorter break. (It should go without saying - except that JUSTICE SCALIA compels us to say it - that political opposition in the Senate would not qualify as an unusual circumstance.)

In sum, we conclude that the phrase "the recess" applies to both intra-session and inter-session recesses. If a Senate recess is so short that it does not require the consent of the House, it is too short to trigger the Recess Appointments Clause. See Art. I, §5, cl. 4. And a recess lasting less than 10 days is presumptively too short as well.

IV

The second question concerns the scope of the phrase "vacancies *that may happen* during the recess of the Senate." Art. II, §2, cl. 3.

All agree that the phrase applies to vacancies that initially occur during a recess. But does it also apply to vacancies that initially occur before a recess and continue to exist during the recess? In our view the phrase applies to both kinds of vacancy.

We believe that the Clause's language, read literally, permits, though it does not naturally favor, our broader interpretation. We concede that the most natural meaning of "happens" as applied to a "vacancy" (at least to a modern ear) is that the vacancy "happens" when it initially occurs…But that is not the only possible way to use the word.

Thomas Jefferson wrote that the Clause is "certainly susceptible of two constructions." It "may mean 'vacancies that may happen to be' or 'may happen to fall'" during a recess…

Similarly, when Attorney General William Wirt advised President Monroe to follow the broader interpretation, he wrote that the "expression seems not perfectly clear. It may mean 'happen to take place:' that is, '*to originate*,'" or it "may mean, also, without violence to the sense, 'happen to exist.'" The broader interpretation, he added, is "most accordant with" the Constitution's "reason and spirit."…

The Clause's purpose strongly supports the broader interpretation. That purpose is to permit the president to obtain the assistance of subordinate officers when the Senate, due to its recess, cannot confirm them. Attorney General Wirt clearly described how the narrower interpretation would undermine this purpose: "Put the case of a vacancy occurring in an office, held in a distant part of the country, on the last day of the Senate's session. Before the vacancy is made known to the president, the Senate rises. The office may be an important one; the vacancy may paralyze a whole line of action

ONE

in some essential branch of our internal police; the public interests may imperiously demand that it shall be immediately filled. But the vacancy happened to occur during the session of the Senate; and if the president's power is to be limited to such vacancies only as happen to occur during the recess of the Senate, the vacancy in the case put must continue, however ruinous the consequences may be to the public."…

> I'm not buying this line. It seems to me that "filling" the "vacancy" with an unqualified person would place him in office for up to two years "however ruinous the consequences may be to the public."

We do not agree with JUSTICE SCALIA's suggestion that the… Congress can always provide for acting officers and the president can always convene a special session of Congress. Acting officers may have less authority than presidential appointments. Moreover, to rely on acting officers would lessen the president's ability to staff the Executive Branch with people of his own choosing, and thereby limit the President's control and political accountability. Special sessions are burdensome (and would have been especially so at the time of the founding). The point of the Recess Appointments Clause was to *avoid* reliance on these inadequate expedients.

At the same time, we recognize one important purpose-related consideration that argues in the opposite direction. A broad interpretation might permit a president to avoid Senate confirmations as a matter of course. If the Clause gives the president the power to "fill up all vacancies" that occur before, and continue to exist during, the Senate's recess, a president might not submit any nominations to the Senate. He might simply wait for a recess and then provide all potential nominees with recess appointments. He might thereby routinely avoid the constitutional need to obtain the Senate's "advice and consent."

Wirt thought considerations of character and politics would prevent presidents from abusing the Clause in this way…In an unusual instance, where a matter is important enough to the Senate, that body can remain in session, preventing recess appointments by refusing to take a recess.

> Justice Breyer doesn't seem to have much faith in this particular "check" on the "balance" of power. Must be pretty important for the Senate to extend its session in order to "insure" the president won't abuse the **primary purpose** of the appointment clause - confirmation by the Senate.

In any event, the Executive Branch has adhered to the broader interpretation for two centuries, and Senate confirmation has always remained the norm for officers that require it.

While we concede that both interpretations carry with them some risk of undesirable consequences, we believe the narrower interpretation risks undermining constitutionally conferred powers more seriously and more often. It would prevent the president from making any recess appointment that arose before a recess, no matter who the official, no matter how dire the need, no matter how uncontroversial the appointment, and no matter how late in the session the office fell vacant. Overall…we believe the broader interpretation more consistent with the Constitution's "reason and spirit."…

The upshot is that the president has consistently and frequently interpreted the Recess Appointments Clause to apply to vacancies that initially occur before, but continue to exist during, a recess of the Senate. The Senate as a body has not countered this practice for nearly three-quarters of a century, perhaps longer…And we are reluctant to upset this traditional practice where doing so would

ONE

seriously shrink the authority that presidents have believed existed and have exercised for so long.

In light of some linguistic ambiguity, the basic purpose of the Clause, and the historical practice we have described, we conclude that the phrase "all vacancies" includes vacancies that come into existence while the Senate is in session.

V

The third question concerns the calculation of the length of the Senate's "recess." On December 17, 2011, the Senate by unanimous consent adopted a resolution to convene *"pro forma* sessions" only, with "no business . . . transacted," on every Tuesday and Friday from December 20, 2011, through January 20, 2012. At the end of each *pro forma* session, the Senate would "adjourn until" the following *pro forma* session. During that period, the Senate convened and adjourned as agreed. It held *pro forma* sessions on December 20, 23, 27, and 30, and on January 3, 6, 10, 13, 17, and 20; and at the end of each *pro forma* session, it adjourned until the time and date of the next.

> Before you get lost, I agree that this discussion is confusing. It is difficult to figure out what is meant by convening a pro forma session "with no business being transacted."

The president made the recess appointments before us on January 4, 2012, in between the January 3 and the January 6 *pro forma* sessions. We must determine the significance of these sessions - that is, whether, for purposes of the Clause, we should treat them as periods when the Senate was in session or as periods when it was in recess. If the former, the period between January 3 and January 6 was a 3-day recess, which is too short to trigger the president's recess-appointment power. If the latter, however, then the 3-day period was part of a much longer recess during which the president did have the power to make recess appointments.

The Solicitor General argues that we must treat the *pro forma* sessions as periods of recess. He says that these "sessions" were sessions in name only because the Senate was in recess as a *functional* matter. The Senate, he contends, remained in a single, unbroken recess from January 3, when the second session of the 112th Congress began by operation of the Twentieth Amendment, until January 23, when the Senate reconvened to do regular business.

In our view, however, the *pro forma* sessions count as sessions, not as periods of recess. We hold that, for purposes of the Recess Appointments Clause, the Senate is in session when it says it is, provided that, under its own rules, it retains the capacity to transact Senate business. The Senate met that standard here.

The standard we apply is consistent with the Constitution's broad delegation of authority to the Senate to determine how and when to conduct its business. The Constitution explicitly empowers the Senate to "determine the Rules of its Proceedings." Art. I, §5, cl. 2. And we have held that "all matters of method are open to the determination" of the Senate, as long as there is "a reasonable relation between the mode or method of proceeding established by the rule and the result which is sought to be attained" and the rule does not "ignore constitutional restraints or violate fundamental rights."

In addition, the Constitution provides the Senate with extensive control over its schedule…The Constitution thus gives the Senate wide latitude to determine whether and when to have a session, as well as how to conduct the session. This suggests that the Senate's determination about what constitutes a session should merit great respect…

ONE

For these reasons, we conclude that we must give great weight to the Senate's own determination of when it is and when it is not in session. But our deference to the Senate cannot be absolute. When the Senate is without the *capacity* to act, under its own rules, it is not in session even if it so declares...The purpose of the Clause is to ensure the continued functioning of the Federal Government while the Senate is unavailable. This purpose would count for little were we to treat the Senate as though it were in session even when it lacks the ability to provide its "advice and consent." Accordingly, we conclude that when the Senate declares that it is in session and possesses the capacity, under its own rules, to conduct business, it is in session for purposes of the Clause.

Applying this standard, we find that the *pro forma* sessions were sessions for purposes of the Clause. First, the Senate said it was in session. The Journal of the Senate and the Congressional Record indicate that the Senate convened for a series of twice-weekly "sessions" from December 20 through January 20. And these reports of the Senate "must be assumed to speak the truth."

Second, the Senate's rules make clear that during its *pro forma* sessions, despite its resolution that it would conduct no business, the Senate retained the power to conduct business...

By way of contrast, we do not see how the Senate could conduct business during a recess. It could terminate the recess and then, when in session, pass a bill. But in that case, of course, the Senate would no longer be in recess. It would be in session. And that is the crucial point. Senate rules make clear that, once in session, the Senate can act even if it has earlier said that it would not.

The Solicitor General argues that more is required. He contends that what counts is not the Senate's *capacity* to conduct business but what the Senate actually does (or here, *did*) during its *pro forma* sessions. And he looks for support to the functional definition of "recess" set forth in the 1905 Senate Report discussed above. That Report describes a "recess" of the Senate as the period of time . . . when its members owe no duty of attendance; when its Chamber is empty; when, because of its absence, it cannot receive communications from the president or participate as a body in making appointments."

Even were we, for argument's sake, to accept all of these criteria as authoritative, they would here be met. Taking the last criterion first, could the Senate, during its *pro forma* sessions, "participate as a body in making appointments"? It could. It could confirm nominees by unanimous consent…

Could the Senate "receive communications from the president"? It could. The Congressional Record indicates that the Senate "received" a message from the president on January 12, during a 3-day adjournment between two *pro forma* sessions. If the Senate could receive presidential messages between two *pro forma* sessions, it could receive them during a *pro forma* session.

Was the Senate's Chamber "empty"? It was not. By its official rules, the Senate operates under the presumption that a quorum is present until a present senator suggests the absence of a quorum and nothing in the Journal of the Senate or the Congressional Record reflects any such suggestion.

Did senators "owe a duty of attendance"? They did. The Senate's rules dictate that senators are under a duty to attend every session… Nothing excused the senators from this duty during the Senate's *pro forma* sessions. If any present senator had raised a question as to the presence of a quorum, and by roll call it had become clear that a

ONE

quorum was missing, the senators in attendance could have directed the Sergeant at Arms to bring in the missing senators.

The Solicitor General asks us to engage in a more realistic appraisal of what the Senate actually did. He argues that, during the relevant *pro forma* sessions, business was not in fact conducted; messages from the president could not be received in any meaningful way because they could not be placed before the Senate; the Senate Chamber was, according to C-SPAN coverage, almost empty; and in practice attendance was not required.

We do not believe, however, that engaging in the kind of factual appraisal that the Solicitor General suggests is either legally or practically appropriate. From a legal perspective, this approach would run contrary to precedent instructing us to "respect . . . coequal and independent departments" by, for example, taking the Senate's report of its official action at its word. From a practical perspective, judges cannot easily determine such matters as who is, and who is not, in fact present on the floor during a particular Senate session. Judicial efforts to engage in these kinds of inquiries would risk undue judicial interference with the functioning of the Legislative Branch.

Finally, the Solicitor General warns that our holding may "disrupt the proper balance between the coordinate branches by preventing the Executive Branch from accomplishing its constitutionally assigned functions." We do not see, however, how our holding could significantly alter the constitutional balance. Most appointments are not controversial and do not produce friction between the branches. Where political controversy is serious, the Senate unquestionably has other methods of preventing recess appointments. As the Solicitor General concedes, the Senate could preclude the president from making recess appointments by holding a series of twice-a-week *ordinary* (not *pro forma*) sessions. And the nature of the business conducted at those ordinary sessions - whether, for example, senators must vote on nominations, or may return to their home States to meet with their constituents - is a matter for the Senate to decide. The Constitution also gives the president (if he has enough allies in Congress) a way to force a recess. Art. II, §3 ("In Case of Disagreement between the Houses, with Respect to the Time of Adjournment, the president may adjourn them to such Time as he shall think proper.") Moreover, the president and senators engage with each other in many different ways and have a variety of methods of encouraging each other to accept their points of view.

Regardless, the Recess Appointments Clause is not designed to overcome serious institutional friction. It simply provides a subsidiary method for appointing officials when the Senate is away during a recess. Here, as in other contexts, friction between the branches is an inevitable consequence of our constitutional structure. That structure foresees resolution not only through judicial interpretation and compromise among the branches but also by the ballot box.

VI

The Recess Appointments Clause responds to a structural difference between the Executive and Legislative Branches: The Executive Branch is perpetually in operation, while the Legislature only acts in intervals separated by recesses. The purpose of the Clause is to allow the Executive to continue operating while the Senate is unavailable. We believe that the Clause's text, standing alone, is ambiguous. It does not resolve whether the president may make appointments during intra-session recesses, or whether he may fill pre-recess vacancies. But the broader reading better serves the Clause's structural function. Moreover, that broader reading is reinforced by centuries of history, which we are hesitant to disturb. We thus hold

ONE

that the Constitution empowers the president to fill any existing vacancy during any recess - intra-session or inter-session - of sufficient length.

JUSTICE SCALIA would render illegitimate thousands of recess appointments reaching all the way back to the founding era. More than that: Calling the Clause an "anachronism," he would basically read it out of the Constitution. He performs this act of judicial excision in the name of liberty. We fail to see how excising the Recess Appointments Clause preserves freedom. In fact, Alexander Hamilton observed in the very first Federalist Paper that "the vigour of government is essential to the security of liberty." And the Framers included the Recess Appointments Clause to preserve the "vigour of government" at times when an important organ of Government, the United States Senate, is in recess. JUSTICE SCALIA's interpretation of the Clause would defeat the power of the Clause to achieve that objective.

> The previous paragraph is perhaps the most disingenuous of any I have ever seen in a Supreme Court opinion. Contact me on our website[17] if you would like to discuss.

The foregoing discussion should refute JUSTICE SCALIA's claim that we have "embraced" an "adverse-possession theory of executive power." Instead, as in all cases, we interpret the Constitution in light of its text, purposes, and "our whole experience" as a nation. And we look to the actual practice of Government to inform our interpretation.

---

17 ellconstitutionclubs.com.

> Without getting into the details of adverse possession, it is basically a legal tool used to gain title to real estate of another by maintaining someone else's ground for many years. Justice Scalia metaphorically refers to this power grab as being similar to adverse possession; i.e., do something "wrong enough" for "long enough" and, voila, you make it your own personal rule of law.

Given our answer to the last question before us, we conclude that the Recess Appointments Clause does not give the president the constitutional authority to make the appointments here at issue. Because the Court of Appeals reached the same ultimate conclusion (though for reasons we reject), its judgment is affirmed.

CONCURRENCE: Scalia/Roberts/Thomas/Alito...

> These four conservative justices all agreed with the outcome of the majority: President Obama's "recess appointments" to the National Labor Relations Board in this case were unconstitutional. However, as you will see, these justices strongly disagree with the majority's interpretation of the meaning of these constitutional provisions.

Except where the Constitution or a valid federal law provides otherwise, all "Officers of the United States" must be appointed by the president "by and with the Advice and Consent of the Senate." U. S. Const., Art. II, §2, cl. 2. That general rule is subject to an exception: "The President shall have Power to fill up all Vacancies that may happen during the Recess of the Senate, by granting Commissions which shall expire at the End of their next Session." This case requires us to decide whether the Recess Appointments Clause authorized three appointments made by President Obama to the National Labor Relations Board in January 2012 without the Senate's consent.

ONE

To prevent the president's recess-appointment power from nullifying the Senate's role in the appointment process, the Constitution [limits] that power in two significant ways. First, it may be exercised only in "the Recess of the Senate," that is, the intermission between two formal legislative sessions. Second, it may be used to fill only those vacancies that "happen during the Recess," that is, offices that become vacant during that intermission. Both conditions are clear from the Constitution's text and structure, and both were well understood at the founding. The Court of Appeals correctly held that the appointments here at issue are invalid because they did not meet either condition.

> Once, again, please understand that the Court of Appeals also struck down these appointments as unconstitutional; however, their reasoning was in line with Scalia, Roberts, Thomas and Alito.

Today's Court agrees that the appointments were invalid, but for the far narrower reason that they were made during a 3-day break in the Senate's session. On its way to that result, the majority sweeps away the key textual limitations on the recess-appointment power. It holds, first, that the president can make appointments without the Senate's participation even during short breaks in the middle of the Senate's session, and second, that those appointments can fill offices that became vacant long before the break in which they were filled. The majority justifies those atextual results on an adverse-possession theory of executive authority: Presidents have long claimed the powers in question, and the Senate has not disputed those claims with sufficient vigor, so the Court should not "upset the compromises and working arrangements that the elected branches of Government themselves have reached."

<u>The Court's decision transforms the recess-appointment power from a tool carefully designed to fill a narrow and specific need into a weapon to be wielded by future presidents against future Senates</u>. To reach that result, the majority casts aside the plain, original meaning of the constitutional text in deference to late-arising historical practices that are ambiguous at best. The majority's insistence on deferring to the Executive's untenably broad interpretation of the power is in clear conflict with our precedent and forebodes a diminution of this Court's role in controversies involving the separation of powers and the structure of government. I concur in the judgment only.

In other words, the minority of four concurs that the NLRB appointments in this case were unconstitutional, but they differ substantially in the reasoning and in the ultimate interpretation of the heretofore clear constitutional limitations of the appointment power.

I. Our Responsibility

Today's majority disregards two overarching principles that ought to guide our consideration of the questions presented here.

First, the Constitution's core, government-structuring provisions are no less critical to preserving liberty than are the later adopted provisions of the Bill of Rights. Indeed, "so convinced were the Framers that liberty of the person inheres in structure that at first they did not consider a Bill of Rights necessary." *Clinton* v. *New York*. Those structural provisions reflect the founding generation's deep conviction that "checks and balances were the foundation of a structure of government that would protect liberty." *Bowsher* v. *Synar*. It is for that reason that "the claims of individuals - not of Government departments - have been the principal source of judicial decisions concerning separation of powers and checks and balances."... Those decisions all rest on the bedrock principle that "the constitutional structure of our Government" is designed first and foremost not to look after the interests of the respective branches, but to "protect individual liberty."

Second and relatedly, when questions involving the Constitution's government-structuring provisions are presented in a justiciable case, it is the solemn responsibility of the Judicial Branch "to say what the law is." *Zivotofsky* v. *Clinton* (quoting *Marbury* v. *Madison**).

This Court does not defer to the other branches' resolution of such controversies; as JUSTICE KENNEDY has previously written, our role is in no way "lessened" because it might be said that "the two political branches are adjusting their own powers between themselves." Since the separation of powers exists for the protection of individual liberty, its vitality "does not depend" on "whether 'the encroached-upon branch approves the encroachment.'" Rather, policing the "enduring structure" of constitutional government when the political branches fail to do so is "one of the most vital functions of this Court." *Public Citizen* v. *Department of Justice*.

Our decision in *Chadha* illustrates that principle. There, we held that a statutory provision authorizing one House of Congress to cancel an executive action taken pursuant to statutory authority - a so-called "legislative veto" - exceeded the bounds of Congress's authority under the Constitution. We did not hesitate to hold the legislative veto unconstitutional even though Congress had enacted, and the president had signed, nearly 300 similar provisions over the course of 50 years. Just the opposite: We said the other branches' enthusiasm for the legislative veto "sharpened rather than blunted" our review. Likewise, when the charge is made that a practice "enhances the president's powers beyond" what the Constitution permits, "it is no answer . . . to say that Congress surrendered its authority by its own hand." *Clinton*. "One Congress cannot yield up its own powers, much less those of other Congresses to follow. Abdication of responsibility is not part of the constitutional design."

Of course, where a governmental practice has been open, widespread, and unchallenged since the early days of the Republic, the practice should guide our interpretation of an ambiguous constitutional provision...But "past practice does not, by itself, create power." That is a necessary corollary of the principle that the political branches cannot by agreement alter the constitutional structure. Plainly, then, a self-aggrandizing practice adopted by one branch well after the founding, often challenged, and never before blessed by this Court - in other words, the sort of practice on which the majority relies in this case - does not relieve us of our duty to interpret the Constitution in light of its text, structure, and original understanding...

II. Intra-Session Breaks

The first question presented is whether "the Recess of the Senate," during which the president's recess-appointment power is active, is (a) the period between two of the Senate's formal sessions, or (b) any break in the Senate's proceedings. I would hold that "the Recess" is the gap between sessions and that the appointments at issue here are invalid because they undisputedly were made *during* the Senate's session. The Court's contrary conclusion - that "the Recess" includes "breaks in the midst of a session" - is inconsistent with the Constitution's text and structure, and it requires judicial fabrication of vague, unadministrable limits on the recess-appointment power (thus defined) that overstep the judicial role. And although the majority relies heavily on "historical practice," no practice worthy of our deference supports the majority's conclusion on this issue.

ONE

A. Plain Meaning

A sensible interpretation of the Recess Appointments Clause should start by recognizing that the Clause uses the term "Recess" in contradistinction to the term "Session." As Alexander Hamilton wrote: "The time within which the power is to operate 'during the recess of the Senate' and the duration of the appointments 'to the end of the next session' of that body, conspire to elucidate the sense of the provision." The Federalist No. 67.

In the founding era, the terms "recess" and "session" had well-understood meanings in the marking-out of legislative time. The life of each elected Congress typically consisted (as it still does) of two or more formal sessions separated by adjournments *"sine die,"* that is, without a specified return date. The period *between* two sessions was known as "the recess."…As one scholar has thoroughly demonstrated, "in government practice the phrase 'the Recess' *always* referred to the gap between sessions." By contrast, other provisions of the Constitution use the verb "adjourn" rather than "recess" to refer to the commencement of breaks *during* a formal legislative session.

To be sure, in colloquial usage both words, "recess" and "session," could take on alternative, less precise meanings. A session could include any short period when a legislature's members were "assembled for business," and a recess could refer to any brief "suspension" of legislative "business." So the Continental Congress could complain of the noise from passing carriages disrupting its "daily Session" and the House could "take a recess" from 4 o'clock to 6 o'clock. But as even the majority acknowledges, the Constitution's use of "the word 'the' in *'the* Recess'" tends to suggest "that the phrase refers to the single break separating formal sessions."

More importantly, neither the Solicitor General nor the majority argues that the Clause uses "session" in its loose, colloquial sense. And if "the next Session" denotes a *formal* session, then "the Recess" must mean the break *between* formal sessions. As every commentator on the Clause until the 20th century seems to have understood, the "Recess" and the "Session" to which the Clause refers are mutually exclusive, alternating states…It is linguistically implausible to suppose - as the majority does - that the Clause uses one of those terms ("Recess") informally and the other ("Session") formally in a single sentence, with the result that an event can occur during *both* the "Recess" *and* the "Session."

Besides being linguistically unsound, the majority's reading yields the strange result that an appointment made during a short break near the beginning of one official session will not terminate until the end of the *following* official session, enabling the appointment to last for up to two years. The majority justifies that result by observing that the process of confirming a nominee "may take several months." But the average duration of the confirmation process is irrelevant. The Clause's self-evident design is to have the president's unilateral appointment last only until the Senate has "had an *opportunity* to act on the subject."

One way to avoid the linguistic incongruity of the majority's reading would be to read both "the Recess" and "the next Session" colloquially, so that the recess-appointment power would be activated during any temporary suspension of Senate proceedings, but appointments made pursuant to that power would last only until the beginning of the next suspension (which would end the next colloquial session). That approach would be more linguistically defensible than the majority's. But it would not cure the most fundamental problem with giving "Recess" its colloquial, rather than its formal, meaning:

Doing so leaves the recess-appointment power without a textually grounded principle limiting the time of its exercise…

The notion that the Constitution empowers the president to make unilateral appointments every time the Senate takes a half-hour lunch break is so absurd as to be self-refuting. But that, in the majority's view, is what the text authorizes…

The majority disregards another self-evident purpose of the Clause: to preserve the Senate's role in the appointment process - which the founding generation regarded as a critical protection against "despotism" - by clearly delineating the times when the president can appoint officers without the Senate's consent. Today's decision seriously undercuts *that* purpose. In doing so, it demonstrates the folly of interpreting constitutional provisions designed to establish "a structure of government that would protect liberty" on the narrow-minded assumption that their only purpose is to make the government run as efficiently as possible. "Convenience and efficiency," we have repeatedly recognized, "are not the primary objectives" of our constitutional framework.

Relatedly, the majority contends that the Clause's supposed purpose of keeping the wheels of government turning demands that we interpret the Clause to maintain its relevance in light of the "new circumstance" of the Senate's taking an increasing number of intra-session breaks that exceed three days. Even if I accepted the canard that courts can alter the Constitution's meaning to accommodate changed circumstances, I would be hard pressed to see the relevance of that notion here. The rise of intra-session adjournments has occurred in tandem with the development of modern forms of communication and transportation that mean the Senate "is always available" to consider nominations, even when its Members are temporarily dispersed for an intra-session break. The Recess Appointments Clause therefore is, or rather, should be, an anachronism - "essentially an historic relic, something whose original purpose has disappeared." The need it was designed to fill no longer exists, and its only remaining use is the ignoble one of enabling the president to circumvent the Senate's role in the appointment process. That does not justify "reading it out of the Constitution" and, contra the majority, I would not do so; but neither would I distort the Clause's original meaning, as the majority does, to ensure a prominent role for the recess-appointment power in an era when its influence is far more pernicious than beneficial.

To avoid the absurd results that follow from its colloquial reading of "the Recess," the majority is forced to declare that some intra-session breaks - though undisputedly within the phrase's colloquial meaning - are simply "too short to trigger the Recess Appointments Clause." But it identifies no textual basis whatsoever for limiting the length of "the Recess," nor does it point to any clear standard for determining how short is too short. **It is inconceivable that the Framers would have left the circumstances in which the president could exercise such a significant and potentially dangerous power so utterly indeterminate.** Other structural provisions of the Constitution that turn on duration are quite specific: Neither House can adjourn "for more than three days" without the other's consent. Art. I, §5, cl. 4. The president must return a passed bill to Congress "within ten Days (Sundays excepted)," lest it become a law. Yet on the majority's view, when the first Senate considered taking a 1-month break, a 3-day weekend, or a half-hour siesta, it had no way of knowing whether the president would be constitutionally authorized to appoint officers in its absence. And any officers appointed in those circumstances would have served under a cloud, unable to determine with any degree of confidence whether their appointments were valid.

ONE

Fumbling for some textually grounded standard, the majority seizes on the Adjournments Clause, which bars either House from adjourning for more than three days without the other's consent. According to the majority, that clause establishes that a 3-day break is *always* "too short" to trigger the Recess Appointments Clause. It goes without saying that nothing in the constitutional text supports that disposition. If (as the majority concludes) "the Recess" means a recess in the colloquial sense, then it necessarily includes breaks shorter than three days. And the fact that the Constitution includes a 3-day limit in one clause but omits it from the other weighs strongly against finding such a limit to be implicit in the clause in which it does not appear. In all events, the dramatically different contexts in which the two clauses operate make importing the 3-day limit from the Adjournments Clause into the Recess Appointments Clause "both arbitrary and mistaken."

And what about breaks longer than three days? The majority says that a break of four to nine days is "presumptively too short" but that the presumption may be rebutted in an "unusual circumstance," such as a "national catastrophe . . . that renders the Senate unavailable but calls for an urgent response." The majority must hope that the *in terrorem* effect of its "presumptively too short" pronouncement will deter future presidents from making any recess appointments during 4-to-9-day breaks and thus save us from the absurd spectacle of unelected judges evaluating (after an evidentiary hearing?) whether an alleged "catastrophe" was sufficiently "urgent" to trigger the recess-appointment power. The majority also says that "political opposition in the Senate would not qualify as an unusual circumstance." So if the Senate should refuse to confirm a nominee whom the president considers highly qualified; or even if it should refuse to confirm any nominee for an office, thinking the office better left vacant for the time being; the president's power would not be triggered during a

4-to-9-day break, no matter how "urgent" the president's perceived need for the officer's assistance. The majority protests that this "should go without saying - except that JUSTICE SCALIA compels us to say it," seemingly forgetting that the appointments at issue in this very case were justified on those grounds and that the Solicitor General has asked us to view the recess-appointment power as a "safety valve" against senatorial "intransigence."

As for breaks of 10 or more days: We are presumably to infer that such breaks do not trigger any "presumption" against recess appointments, but does that mean the president has an utterly free hand? Or can litigants seek invalidation of an appointment made during a 10-day break by pointing to an absence of "unusual" or "urgent" circumstances necessitating an immediate appointment, albeit without the aid of a "presumption" in their favor? Or, to put the question as it will present itself to lawyers in the Executive Branch: Can the president make an appointment during a 10-day break simply to overcome "political opposition in the Senate" despite the absence of any "national catastrophe," even though it "goes without saying" that he cannot do so during a 9-day break? Who knows? The majority does not say, and neither does the Constitution.

Even if the many questions raised by the majority's failure to articulate a standard could be answered, a larger question would remain: If the Constitution's text empowers the president to make appointments during any break in the Senate's proceedings, by what right does the majority subject the president's exercise of that power to vague, court-crafted limitations with no textual basis? The majority claims its temporal guideposts are informed by executive practice, but a president's self-restraint cannot "bind his successors by diminishing their powers." *Clinton* v. *Jones** (BREYER, J., concurring in judgment) ("voluntary actions" by past presidents "tell us little about what the Constitution commands.")

ONE

An interpretation that calls for this kind of judicial adventurism cannot be correct. Indeed, if the Clause really did use "Recess" in its colloquial sense, then there would be no "judicially discoverable and manageable standard for resolving" whether a particular break was long enough to trigger the recess-appointment power, making that a nonjusticiable political question.

B. Historical Practice

For the foregoing reasons, the Constitution's text and structure unambiguously refute the majority's freewheeling interpretation of "the Recess." It is not plausible that the Constitution uses that term in a sense that authorizes the president to make unilateral appointments during *any* break in Senate proceedings, subject only to hazy, atextual limits crafted by this Court centuries after ratification. The majority, however, insists that history "offers strong support" for its interpretation. The historical practice of the political branches is, of course, irrelevant when the Constitution is clear. But even if the Constitution were thought ambiguous on this point, history does not support the majority's interpretation.

1. 1789 to 1866

To begin, the majority dismisses the 78 years of history from the founding through 1866 as "not helpful" because during that time Congress took hardly any "significant" intra-session breaks, by which the majority evidently means breaks longer than three days. In fact, Congress took 11 intra-session breaks of more than three days during that time and it appears presidents made recess appointments during none of them.

More importantly, during those eight decades, Congress must have taken thousands of breaks that were three days or shorter. On the majority's reading, every one of those breaks would have been within the Clause's text - the majority's newly minted limitation not yet having been announced. Yet there is no record of anyone, ever, having so much as *mentioned the possibility* that the recess-appointment power was activated during those breaks. That would be surprising indeed if the text meant what the majority thinks it means.

2. 1867 and 1868

The first intra-session recess appointments in our history almost certainly were made by President Andrew Johnson in 1867 and 1868. That was, of course, a period of dramatic conflict between the Executive and Congress that saw the first-ever impeachment of a sitting president. The Solicitor General counts 57 intra-session recess appointments during those two years. But the precise nature and historical understanding of many of those appointments is subject to debate. It seems likely that at least 36 of the 57 appointments were made with the understanding that they took place during a recess *between sessions...*

3. 1869 to 1920

More than half a century went by before any other president made an intra-session recess appointment, and there is strong reason to think that during that period neither the Executive nor the Senate believed such a power existed…

4. 1921 to the Present

It is necessary to skip over the first 13 decades of our nation's history in order to find a presidential legal adviser arguably embracing the majority's interpretation of "the Recess." In 1921 President Harding's Attorney General, Harry Daugherty, advised Harding that he could make recess appointments while the Senate stood adjourned for 28 days during the session because "the term 'recess' must be given a practical construction." Daugherty acknowledged Knox's 1901 opinion to the contrary, but he (committing the same fallacy as today's majority) thought the 1905 Judiciary Committee report had come to the opposite conclusion. He also recognized the fundamental flaw in this interpretation: that it would be impossible to "accurately draw" a line between intra-session breaks that constitute "the Recess" and those that do not. But he thought the absence of a standard gave the president "discretion to determine when there is a real and genuine recess." While a "palpable abuse of discretion might subject his appointment to review," Daugherty thought that "every presumption should be indulged in favor of the validity of whatever action he may take."

Only after Daugherty's opinion did the flow of intra-session recess appointments start, and for several years it was little more than a trickle. The Solicitor General has identified 22 such appointments made by Presidents Harding, Coolidge, Hoover, and Franklin Roosevelt between 1921 and 1944. Intra-session recess appointments experienced a brief heyday after World War II, with President Truman making about 150 such appointments to civilian positions and several thousand to military posts from 1945 through 1950. (The majority's impressive-sounding claim that "presidents have made thousands of intra-session recess appointments" depends entirely on post-war military appointments that Truman made in just two years, 1947 and 1948.) President Eisenhower made only 43 intra-session recess appointments, after which the practice sank back into relative obscurity. Presidents Kennedy, Lyndon Johnson, and Ford made none, while Nixon made just 7. The practice rose again in the last decades of the 20th century: President Carter made 17 intra-session recess appointments, Reagan 72, George H. W. Bush 37, Clinton 53, and George W. Bush 135. When the Solicitor General filed his brief,

President Obama had made 26. Even excluding Truman's military appointments, roughly 90 percent of all the intra-session recess appointments in our history have been made since 1945.

> The number of intra-session appointments made by various presidents doesn't impress me. The significance of the appointments is the issue when comparing prior administrations. Are we talking figure-head appointments or appointments that come with significant power?

Legal advisers in the Executive Branch during this period typically endorsed the president's authority to make intra-session recess appointments by citing Daugherty's opinion with little or no additional analysis. The majority's contention that "opinions of presidential legal advisers . . . are nearly unanimous in determining that the Clause authorizes intra-session recess appointments" is thus true but misleading: No presidential legal adviser approved that practice before 1921, and subsequent approvals have rested more on precedent than on independent examination.

The majority is correct that during this period, the Senate "as a body" did not formally repudiate the emerging executive practice. And on one occasion, Comptroller General Lindsay Warren cited Daugherty's opinion as representing "the accepted view" on the question, although there is no evidence he consulted any senators or that his statement reflected their views. But the rise of intra-session recess appointments in the latter half of the 20th century drew sharp criticism from a number of senators on both sides of the aisle. At first, their objections focused on the length of the intra-session breaks at issue. 130 Cong. Rec. (decrying recess appointment during a 3-week intra-session adjournment as "a circumvention of the Senate confirmation power"); (resolution offered by Sen. Byrd, with

ONE

39 cosponsors, urging that no recess appointments occur during intra-session breaks of fewer than 30 days)...

What does all this amount to? In short: Intra-session recess appointments were virtually unheard of for the first 130 years of the Republic, were deemed unconstitutional by the first Attorney General to address them, were not openly defended by the Executive until 1921, were not made in significant numbers until after World War II, and have been repeatedly criticized as unconstitutional by senators of both parties. It is astonishing for the majority to assert that this history lends "strong support" to its interpretation of the Recess Appointments Clause. And the majority's contention that recent executive practice in this area merits deference because the Senate has not done more to oppose it is utterly divorced from our precedent. "The structural interests protected by the Appointments Clause are not those of any one branch of Government but of the entire Republic" and the Senate could not give away those protections even if it wanted to.

Moreover, the majority's insistence that the Senate gainsay an executive practice "as a body" in order to prevent the Executive from acquiring power by adverse possession, will systematically favor the expansion of executive power at the expense of Congress. In any controversy between the political branches over a separation-of-powers question, staking out a position and defending it over time is far easier for the Executive Branch than for the Legislative Branch. All presidents have a high interest in expanding the powers of their office, since the more power the president can wield, the more effectively he can implement his political agenda; whereas individual senators may have little interest in opposing presidential encroachment on legislative prerogatives, especially when the encroacher is a president who is the leader of their own party. (The majority would not be able to point to a lack of "formal action" by the Senate "as a body" challenging intra-session recess appointments, had the appointing president's party in the Senate not blocked such action on multiple occasions.) And when the president wants to assert a power and establish a precedent, he faces neither the collective-action problems nor the procedural inertia inherent in the legislative process. The majority's methodology thus all but guarantees the continuing aggrandizement of the Executive Branch.

III. Pre-Recess Vacancies

The second question presented is whether vacancies that "happen during the Recess of the Senate," which the president is empowered to fill with recess appointments, are (a) vacancies that *arise* during the recess, or (b) all vacancies that *exist* during the recess, regardless of when they arose. I would hold that the recess-appointment power is limited to vacancies that arise during the recess in which they are filled, and I would hold that the appointments at issue here - which undisputedly filled pre-recess vacancies - are invalid for that reason as well as for the reason that they were made during the session. The Court's contrary conclusion is inconsistent with the Constitution's text and structure, and it further undermines the balance the Framers struck between presidential and senatorial power. Historical practice also fails to support the majority's conclusion on this issue.

A. Plain Meaning

As the majority concedes, "the most natural meaning of 'happens' as applied to a 'vacancy' . . . is that the vacancy 'happens' when it initially occurs." The majority adds that this meaning is most natural "to a modern ear," but it fails to show that founding-era ears heard it differently. "Happen" meant then, as it does now, "to fall out; to chance; to come to pass." Thus, a vacancy that *happened* during the

ONE

Recess was most reasonably understood as one that *arose* during the recess. It was, of course, possible in certain contexts for the word "happen" to mean "happen to be" rather than "happen to occur," as in the idiom "it so happens." But that meaning is not at all natural when the subject is a vacancy, a state of affairs that comes into existence at a particular moment in time.

In any event, no reasonable reader would have understood the Recess Appointments Clause to use the word "happen" in the majority's "happen to be" sense, and thus to empower the president to fill all vacancies that might *exist* during a recess, regardless of when they arose…

For another thing, the majority's reading not only strains the Clause's language but distorts its constitutional role, which was meant to be subordinate. As Hamilton explained, appointment with the advice and consent of the Senate was to be "the general mode of appointing officers of the United States." The Federalist No. 67. The Senate's check on the president's appointment power was seen as vital because "manipulation of official appointments had long been one of the American revolutionary generation's greatest grievances against executive power." The unilateral power conferred on the president by the Recess Appointments Clause was therefore understood to be "nothing more than a supplement" to the "general method" of advice and consent. The Federalist No. 67…

On the majority's reading, the president would have had no need *ever* to seek the Senate's advice and consent for his appointments: Whenever there was a fair prospect of the Senate's rejecting his preferred nominee, the president could have appointed that individual unilaterally during the recess, allowed the appointment to expire at the end of the next session, renewed the appointment the following day, and so on *ad infinitum*. (Circumvention would have been especially easy if, as the majority also concludes, the president was authorized to make such appointments during any intra-session break of more than a few days.) It is unthinkable that such an obvious means for the Executive to expand its power would have been overlooked during the ratification debates...

The majority, however, relies heavily on a contrary account of the Clause given by Attorney General William Wirt in 1823. Wirt notably began - as does the majority - by acknowledging that his predecessors' reading was "most accordant with the letter of the constitution." But he thought the "most natural" reading had to be rejected because it would interfere with the "substantial purpose of the constitution," namely, "keeping . . . offices filled." He was chiefly concerned that giving the Clause its plain meaning would produce "embarrassing inconveniences" if a distant office were to become vacant during the Senate's session, but news of the vacancy were not to reach the president until the recess. The majority fully embraces Wirt's reasoning.

Wirt's argument is doubly flawed. To begin, the Constitution provides ample means, short of rewriting its text, for dealing with the hypothetical dilemma Wirt posed. Congress can authorize "acting" officers to perform the duties associated with a temporarily vacant office - and has done that, in one form or another, since 1792. And on "extraordinary Occasions" the president can call the Senate back into session to consider a nomination. Art. II, §3. If the Framers had thought those options insufficient and preferred to authorize the president to make recess appointments to fill vacancies arising late in the session, they would have known how to do so. Massachusetts, for example, had authorized its Governor to make certain recess appointments "in case a vacancy shall happen . . . in the recess of the

ONE

General Court [*i.e.,* the state legislature], *or at so late a period in any session of the same Court, that the vacancy . . . shall not be supplied in the same session thereof."*

The majority protests that acting appointments, unlike recess appointments, are an "inadequate" solution to Wirt's hypothetical dilemma because acting officers "may have less authority than presidential appointments." It cites an OLC opinion which states that "an acting officer . . . is frequently considered merely a caretaker without a mandate to take far-reaching measures." But just a few lines later, the majority says that "the lack of Senate approval . . . may diminish the recess appointee's ability, as a practical matter, to get a controversial job done." The majority does not explain why an acting officer would have less authority "as a practical matter" than a recess appointee. The majority also objects that requiring the president to rely on acting officers would "lessen the president's ability to staff the Executive Branch with people of his own choosing" - a surprising charge, since that is the very purpose of the Constitution's advice-and-consent requirement. As for special sessions, the majority thinks it a sufficient answer to say that they are "burdensome," an observation that fails to distinguish them from many procedures required by our structural Constitution.

More fundamentally, Wirt and the majority are mistaken to say that the Constitution's "substantial purpose" is to "keep . . . offices filled." The Constitution is not a road map for maximally efficient government, but a system of "carefully crafted restraints" designed to "protect the people from the improvident exercise of power." Wirt's and the majority's *argumentum ab inconvenienti* thus proves far too much. There are many circumstances other than a vacancy that can produce similar inconveniences if they arise late in the session: For example, a natural disaster might occur to which the

Executive cannot respond effectively without a supplemental appropriation. But in those circumstances, the Constitution would not permit the president to appropriate funds himself. See Art. I, §9, cl. 7. Congress must either anticipate such eventualities or be prepared to be haled back into session. The troublesome need to do so is not a bug to be fixed by this Court, but a calculated feature of the constitutional framework. As we have recognized, while the Constitution's government-structuring provisions can seem "clumsy" and "inefficient," they reflect "hard choices . . . consciously made by men who had lived under a form of government that permitted arbitrary governmental acts to go unchecked."

> Argumentum ab inconvenienti: an argument arising from the inconvenience a construction of the law would create.

B. Historical Practice

For the reasons just given, it is clear that the Constitution authorizes the president to fill unilaterally only those vacancies that arise during a recess, not every vacancy that happens to exist during a recess. Again, however, the majority says "historical practice" requires the broader interpretation. And again the majority is mistaken. Even if the Constitution were wrongly thought to be ambiguous on this point, a fair recounting of the relevant history does not support the majority's interpretation...

In sum: Washington's and Adams' Attorneys General read the Constitution to restrict recess appointments to vacancies arising during the recess, and there is no evidence that any of the first four presidents consciously departed from that reading. The contrary reading was first defended by an executive official in 1823, was vehemently rejected by the Senate in 1863, was vigorously resisted by legislation in place from 1863 until 1940, and is arguably inconsistent with legislation in place from 1940 to the present. The Solicitor General has identified only about 100 appointments that have ever been made under the broader reading, and while it seems likely that a good deal more have been made in the last few decades, there is good reason to doubt that many were made before 1940 (since the appointees could not have been compensated). I can conceive of no sane constitutional theory under which this evidence of "historical practice" - which is actually evidence of a long-simmering inter-branch conflict - would require us to defer to the views of the Executive Branch.

IV. Conclusion

What the majority needs to sustain its judgment is an ambiguous text and a clear historical practice. What it has is a clear text and an at-best-ambiguous historical practice. Even if the Executive could accumulate power through adverse possession by engaging in a *consistent* and *unchallenged* practice over a long period of time, the oft-disputed practices at issue here would not meet that standard. Nor have those practices created any justifiable expectations that could be disappointed by enforcing the Constitution's original meaning. There is thus no ground for the majority's deference to the unconstitutional recess-appointment practices of the Executive Branch.

The majority replaces the Constitution's text with a new set of judge-made rules to govern recess appointments. Henceforth, the Senate can avoid triggering the president's now-vast recess-appointment power by the odd contrivance of never adjourning for more than three days without holding a *pro forma* session at which it is understood that no business will be conducted. How this new regime will work in practice remains to be seen.

Perhaps it will reduce the prevalence of recess appointments. But perhaps not: Members of the president's party in Congress may be able to prevent the Senate from holding *pro forma* sessions with the necessary frequency, and if the House and Senate disagree, the president may be able to adjourn both "to such Time as he shall think proper." U. S. Const., Art. II, §3. In any event, the limitation upon the president's appointment power is there not for the benefit of the Senate, but for the protection of the people; it should not be dependent on Senate action for its existence.

The real tragedy of today's decision is not simply the abolition of the Constitution's limits on the recess-appointment power and the substitution of a novel framework invented by this Court. It is the damage done to our separation-of-powers jurisprudence more generally. It is not every day that we encounter a proper case or controversy requiring interpretation of the Constitution's structural provisions. Most of the time, the interpretation of those provisions is left to the political branches - which, in deciding how much respect to afford the constitutional text, often take their cues from this Court. We should therefore take every opportunity to affirm the primacy of the Constitution's enduring principles over the politics of the moment. Our failure to do so today will resonate well beyond the particular dispute at hand. Sad, but true: The Court's embrace of the adverse-possession theory of executive power (a characterization the majority resists but does not refute) will be cited in diverse contexts, including those presently unimagined, and will have the effect of aggrandizing the Presidency beyond its constitutional bounds and undermining respect for the separation of powers.

I concur in the judgment only.

ONE

SUMMARY: President Obama went too far with these three "recess appointments" to the National Labor Relations Board - **all nine robes** agree with that much. That means that the NLRB ruling against Pepsi distributor, Noel Canning, is void, as well as all other rulings where it took one of the invalid appointees to decide the question. However, only five of the nine agree with the expanded interpretation of the Appointment Clause and the Recess Appointment Clause. The other four lament yet another assault on the original intent of the Framers.

COMMENT: The D.C. Circuit Court of Appeals, then, was affirmed – at least as far as the outcome is concerned. But, that lower court opinion is in line with the concurring opinion you just read. The Court of Appeals decision is a much easier read. A majority of the High Court should have adopted it here. If you want to read it (and, I strongly suggest you do) you can get the ELLionized lower court opinion on our website under the name of *Canning v. NLRB*. See the Appendix for instructions.

PLEA: This case, and decisions like them that fall within the subset of cases that decide the "structure of our republic," is one of the most important in this book. When an overreaching majority in the judiciary amends the Constitution with their pen (i.e., with their vote on the Court), "We, the People" lose more than the future impact of the case on the issues at hand. We lose control of a government designed to be controlled by us. We lose our freedom. We can get it back, but only if we vote for presidents and senators that want us to have it back. Only they can help assure that future elite members of the most powerful group of men and women in the world will preserve the blood-bought freedoms of our Constitution when called upon to do so. **One vote** can make all the difference in who gets that **one robe** that sets our course for freedom. Don't stay home next time; in fact, consider helping others of like mind get to the polls.

Chapter Fifteen

ONE ROBE LONG ON JUNE 30, 2014, PRESERVED RELIGIOUS FREEDOM!

WHAT BROUGHT US TO JUNE 30, 2014,
A MONUMENTAL DAY IN THE HISTORY OF AMERICA ---
THE DAY *BURWELL V. HOBBY LOBBY STORES, INC.**
WAS DECIDED ---
THE DAY FREEDOM WAS CELEBRATED?
AND, WHAT IS THE TRUE HOLDING
(AS OPPOSED TO AGENDA-DRIVEN MEDIA HYPE)?

I contend this case is right at the top in importance for our nation. Had it been lost by just **one robe**, the impact to our society – to our freedom – would have been monumental.

No president prior to Obama has ever sought to divide us along the battle lines of abortion versus religion. When the Affordable Health Care Act (Obamacare) was being thrust upon us, I distinctly remember all of the promises that were made in order to "pole vault" it over the total votes necessary to pass. I remember a promise of $2,500 less per year in premiums for a family of four. I remember the promise of doctors we could keep and plans we could keep. And, oh yes, I vividly remember the promise of one of his famous executive orders that would guarantee his plan would not fund abortion. He reneged on his promises. He intended to divide us along religious lines - outrageous for any leader of this nation!

So, by **one robe**, as you will see, the Supreme Court thankfully told this administration that in America, the executive branch cannot require a faith-based, closely held corporation to choose between (1) violating its beliefs by forcing it to provide a metaphorical gun to employees desiring to kill their babies or (2) to pay a fine so large it would effectively put them out of business. For any president to put that choice before freedom-loving American employers is flat unAmerican!

He did it because he felt that, on balance, it would garner him more votes than he would lose. And, it appears he was right, for you Christians who just could not bring yourselves to vote for a Morman in 2012 either stayed home or voted for a third party candidate, enabling him to gain office for a second term - a second term <u>after</u> you already had a taste of Obamacare!

ONE

If you fail to vote for constitutional conservatives for president or for the Senate and the balance of power shifts the wrong way in the Supreme Court, you will own the reversal of this freedom-preserving decision and you will help bring religious persecution to our doorstep. Don't let that happen! Let's explore *Burwell v. Hobby Lobby Stores, Inc.* as we thank God for its result.

BURWELL v. HOBBY LOBBY STORES, INC.
SUPREME COURT OF THE UNITED STATES
June 30, 2014
[5 – 4]

OPINION: Alito/Roberts/Thomas/Scalia/Kennedy … We must decide in these cases whether the Religious Freedom Restoration Act of 1993 (RFRA) permits the United States Department of Health and Human Services (HHS) to demand that three closely held corporations provide health-insurance coverage for methods of contraception that violate the sincerely held religious beliefs of the companies' owners. [We hold that these HHS regulations violate RFRA. The Federal Government has violated the freedoms that RFRA protects.]

Religious Freedom Restoration Act of 1993? What? Who knew that religious freedom needed restoring in 1993 in the land of the free? After all, we have had 1st Amendment free exercise of religion for over 200 years! What gives? Stay with me on this. Just when you may think you are lost, a textbox will appear and the sun will shine! Also, let's start off with clarity. These faith-based corporations were not objecting to providing contraceptive insurance coverage - they were objecting to providing coverage for 2 drugs and 2 devices that kill fertilized eggs. This case is about abortifacients, not contraceptives, although the media would have you believe otherwise.

…The owners of [these] businesses have religious objections to abortion, and according to their religious beliefs, the four contraceptive methods at issue are abortifacients. If the owners comply with the HHS mandate, they believe they will be facilitating abortions, and if they do not comply, they will pay a very heavy price - as much as $1.3 million per day, or about $475 million per year, in the case of one of the companies…

For now, Justice Alito is giving you an overview of the landscape.

He first informs that RFRA protects for-profit corporate religious freedom. Next, he informs that the HHS abortifacient mandate "substantially burdens" the employers' exercise of religion.

In order for these folks to prevail, they must first prove that the law they complain of "substantially burdens" their religion. Justice Alito is informing you that the majority agrees that this insurance coverage mandate does, indeed, substantially burden their religious beliefs. You may remember that President Obama signed an executive order before passage of the Affordable Care Act promising that the ACA would not - would not - provide federal funds to subsidize abortion. Mandating that employers provide the method to abort should never have even been considered. He lied again.

When you are not used to using acronyms, especially when reading legal opinions, it can be confusing. So, once more, remember that RFRA stands for the Religious Freedom Restoration Act. We are going to learn why religious freedom needed restoring and what the Act provided - one step at a time.

One

Under RFRA, a Government action that imposes a substantial burden on religious exercise must serve a compelling government interest, and we assume that the HHS regulations satisfy this requirement. But in order for the HHS mandate to be sustained, it must also constitute the least restrictive means of serving that interest, and the mandate plainly fails that test. There are other ways in which Congress or HHS could equally ensure that every woman has cost-free access to the particular contraceptives at issue here and, indeed, to all FDA-approved contraceptives.

> OK. We will be going over this again, but to summarize: If government passes a law that substantially burdens religion, that alone is not enough to overcome it. If the law does not serve a "compelling government interest," then it can be overcome, but, if it does, the government must still show that the law is the least restrictive means of serving that interest. This will become more apparent as we proceed.

In fact, HHS has already devised and implemented a system that seeks to respect the religious liberty of religious nonprofit corporations while ensuring that the employees of these entities have precisely the same access to all FDA-approved contraceptives as employees of companies whose owners have no religious objections to providing such coverage. The employees of these religious nonprofit corporations still have access to insurance coverage without cost sharing for all FDA-approved contraceptives; and according to HHS, this system imposes no net economic burden on the insurance companies that are required to provide or secure the coverage.

Although HHS has made this system available to religious nonprofits that have religious objections to the contraceptive mandate, HHS has provided no reason why the same system cannot be made available when the owners of for-profit corporations have similar religious objections. We therefore conclude that this system constitutes an alternative that achieves all of the Government's aims while providing greater respect for religious liberty. And under RFRA, that conclusion means that enforcement of the HHS contraceptive mandate against the objecting parties in these cases is unlawful.

The additional question, then, is whether the government's method of imposing the mandate is the least restrictive method available. After all, if there are other ways to get these four abortifacients to employees for free without demanding that employers violate their conscience, no woman loses - right?

Hillary, why are you so angry? Do you care so little for the religious beliefs of American citizens that you would demand they bow down to your idea of fairness even when there is no unfairness? It's all about riding ignorance to the polls, isn't it? It's all about feigned revulsion to the mythical Republican "war on women," isn't it?

…We do not hold, as the [dissent] alleges, that for-profit corporations and other commercial enterprises can "opt out of any law… they judge incompatible with their sincerely held religious beliefs." Nor do we hold, as the dissent implies, that such corporations have free rein to take steps that impose "disadvantages…on others" or that require "the general public to pick up the tab." And we certainly do not hold or suggest that "RFRA demands accommodation of a for-profit corporation's religious beliefs no matter the impact that accommodation may have on…thousands of women employed by Hobby Lobby." The effect of the HHS-created accommodation on the women employed by Hobby Lobby and the other companies involved in these cases would be precisely **zero**. Under that accommodation, these women would still be entitled to all FDA-approved contraceptives without cost sharing.

> Justice Alito lays to rest all of the hysterical and misleading allegations of Justice Ginsburg in her dissent. Justice Kennedy will do so, as well, in his concurring opinion, below.

I
A

> I will try to explain why it was necessary to enact RFRA in 1993.

> Prior to a case that was decided in 1990 by the name of *Employment Division v. Smith**, when challenges were made to government laws that impacted the free exercise of religion, the tests we have discussed thus far were the same tests the Supreme Court used to answer those challenges. They had interpreted the First Amendment free exercise of religion in fundamentally the same manner as RFRA does. For example, in order to get relief from a law that impacted religion before *Smith* was decided, the burden on religion had to be substantial and, if the government interest in enforcing the law was not compelling, religion won. If it was compelling, religion also won if government could accomplish the purpose of the law by a lesser restrictive means. In other words, the law prior to the *Smith* decision was, for all practical purposes, identical to RFRA. RFRA was enacted to cure the problems caused by the *Smith* decision in 1990. We need to look at the *Smith* decision now to understand why Congress thought that was necessary.

...*Smith* concerned two members of the Native American Church who were fired for ingesting peyote for sacramental purposes. When they sought unemployment benefits, the State of Oregon rejected their claims on the ground that consumption of peyote was a crime, but the Oregon Supreme Court, applying the [law as explained in the above textbox], held that the denial of benefits violated the Free Exercise Clause.

This Court [the Supreme Court] then reversed, observing that use of [the old tests] whenever a person objected on religious grounds to the enforcement of a generally applicable law "would open the prospect of constitutionally required religious exemptions from civic obligations of almost every conceivable kind." The Court therefore held that, under the 1st Amendment, "neutral generally applicable laws may be applied to religious practices even when not supported by a compelling governmental interest."

> The *Smith* decision served to limit religious freedom. Congress overwhelmingly believed the Religious Freedom Restoration Act was necessary to bring the protection of religious freedom more in line with the Court's rulings prior to the *Smith* decision. There is a movement on (after this decision) to repeal RFRA. That must not happen.

Congress responded to *Smith* by enacting RFRA. "Laws that are 'neutral' toward religion," Congress found, "may burden religious exercise as surely as laws intended to interfere with religious exercise." In order to ensure broad protection for religious liberty, RFRA provides that "Government shall not substantially burden a person's exercise of religion even if the burden results from a rule of general applicability." If the Government substantially burdens a person's exercise of religion, under the Act that person is entitled to an exemption from the rule unless the Government "demonstrates that application of the burden to the person - (1) is in furtherance of a compelling governmental interest; and (2) is the least restrictive means of furthering that compelling governmental interest."...

One

B

At issue in these cases are HHS regulations promulgated under the Patient Protection and Affordable Care Act of 2010. ACA generally requires employers with 50 or more full-time employees to offer "a group health plan or group health insurance coverage" that provides "minimum essential coverage." Any covered employer that does not provide such coverage must pay a substantial price. Specifically, if a covered employer provides group health insurance but its plan fails to comply with ACA's group-health-plan requirements, the employer may be required to pay $100 per day for each affected "individual." And if the employer decides to stop providing health insurance altogether and at least one full-time employee enrolls in a health plan and qualifies for a subsidy on one of the government-run ACA exchanges, the employer must pay $2,000 per year for each of its fulltime employees.

Unless an exception applies, ACA requires an employer's group health plan or group-health-insurance coverage to furnish "preventive care and screenings" for women without "any cost sharing requirements." Congress itself, however, did not specify what types of preventive care must be covered. Instead, Congress authorized the Health Resources and Services Administration (HRSA), a component of HHS, to make that important and sensitive decision. The HRSA in turn consulted the Institute of Medicine, a nonprofit group of volunteer advisers, in determining which preventive services to require.

In August 2011, based on the Institute's recommendations, the HRSA promulgated the Women's Preventive Services Guidelines. The Guidelines provide that nonexempt employers are generally required to provide "coverage, without cost sharing" for "all Food and Drug Administration (FDA) approved contraceptive methods, sterilization procedures, and patient education and counseling." Although many of the required, FDA-approved methods of contraception work by preventing the fertilization of an egg, four of those methods (those specifically at issue in these cases) may have the effect of preventing an already fertilized egg from developing any further by inhibiting its attachment to the uterus.

> These are the only four "FDA approved" methods to which these faith-based corporations object. They believe these four drugs/devices kill human beings. You see, religious freedom is still protected in America --- **by one robe**! Why would anyone demand of others (against their sincere religious convictions) that they must participate in the destruction of human life or go out of business in the land of the free? Hillary, even if you don't believe as others do, how can you respect a government that forces their compliance? No, you and your party are the ones who foster intolerance, discrimination, loss of freedom and hate.

HHS also authorized the HRSA to establish exemptions from the contraceptive mandate for "religious employers." That category encompasses "churches, their integrated auxiliaries, and conventions or associations of churches," as well as "the exclusively religious activities of any religious order." In its Guidelines, HRSA exempted these organizations from the requirement to cover contraceptive services.

In addition, HHS has effectively exempted certain religious non-profit organizations, described under HHS regulations as "eligible organizations," from the contraceptive mandate. An "eligible organization" means a nonprofit organization that "holds itself out as a religious organization" and "opposes providing coverage for some or all of any contraceptive services required to be covered . . . on account of religious objections." To qualify for this accommodation, an employer must certify that it is such an organization. When a group-health-insurance issuer receives notice that one of its clients has invoked this provision, the issuer must then exclude contraceptive coverage from the employer's plan and provide separate payments for contraceptive services for plan participants without imposing any cost-sharing requirements on the eligible organization, its insurance plan, or its employee beneficiaries. Although this procedure requires the issuer to bear the cost of these services, HHS has determined that this obligation will not impose any net expense on issuers because its cost will be less than or equal to the cost savings resulting from the services.

In addition to these exemptions for religious organizations, ACA exempts a great many employers from most of its coverage requirements. Employers providing "grandfathered health plans" - those that existed prior to March 23, 2010, and that have not made specified changes after that date - need not comply with many of the Act's requirements, including the contraceptive mandate. And employers with fewer than 50 employees are not required to provide health insurance at all.

All told, the contraceptive mandate "presently does not apply to tens of millions of people." This is attributable, in large part, to grandfathered health plans: Over one-third of the 149 million nonelderly people in America with employer-sponsored health plans were enrolled in grandfathered plans in 2013. The count for employees working for firms that do not have to provide insurance at all because they employ fewer than 50 employees is 34 million workers.

> What will the "poor" women who work for churches, whose employer has fewer than 50 employees, whose employer's policies are grandfathered or who work for religious not-for-profits do when faced with no free abortifacients? These self-imposed exemptions by the Obama administration encompass vast millions of female employees. So, Hillary, why aren't you upset with the President for his so-called "war on women"? How will these millions survive without the first-ever statutorily mandated abortifacient give-away in our nation's history - all at the hand of President Obama?

II
A

> Please meet the Hahns a/k/a Conestoga Wood Specialties, a closely held for-profit (gasp) corporation. I am sure you will agree these "mean-spirited stockholders" just don't care about women – except, that is, for the millions upon millions that didn't have the chance to become women at the hands of a government that permits (even celebrates) the early demise of baby girls.

Norman and Elizabeth Hahn and their three sons are devout members of the Mennonite Church, a Christian denomination. The Mennonite Church opposes abortion and believes that "the fetus in its earliest stages . . . shares humanity with those who conceived it."

Fifty years ago, Norman Hahn started a wood-working business in his garage, and since then, this company, Conestoga Wood Specialties, has grown and now has 950 employees. Conestoga is organized under Pennsylvania law as a for-profit corporation. The Hahns exercise sole ownership of the closely held business; they control its board of directors and hold all of its voting shares. One of the Hahn sons serves as the president and CEO.

ONE

The Hahns believe that they are required to run their business "in accordance with their religious beliefs and moral principles." To that end, the company's mission, as they see it, is to "operate in a professional environment founded upon the highest ethical, moral, and Christian principles." The company's "Vision and Values Statements" affirms that Conestoga endeavors to "ensure a reasonable profit in a manner that reflects the Hahns' Christian heritage."

As explained in Conestoga's board-adopted "Statement on the Sanctity of Human Life," the Hahns believe that "human life begins at conception." It is therefore "against their moral conviction to be involved in the termination of human life" after conception, which they believe is a "sin against God to which they are held accountable." The Hahns have accordingly excluded from the group-health-insurance plan they offer to their employees certain contraceptive methods that they consider to be abortifacients.

The Hahns and Conestoga sued HHS and other federal officials and agencies under RFRA and the Free Exercise Clause of the First Amendment, seeking to enjoin application of ACA's contraceptive mandate insofar as it requires them to provide health-insurance coverage for four FDA-approved contraceptives that may operate after the fertilization of an egg. These include two forms of emergency contraception commonly called "morning-after" pills and two types of intrauterine devices.

In opposing the requirement to provide coverage for the contraceptives to which they object, the Hahns argued that "it is immoral and sinful for them to intentionally participate in, pay for, facilitate, or otherwise support these drugs." The District Court denied a preliminary injunction and the Third Circuit affirmed in a divided opinion, holding that "for-profit, secular corporations cannot engage in religious exercise" within the meaning of RFRA or the First Amendment. The Third Circuit also rejected the claims brought by the Hahns themselves because it concluded that the HHS "mandate does not impose any requirements on the Hahns" in their personal capacity.

B

> Please meet the Greens a/k/a Hobby Lobby Stores, Inc. and Mardel, closely held for-profit (shudder) corporations. Ditto as for their "mean-spirited" attitude about "women."

David and Barbara Green and their three children are Christians who own and operate two family businesses. Forty-five years ago, David Green started an arts-and-crafts store that has grown into a nationwide chain called Hobby Lobby…[It] is organized as a for-profit corporation under Oklahoma law.

One of David's sons started an affiliated business, Mardel, which operates 35 Christian bookstores and…is also organized as a for-profit corporation under Oklahoma law.

Though these two businesses have expanded over the years, they remain closely held, and David, Barbara, and their children retain exclusive control of both companies. David serves as the CEO of Hobby Lobby, and his three children serve as the president, vice president, and vice CEO.

> Fundamentally, a "closely-held corporation" is a corporation where more than 50% of its outstanding stock is owned by five or fewer individuals.

ONE

Hobby Lobby's statement of purpose commits the Greens to "honoring the Lord in all they do by operating the company in a manner consistent with Biblical principles." Each family member has signed a pledge to run the businesses in accordance with the family's religious beliefs and to use the family assets to support Christian ministries. In accordance with those commitments, Hobby Lobby and Mardel stores close on Sundays, even though the Greens calculate that they lose millions in sales annually by doing so. The businesses refuse to engage in profitable transactions that facilitate or promote alcohol use; they contribute profits to Christian missionaries and ministries; and they buy hundreds of full-page newspaper ads inviting people to "know Jesus as Lord and Savior."

Like the Hahns, the Greens believe that life begins at conception and that it would violate their religion to facilitate access to contraceptive drugs or devices that operate after that point. They specifically object to the same four contraceptive methods as the Hahns and, like the Hahns, they have no objection to the other 16 FDA-approved methods of birth control. Although their group-health-insurance plan predates the enactment of ACA, it is not a grandfathered plan because Hobby Lobby elected not to retain grandfathered status before the contraceptive mandate was proposed…We granted certiorari.

> The Hahns lost in the lower court. The Greens won. The Supreme Court agreed to hear these cases, in part, because of these conflicting lower court rulings from different jurisdictions.

III
A

RFRA prohibits the "Government from substantially burdening *a person's* exercise of religion even if the burden results from a rule of general applicability" unless the Government "demonstrates that application of the burden to *the person* - (1) is in furtherance of a compelling governmental interest; and (2) is the least restrictive means of furthering that compelling governmental interest." The first question that we must address is whether this provision applies to regulations that govern the activities of for-profit corporations like Hobby Lobby, Conestoga, and Mardel...

> Now the Court is getting down to the business of interpreting RFRA. Justice Alito will be covering the foregoing concepts in much more detail.

According to HHS, the companies cannot sue because they seek to make a profit for their owners, and the owners cannot be heard because the regulations, at least as a formal matter, apply only to the companies and not to the owners as individuals. HHS's argument would have dramatic consequences...

HHS would put [sole proprietors and partnerships wishing to become closely-held corporations] to a difficult choice: either give up the right to seek judicial protection of their religious liberty or forgo the benefits, available to their competitors, of operating as corporations.

As we have seen, RFRA was designed to provide very broad protection for religious liberty. By enacting RFRA, Congress went far beyond what this Court has held is constitutionally required. Is there any reason to think that the Congress that enacted such sweeping protection put small-business owners to the choice that HHS suggests? An examination of RFRA's text, to which we turn in the next part of this opinion, reveals that Congress did no such thing.

As we will show, Congress provided protection for people like the

ONE

Hahns and Greens by employing a familiar legal fiction: It included corporations within RFRA's definition of "persons." But it is important to keep in mind that the purpose of this fiction is to provide protection for human beings. A corporation is simply a form of organization used by human beings to achieve desired ends. An established body of law specifies the rights and obligations of the *people* (including shareholders, officers, and employees) who are associated with a corporation in one way or another. When rights, whether constitutional or statutory, are extended to corporations, the purpose is to protect the rights of these people…Protecting the free-exercise rights of corporations like Hobby Lobby, Conestoga, and Mardel protects the religious liberty of the humans who own and control those companies.

In holding that Conestoga, as a "secular, for-profit corporation," lacks RFRA protection, the Third Circuit wrote as follows: "General business corporations do not, *separate and apart from the actions or belief systems of their individual owners or employees,* exercise religion. They do not pray, worship, observe sacraments or take other religiously-motivated actions separate and apart from the intention and direction of their individual actors."

All of this is true - but quite beside the point. Corporations, "separate and apart from" the human beings who own, run, and are employed by them, cannot do anything at all.

B
1

As we noted above, RFRA applies to "a person's" exercise of religion and RFRA itself does not define the term "person." We therefore look to the Dictionary Act, which we must consult "in determining the meaning of any Act of Congress, unless the context indicates otherwise."

> In other words, if the context of an Act of Congress makes the definition of a word it uses clear, then no need to look elsewhere. But, where it does not, then Congress has adopted the Dictionary Act where words are defined and applied in those circumstances.

Under the Dictionary Act, "the word 'person'…includes corporations, companies, associations, firms, partnerships, societies, and joint stock companies, as well as individuals."…Thus, unless there is something about the RFRA context that "indicates otherwise," the Dictionary Act provides a quick, clear, and affirmative answer to the question whether the companies involved in these cases may be heard.

We see nothing in RFRA that suggests a congressional intent to depart from the Dictionary Act definition, and HHS…concedes that a nonprofit corporation can be a "person" within the meaning of RFRA.

This concession effectively dispatches any argument that the term "person" as used in RFRA does not reach the closely held corporations involved in these cases. No known understanding of the term "person" includes *some* but not all corporations. The term "person" sometimes encompasses artificial persons (as the Dictionary Act instructs), and it sometimes is limited to natural persons. But no conceivable definition of the term includes natural persons and non-profit corporations, but not for-profit corporations…

2

The principal argument advanced by HHS…focuses not on the statutory term "person," but on the phrase "exercise of religion." According to HHS and the dissent, these corporations are not protected by RFRA because they cannot <u>exercise</u> religion. Neither HHS nor the dissent, however, provides any persuasive explanation for this conclusion…

ONE

Some lower court judges have suggested that RFRA does not protect for-profit corporations because the purpose of such corporations is simply to make money. This argument flies in the face of modern corporate law...For-profit corporations, with ownership approval, support a wide variety of charitable causes, and it is not at all uncommon for such corporations to further humanitarian and other altruistic objectives...So long as its owners agree, a for-profit corporation may take costly pollution-control and energy-conservation measures that go beyond what the law requires. A for-profit corporation that operates facilities in other countries may exceed the requirements of local law regarding working conditions and benefits. If for-profit corporations may pursue such worthy objectives, there is no apparent reason why they may not further religious objectives as well.

HHS would draw a sharp line between nonprofit corporations (which, HHS concedes, are protected by RFRA) and for-profit corporations (which HHS would leave unprotected), but the actual picture is less clear-cut. Not all corporations that decline to organize as nonprofits do so in order to maximize profit. For example, organizations with religious and charitable aims might organize as for-profit corporations because of the potential advantages of that corporate form, such as the freedom to participate in lobbying for legislation or campaigning for political candidates who promote their religious or charitable goals...

The objectives that may properly be pursued by the companies in these cases are governed by the laws of the States in which they were incorporated - Pennsylvania and Oklahoma - and the laws of those States permit for-profit corporations to pursue "any lawful purpose" or "act," including the pursuit of profit in conformity with the owners' religious principles...

4

Finally, HHS contends that Congress could not have wanted RFRA to apply to for-profit corporations because it is difficult as a practical matter to ascertain the sincere "beliefs" of a corporation. HHS goes so far as to raise the specter of "divisive, polarizing proxy battles over the religious identity of large, publicly traded corporations such as IBM or General Electric."

These cases, however, do not involve publicly traded corporations, and it seems unlikely that the sort of corporate giants to which HHS refers will often assert RFRA claims...The companies in the cases before us are closely held corporations, each owned and controlled by members of a single family, and no one has disputed the sincerity of their religious beliefs...

And if, as HHS seems to concede, Congress wanted RFRA to apply to nonprofit corporations, what reason is there to think that Congress believed that spotting insincere claims would be tougher in cases involving for-profits?

HHS and the principal dissent express concern about the possibility of disputes among the owners of corporations, but that is not a problem that arises because of RFRA or that is unique to this context. The owners of closely held corporations may - and sometimes do - disagree about the conduct of business. And even if RFRA did not exist, the owners of a company might well have a dispute relating to religion. For example, some might want a company's stores to remain open on the Sabbath in order to make more money, and others might want the stores to close for religious reasons. State corporate law provides a ready means for resolving any conflicts by, for example, dictating how a corporation can establish its governing structure...

One

For all these reasons, we hold that a federal regulation's restriction on the activities of a for-profit closely held corporation must comply with RFRA.

IV

Because RFRA applies in these cases, we must next ask whether the HHS contraceptive mandate "substantially burdens" the exercise of religion. We have little trouble concluding that it does.

A

As we have noted, the Hahns and Greens have a sincere religious belief that life begins at conception. They therefore object on religious grounds to providing health insurance that covers methods of birth control that, as <u>HHS acknowledges,</u> may result in the destruction of an embryo. By requiring the Hahns and Greens and their companies to arrange for such coverage, the HHS mandate demands that they engage in conduct that seriously violates their religious beliefs.

> I have seen numerous articles insisting that the four drugs/devices the Hahns and Greens complain of do not cause the demise of an embryo. However, the government (HHS) acknowledges they may and I am betting the manufacturer of the drugs warns of at least the possibility of an abortion on the labels.

If the Hahns and Greens and their companies do not yield to this demand, the economic consequences will be severe...

It is true that the plaintiffs could avoid these assessments by dropping insurance coverage altogether and thus forcing their employees to obtain health insurance on one of the exchanges established under ACA. But if at least one of their full-time employees were to qualify for a subsidy on one of the government-run exchanges, this course would also entail substantial economic consequences...

B

Although these totals are high, *amici* supporting HHS have suggested that the $2,000 per-employee penalty is actually less than the average cost of providing health insurance and therefore, they claim, the companies could readily eliminate any substantial burden by forcing their employees to obtain insurance in the government exchanges...

As an initial matter, it entirely ignores the fact that the Hahns and Greens and their companies have religious reasons for providing health-insurance coverage for their employees. Before the advent of ACA, they were not legally compelled to provide insurance, but they nevertheless did so - in part, no doubt, for conventional business reasons, but also in part because their religious beliefs govern their relations with their employees.

Putting aside the religious dimension of the decision to provide insurance, moreover, it is far from clear that the net cost to the companies of providing insurance is more than the cost of dropping their insurance plans and paying the ACA penalty. Health insurance is a benefit that employees value. If the companies simply eliminated that benefit and forced employees to purchase their own insurance on the exchanges, without offering additional compensation, it is predictable that the companies would face a competitive disadvantage in retaining and attracting skilled workers.

The companies could attempt to make up for the elimination of a group health plan by increasing wages, but this would be costly. Group health insurance is generally less expensive than comparable individual coverage, so the amount of the salary increase needed to fully compensate for the termination of insurance coverage may well exceed the cost to the companies of providing the insurance. In addition, any salary increase would have to take into account the fact that employees must pay income taxes on wages but not on the value of employer-provided health insurance. Likewise, employers can deduct the cost of providing health insurance, but apparently cannot deduct the amount of the penalty that they must pay if insurance is not provided; that difference also must be taken into account. Given these economic incentives, it is far from clear that it would be financially advantageous for an employer to drop coverage and pay the penalty.

In sum, we refuse to sustain the challenged regulations on the ground - never maintained by the Government - that dropping insurance coverage eliminates the substantial burden that the HHS mandate imposes. We doubt that the Congress that enacted RFRA - or, for that matter, ACA - would have believed it a tolerable result to put family-run businesses to the choice of violating their sincerely held religious beliefs or making all of their employees lose their existing healthcare plans.

C

In taking the position that the HHS mandate does not impose a substantial burden on the exercise of religion, HHS's main argument (echoed by the principal dissent) is basically that the connection between what the objecting parties must do (provide health-insurance coverage for four methods of contraception that may operate after the fertilization of an egg) and the end that they find to be morally wrong (destruction of an embryo) is simply too attenuated. HHS and the dissent note that providing the coverage would not itself result in the destruction of an embryo; that would occur only if an employee chose to take advantage of the coverage and to use one of the four methods at issue.

This argument dodges the question that RFRA presents (whether the HHS mandate imposes a substantial burden on the ability of the objecting parties to conduct business in accordance with *their religious beliefs*) and instead addresses a very different question that the federal courts have no business addressing (whether the religious belief asserted in a RFRA case is reasonable). The Hahns and Greens believe that providing the coverage demanded by the HHS regulations is connected to the destruction of an embryo in a way that is sufficient to make it immoral for them to provide the coverage. This belief implicates a difficult and important question of religion and moral philosophy, namely, the circumstances under which it is wrong for a person to perform an act that is innocent in itself but that has the effect of enabling or facilitating the commission of an immoral act by another.

[Assuming themselves to be] the authority to provide a binding national answer to this religious and philosophical question, HHS and the principal dissent in effect tell the plaintiffs that their beliefs are flawed. For good reason, we have repeatedly refused to take such a step. "Repeatedly and in many different contexts, we have warned that courts must not presume to determine . . . the plausibility of a religious claim"; *Hernandez v. Commissioner**; *Presbyterian Church in U. S. v. Mary Elizabeth Blue Hull Memorial Presbyterian Church*.

I will admit (and so would Justice Alito) that somewhere there is a line beyond which a religious belief will not prevail because it is not judicially recognized; i.e., the Court is not going to honor the Church of Nontaxpayers even if its members sincerely believe they are forbidden by God from contributing to government coffers. Perhaps the dividing line will find more definition in future cases. However, the issues <u>in this case</u> cannot (or should not) be second-guessed by members of the Court who wish to decide for others that enabling an employee to kill her child by metaphorically providing her the gun to accomplish it isn't a belief worthy of holding.

ONE

Moreover, in *Thomas v. Review Bd.* *, we considered and rejected an argument that is nearly identical to the one now urged by HHS and the dissent. In *Thomas,* a Jehovah's Witness was initially employed making sheet steel for a variety of industrial uses, but he was later transferred to a job making turrets for tanks. Because he objected on religious grounds to participating in the manufacture of weapons, he lost his job and sought unemployment compensation. Ruling against the employee, the state court had difficulty with the line that the employee drew between work that he found to be consistent with his religious beliefs (helping to manufacture steel that was used in making weapons) and work that he found morally objectionable (helping to make the weapons themselves). This Court, however, held that "it is not for us to say that the line he drew was an unreasonable one."

> Hillary says: "Hobby Lobby should not be permitted to impose their religious beliefs on women." Of course, they are not doing so. Their employees are free to use abortifacients. No, this administration is attempting to force its views on these employers.

Similarly, in these cases, the Hahns and Greens and their companies sincerely believe that providing the insurance coverage demanded by the HHS regulations lies on the forbidden side of the line, and it is not for us to say that their religious beliefs are mistaken or insubstantial. Instead, our "narrow function . . . in this context is to determine" whether the line drawn reflects "an honest conviction" and there is no dispute that it does…

V

Since the HHS contraceptive mandate imposes a substantial burden on the exercise of religion, we must move on and decide whether HHS has shown that the mandate both "(1) is in furtherance of a compelling governmental interest; and (2) is the least restrictive means of furthering that compelling governmental interest."

A

HHS asserts that the contraceptive mandate serves a variety of important interests, but many of these are couched in very broad terms, such as promoting "public health" and "gender equality."...

In addition to asserting these very broadly framed interests, HHS maintains that the mandate serves a compelling interest in ensuring that all women have access to all FDA-approved contraceptives without cost sharing. Under our cases, women (and men) have a constitutional right to obtain contraceptives, see *Griswold v. Connecticut**, and HHS tells us that "studies have demonstrated that even moderate copayments for preventive services can deter patients from receiving those services."

> A "right to obtain contraceptives" isn't precisely accurate. One is left with the impression that the *Griswold* case supports the "right" to get contraceptives for free. Not so. It simply was the first of two decisions ultimately holding that the Constitution prohibits government from making the possession or use of contraceptives illegal.

The objecting parties contend that HHS has not shown that the mandate serves a compelling government interest, and it is arguable that there are features of ACA that support that view. As we have noted, many employees - those covered by grandfathered plans and those who work for employers with fewer than 50 employees - may have no contraceptive coverage without cost sharing at all...

> Justice Alito is going to wisely avoid ruling on whether the government's interest in this mandate is compelling because that discussion would engender unjustified allegations of a war on women. However, it is truly hard to argue that this mandate is seriously compelling when countless millions are exempted from its "benefits" by President Obama's exemptions. Must not be so compelling for women who work for an employer with under 50 employees. As the argument goes, if not compelling for them, what makes it compelling on the day the employer hires number 50?

<u>We find it unnecessary to adjudicate this issue. We will assume that the interest in guaranteeing cost-free access to the four challenged contraceptive methods is compelling</u> within the meaning of RFRA, and we will proceed to consider the final prong of the RFRA test, *i.e.,* whether HHS has shown that the contraceptive mandate is "the least restrictive means of furthering that compelling governmental interest."

B

The least-restrictive-means standard is exceptionally demanding and it is not satisfied here. HHS has not shown that it lacks other means of achieving its desired goal without imposing a substantial burden on the exercise of religion by the objecting parties in these cases…

The most straightforward way of doing this would be for the Government to assume the cost of providing the four contraceptives at issue to any women who are unable to obtain them under their health-insurance policies due to their employers' religious objections. This would certainly be less restrictive of the plaintiffs' religious liberty, and HHS has not shown that this is not a viable alternative. HHS has not provided any estimate of the average cost per employee of providing access to these contraceptives, two of which, according to the FDA, are designed primarily for emergency use. Nor has HHS provided any statistics regarding the number of employees who might be affected because they work for corporations like Hobby Lobby, Conestoga, and Mardel. Nor has HHS told us that it is unable to provide such statistics. It seems likely, however, that the cost of providing the forms of contraceptives at issue in these cases (if not all FDA-approved contraceptives) would be minor when compared with the overall cost of ACA. According to one of the Congressional Budget Office's most recent forecasts, ACA's insurance-coverage provisions will cost the Federal Government more than $1.3 trillion through the next decade. If, as HHS tells us, providing all women with cost-free access to all FDA-approved methods of contraception is a Government interest of the highest order, it is hard to understand HHS's argument that it cannot be required under RFRA to pay *anything* in order to achieve this important goal…

HHS's view that RFRA can never require the Government to spend even a small amount reflects a judgment about the importance of religious liberty that was not shared by the Congress that enacted that law.

> The hysterical reaction to this case has already suggested a movement to repeal RFRA. Twenty-one years ago, Congress had a much different view about the importance of religious freedom. Where do they stand today?

In the end, however, we need not rely on the option of a new, government-funded program in order to conclude that the HHS regulations fail the least-restrictive-means test. HHS itself has demonstrated that it has at its disposal an approach that is less restrictive than requiring employers to fund contraceptive methods that violate their religious beliefs. As we explained above, HHS has already established an accommodation for nonprofit organizations with religious objections. Under that accommodation, the organization can self-certify that it opposes providing coverage for particular contraceptive services. If the organization makes such a certification, the organization's insurance issuer or third-party administrator must "expressly exclude contraceptive coverage from the group health insurance coverage provided in connection with the group health plan" and "provide separate payments for any contraceptive services required to be covered" without imposing "any cost-sharing requirements . . . on the eligible organization, the group health plan, or plan participants or beneficiaries."

We do not decide today whether an approach of this type complies with RFRA for purposes of all religious claims. At a minimum, however, it does not impinge on the plaintiffs' religious belief that providing insurance coverage for the contraceptives at issue here violates their religion, and it serves HHS's stated interests equally well.

The principal dissent identifies no reason why this accommodation would fail to protect the asserted needs of women as effectively as the contraceptive mandate, and there is none. Under the accommodation, the plaintiffs' female employees would continue to receive contraceptive coverage without cost sharing for all FDA-approved contraceptives, and they would continue to "face minimal logistical and administrative obstacles," because their employers' insurers would be responsible for providing information and coverage. Ironically, it is the dissent's approach that would "impede women's receipt of benefits by 'requiring them to take steps to learn about, and to sign up for, a new government funded and administered health benefit,'" because the dissent would effectively compel religious employers to drop health-insurance coverage altogether, leaving their employees to find individual plans on government-run exchanges or elsewhere. This is indeed "scarcely what Congress contemplated."

C

HHS and the principal dissent argue that a ruling in favor of the objecting parties in these cases will lead to a flood of religious objections regarding a wide variety of medical procedures and drugs, such as vaccinations and blood transfusions, but HHS has made no effort to substantiate this prediction...

Under HHS's view, RFRA would permit the Government to require all employers to provide coverage for any medical procedure allowed by law in the jurisdiction in question - for instance, third-trimester abortions or assisted suicide. The owners of many closely held corporations could not in good conscience provide such coverage, and thus HHS would effectively exclude these people from full participation in the economic life of the nation. RFRA was enacted to prevent such an outcome.

In any event, our decision in these cases is concerned solely with the contraceptive mandate. Our decision should not be understood to hold that an insurance-coverage mandate must necessarily fall if it conflicts with an employer's religious beliefs. Other coverage requirements, such as immunizations, may be supported by different interests (for example, the need to combat the spread of infectious diseases) and may involve different arguments about the least restrictive means of providing them.

The principal dissent raises the possibility that discrimination in hiring, for example on the basis of race, might be cloaked as religious practice to escape legal sanction. Our decision today provides no such shield. The Government has a compelling interest in providing an equal opportunity to participate in the workforce without regard to race, and prohibitions on racial discrimination are precisely tailored to achieve that critical goal.

...In its final pages, the principal dissent reveals that its fundamental objection to the claims of the plaintiffs is an objection to RFRA itself. The dissent worries about forcing the federal courts to apply RFRA to a host of claims made by litigants seeking a religious exemption from generally applicable laws, and the dissent expresses a desire to keep the courts out of this business...But Congress, in enacting RFRA, took the position that "the compelling interest test as set forth in prior Federal court rulings is a workable test for striking sensible balances between religious liberty and competing prior governmental interests." **The wisdom of Congress's judgment on this matter is not our concern. Our responsibility is to enforce RFRA as written, and under the standard that RFRA prescribes, the HHS contraceptive mandate is unlawful.**

> **That's how an oath-taker looks at his role!**

The contraceptive mandate, as applied to closely held corporations, violates RFRA. Our decision on that statutory question makes it unnecessary to reach the First Amendment claim raised by Conestoga and the Hahns.

> If the Court had determined that RFRA did not protect Hobby Lobby, then First Amendment freedom of religion would have come into play and the Court would have set about determining whether the Constitution itself protects Hobby Lobby.
>
> Since they did not have to go that far, this case is not about the Constitution - it is about the statutory interpretation of RFRA.

The judgment of the Tenth Circuit in [favor of Hobby Lobby] is affirmed; the judgment of the Third Circuit [against the Hahns] is reversed, and that case is remanded for further proceedings consistent with this opinion.

CONCURRENCE: Kennedy...The Court's opinion does not have the breadth and sweep ascribed to it by the respectful and powerful dissent. The Court and the dissent disagree on the proper interpretation of the Religious Freedom and Restoration Act of 1993 (RFRA), but do agree on the purpose of that statute. It is to ensure that interests in religious freedom are protected.

In our constitutional tradition, freedom means that all persons have the right to believe or strive to believe in a divine creator and a divine law. For those who choose this course, free exercise is essential in preserving their own dignity and in striving for a self-definition shaped by their religious precepts. Free exercise in this sense implicates more than just freedom of belief. It means, too, the right to express those beliefs and to establish one's religious (or nonreligious) self-definition in the political, civic, and economic life of our larger community.

> The Court, rightly so, has never bought into this new philosophy that the "free exercise of religion" is limited to "worship" inside the church building. We are living in very dangerous times for our most cherished freedom. **One more liberal justice on the Court** will likely destroy the breadth of religious freedom we have enjoyed since our founding. Voting is important!

But in a complex society and an era of pervasive governmental regulation, defining the proper realm for free exercise can be difficult. In these cases the plaintiffs deem it necessary to exercise their religious beliefs within the context of their own closely held, for-profit corporations. They claim protection under RFRA...

As the Court notes, under our precedents, RFRA imposes a "stringent test." The Government must demonstrate that the application of a substantial burden to a person's exercise of religion "(1) is in furtherance of a compelling governmental interest; and (2) is the least restrictive means of furthering that compelling governmental interest."

As to RFRA's first requirement, the Department of Health and Human Services (HHS) makes the case that the mandate serves the Government's compelling interest in providing insurance coverage that is necessary to protect the health of female employees, coverage that is significantly more costly than for a male employee. There are many medical conditions for which pregnancy is contraindicated. It is important to confirm that a premise of the Court's opinion is its assumption that the HHS regulation here at issue furthers a legitimate and compelling interest in the health of female employees.

But the Government has not made the second showing required by RFRA, that the means it uses to regulate is the least restrictive way to further its interest. As the Court's opinion explains, the record in these cases shows that there is an existing, recognized, workable, and already-implemented framework to provide coverage. That framework is one that HHS has itself devised, that the plaintiffs have not criticized with a specific objection that has been considered in detail by the courts in this litigation, and that is less restrictive than the means challenged by the plaintiffs in these cases.

The means the Government chose is the imposition of a direct mandate on the employers in these cases. But in other instances the Government has allowed the same contraception coverage in issue here to be provided to employees of nonprofit religious organizations, as an accommodation to the religious objections of those entities. The accommodation works by requiring insurance companies to cover, without cost sharing, contraception coverage for female employees who wish it. That accommodation equally furthers the Government's interest but does not impinge on the plaintiffs' religious beliefs.

On this record and as explained by the Court, the Government has not met its burden of showing that it cannot accommodate the plaintiffs' similar religious objections under this established framework. RFRA is inconsistent with the insistence of an agency such as HHS on distinguishing between different religious believers - burdening one while accommodating the other - when it may treat both equally by offering both of them the same accommodation.

As clearly established by Justice Alito and Justice Kennedy, all interested parties in this case can be accommodated. All the president needs to do is what he did for religious not-for-profits: require the insurance companies to provide the abortifacients for free. He will not likely do that because he believes he can make more political hay with division, as opposed to unity. I have never seen anything like this in our country.

...For these reasons and others put forth by the Court, I join its opinion.

DISSENT: Ginsburg/Sotomayor/Kagan/Breyer...In a decision of startling breadth, the Court holds that commercial enterprises, including corporations, along with partnerships and sole proprietorships,

ONE

can opt out of any law...they judge incompatible with their sincerely held religious beliefs. Compelling governmental interests in uniform compliance with the law, and disadvantages that religion-based opt-outs impose on others, hold no sway, the Court decides, at least when there is a "less restrictive alternative." And such an alternative, the Court suggests, there always will be whenever, in lieu of tolling an enterprise claiming a religion-based exemption, the government, *i.e.,* the general public, can pick up the tab.

"Startling"? "Can opt out of any law"? "Hold no sway"? As carefully said by Justices Alito and Kennedy, these allegations are simply false. The country is not benefitted by hysteria.

The Court does not pretend that the First Amendment's Free Exercise Clause demands religion-based accommodations so extreme, for our decisions leave no doubt on that score. Instead, the Court holds that Congress, in the Religious Freedom Restoration Act of 1993 (RFRA), dictated the extraordinary religion-based exemptions today's decision endorses. In the Court's view, RFRA demands accommodation of a for-profit corporation's religious beliefs no matter the impact that accommodation may have on third parties who do not share the corporation owners' religious faith - in these cases, thousands of women employed by Hobby Lobby and Conestoga or dependents of persons those corporations employ. Persuaded that Congress enacted RFRA to serve a far less radical purpose, and mindful of the havoc the Court's judgment can introduce, I dissent.

I

"The ability of women to participate equally in the economic and social life of the nation has been facilitated by their ability to control their reproductive lives." *Planned Parenthood* v. *Casey*...*

A

> Although Justice Alito dramatically proves that no women need be affected by this ruling, the universe of women so affected (assuming he is wrong) continues to dwindle. Let's see, the pool of women in this universe <u>does not include</u> employees in an under 50 employee workforce. And, it does not include employees where grandfathered policies are in place, employees of religious not-for-profits, or employees of churches.
>
> It does not include employees beyond reproductive age. It does not include employees of all employers who have no religious objection to supplying abortifacients, employees who are just fine with the other 16 free contraceptives, and, lest we forget, employees who themselves have religious convictions against abortion. My, oh my, this war on women allegation isn't very serious, is it? Fascinating. No one seems to be complaining about co-pays for medication or treatment of childhood disease, but drugs/devices to kill babies has to be free or the sky will fall.
>
> I use non-politically correct terminology to save time and cut to the chase, for it matters not whether **you** believe babies die in the process or whether **you** believe that is wrong, regardless of your position on whether a fetus is a person. What matters **in *this* nation** are the religious beliefs of **those with whom you disagree**. It's called America.

B

While the Women's Health Amendment succeeded, a countermove proved unavailing. The Senate voted down the so-called "conscience amendment," which would have enabled any employer or insurance provider to deny coverage based on its asserted "religious beliefs or

One

moral convictions." That amendment, Senator Mikulski observed, would have "put the personal opinion of employers and insurers over the practice of medicine." Rejecting the "conscience amendment," Congress left health care decisions - including the choice among contraceptive methods - in the hands of women, with the aid of their health care providers.

> This decision does not affect any choice a woman had before the decision. That is still "in the hands" of women.

II

Any First Amendment Free Exercise Clause claim Hobby Lobby or Conestoga might assert is foreclosed by this Court's decision in *Employment Div. v. Smith*...

> As previously stated, the Court did not reach and, therefore, did not rule upon any First Amendment question. Why Justice Ginsburg feels compelled to address it is a mystery. However, I do not believe the *Smith* decision would necessarily result in a government win even if the issue were addressed in this case.

The exemption sought by Hobby Lobby and Conestoga would override significant interests of the corporations' employees and covered dependents...In sum, with respect to free exercise claims no less than free speech claims, "your right to swing your arms ends just where the other man's nose begins."

> Clever slogans will not overcome the truth.

> In this case, the "other man" is Hobby Lobby and its nose begins just short of government imposed participation in death. Shame on any administration that would dare divide us along gender or religious lines. None of this was necessary. No one ever heard of free abortifacients before this administration set up the great divide.

III
A

Lacking a tenable claim under the Free Exercise Clause, Hobby Lobby and Conestoga rely on RFRA…In RFRA, Congress "adopted a statutory rule comparable to the constitutional rule rejected in *Smith.*"…

> It is just sad when a Supreme Court justice resorts to the dirty game of misleading politics. "Lacking a tenable claim under the Free Exercise Clause?" Utter nonsense. It was the majority, not Hobby Lobby and Conestoga, who decided it was not necessary to address the First Amendment and they most definitely did not decide the First Amendment question. I disagree with Justice Kennedy. This dissent is neither powerful nor respectful. It is false and misleading.

3

Even if one were to conclude that Hobby Lobby and Conestoga meet the substantial burden requirement, the Government has shown that the contraceptive coverage for which the ACA provides furthers compelling interests in public health and women's well-being…

> Personally, I believe Justice Ginsburg's ranting is embarrassing. The majority assumed the government interest in the mandate is compelling. That is a non-issue.

One

The Court's reasoning appears to permit commercial enterprises like Hobby Lobby and Conestoga to exclude from their group health plans all forms of contraceptives…

> Yes, indeed, there are those who believe that all contraceptives are sinful. And, yes, I believe this decision would protect them, as well. The truth is, constitutional freedom of religion should trump the statutory right to "free stuff" every time.

The cost of an IUD is nearly equivalent to a month's full-time pay for workers earning the minimum wage…

> Justice Ginsburg, what price would you put on freedom?

The Court ultimately acknowledges a critical point: RFRA's application *"must* take adequate account of the burdens a requested accommodation may impose on non-beneficiaries." No tradition, and no prior decision under RFRA, allows a religion-based exemption when the accommodation would be harmful to others - here, the very persons the contraceptive coverage requirement was designed to protect…

> Justice Ginsburg, you, of all people, surely know that we are not dealing with any "liberties" of employees. The statutory "right" to free stuff created by the ACA doesn't come close to being a cherished "liberty" protected by the First Amendment. And, how can you possibly compare the "harm" to women who may have to come out-of-pocket a few bucks per month (which they have had to do since such products were invented) with forcing an employer to violate their faith or practically go out of business?

IV

...For the reasons stated, I would reverse the judgment of the Court of Appeals for the Tenth Circuit and affirm the judgment of the Court of Appeals for the Third Circuit.

DISSENT: Breyer/Kagan ... We agree with JUSTICE GINSBURG that the plaintiffs' challenge to the contraceptive coverage requirement fails on the merits. We need not and do not decide whether either for-profit corporations or their owners may bring claims under the Religious Freedom Restoration Act of 1993...

SUMMARY: We came perilously close to losing the very foundation of this country – the bedrock of our nation – religious freedom. In fact, it is the first of the freedoms mentioned in the First Amendment for a reason. Religious freedom is what sets us apart from other nations of the world. **"One robe"** saved us. The Supreme Court told this administration that the Religious Freedom Restoration Act protects closely-held faith-based corporations from its abortifacient mandate.

COMMENT: While it is true that the 1973 Supreme Court decision in *Roe v. Wade** has divided this nation ever since, at least the cause of the divide was the judiciary. This attempted abortifacient mandate was an intentional act of President Obama – a president who said he would bring us together. I cannot think of anything he has done to bring us together.

Think about it. Prior to this mandate, we didn't have a college student, Sandra Fluke, making her claim to fame by embarrassing herself over her outrage that people of faith found it a sin to comply.

ONE

What on earth would college students do without their free contraceptives? More importantly, what had they done before the president oversaw this insult to religious freedom? I suppose they abstained, paid for it themselves or acted irresponsibly and became pregnant.

He has successfully divided us over religion, money, race, immigration, marriage…the list is too long to complete. **One more robe** on the High Court is all he needs to complete the task of transforming America for generations to come.

PLEA: "One less robe" in the future will bring back religious tyranny. In fact, go back and read the *Burwell* case very carefully. One more liberal on the bench could easily mean a diminishment of religious freedom so great that Christians will only be able to exercise their faith during "worship" at "church" - no more mention of God in the public square. That is how important your vote is. The next time you decide it is too inconvenient to vote, think again!

Chapter Sixteen

ONE ROBE SHORT - ONE ROBE LONG - TEN ADDITIONAL CASES THAT, LIKE IT OR NOT, DEFINE WHAT WE PRESENTLY STAND FOR AS A NATION

Space limitations prevent me from exploring these ten additional selected 5-4 decisions in detail. Of course, the decisions in this book do not comprise all of the 5-4 decisions from the Rehnquist era forward, but they do cover the major ones, at least in my opinion.

I thought you might want to know the holding of these additional cases and then perhaps read them on our website. See the Appendix for instructions on how to find them.

One Robe Long:
Five additional victories decided by one robe.

1995: In *Rosenberger v. Rector and Visitors of the University of Virginia**, printing costs paid for by mandatory student fees at the University of Virginia for an independent student-based Christian organization's publications were upheld as protected free speech and also withstood an attack on establishment clause grounds.

2000: In *United States v. Morrison**, a federal statute providing a civil remedy for victims of gender-motivated violence was held to be an unconstitutional overreach of congressional commerce power.

2000: In *Boy Scouts of America v. Dale**, applying New Jersey's public accommodations law to require the Boy Scouts to admit a gay leader was held to violate the Boy Scouts' First Amendment right of expressive association.

2005: In *Van Orden v. Perry**, a Ten Commandments monument on the grounds of the Texas state capitol was held not to be an unconstitutional establishment of religion.

2007: In *Morse v. Frederick**, the First Amendment did not protect a high school student's alleged free speech rights when he, out of disrespect for his school principal, refused to take down a banner he brought to a field trip which read "Bong Hits 4 Jesus."

ONE

<u>One Robe Short</u>:
Five additional losses decided by one robe.

2000: In *Stenberg v. Carhart**, a Nebraska statute that sought to criminalize partial-birth abortion was held unconstitutional.

2004: In *Missouri v. Seibert**, Missouri's method of questioning criminal suspects without a Miranda warning, then providing a Miranda warning and questioning the suspect again hoping to arrive at the same answers was held unconstitutional.

2005: In *Roper v. Simmons**, Missouri's law supporting the death penalty for a murder committed by a person 17 years of age at the time of the crime was held unconstitutional.

2005: In *McCreary County v. ACLU**, Kentucky's display of the Ten Commandments at a courthouse was held unconstitutional.

2008: In *Kennedy v. Louisiana**, Louisiana's attempt to enforce the death penalty for the rape of an eight year old child was held unconstitutional.

Chapters Seventeen and Eighteen will wrap all of this up in a manner I hope you will long remember – especially in the voting booth!

Chapter Seventeen

ONE SACRIFICE OUGHT TO BE ENOUGH!

Donald W. Bornman, Ronald D. Keller, Gerald E. Henry, Ronald E. Rohrkaste, Sherlin A. Heiman, and Michael J. Tessaro have at least two things in common. They all hailed from Edwardsville, Illinois, the town where I grew up, and they all lost their lives from 1968 to 1969 fighting for this country – fighting for you and me.[18] I didn't know any of them. Their names are engraved on the Vietnam War Memorial in Washington, D.C., along with 2,932 other Illinois names and 55,271 names from other hometowns in other parts of America! 58,209 American military men and women died in the Vietnam War. Well, I don't suppose we will ever know the true total. Many are unknown.

In 1969, Richard M. Nixon was inaugurated as our 37th president, Neil Armstrong walked on the moon, Woodstock became a household word, the Texas Longhorns were undefeated in football, and President Eisenhower died. "Sugar, Sugar" by the Archies was the top hit even though it should have been **"One"** by Three Dog Night.

I turned 18 that year, registered with my draft board, graduated from Edwardsville High School and awaited my lottery number for a chance at winning a free one-way ticket to Vietnam with the promise of a return flight if things worked out better than they had for Donald W. Bornman.

My number was never called.

Oh, I would have gone and would like to think I would have made a good soldier, but failing to enlist is one of my life's greatest regrets in spite of every Vietnam veteran I know telling me I'm crazy to fret over that. Yet, I do.

---

18 http://vietnam-casualties.mooseroots.com/d/b/Illinois/Edwardsville.

One

We lost over 405,000 of our military in World War II and over 625,000 in the Civil War. These numbers are difficult to comprehend, yet one sacrifice ought to be enough to motivate us to preserve freedom for our posterity.

Beginning with this book, every book I write will be dedicated to one warrior who gave his life to enable us to live in freedom.

I dedicate this book to Amos Humiston.

The following is quoted from an article by Mark H. Dunkelman on History Net[19]:

> Amos Humiston: Union Soldier Who Died at the Battle of Gettysburg. Mark H. Dunkelman.
>
> "Of all the fallen heroes of the epic, three-day Civil War Battle of Gettysburg in July 1863, this Union soldier was unique. He had not led a charge, nor captured an enemy flag, nor rescued a comrade under fire. Instead, his fame rested on his dying act of devotion and love; his death pose made his story special. Found after the battle, in a secluded spot in the town near the intersection of Stratton and York Streets, the soldier bore nothing on his person to identify him. But clutched in his hand was an ambrotype photograph of three young children. In his final moments, he had fixed his gaze on the image of his beloved little ones, and carried the sight with him into death. The picture was freed from his frozen grip, and he was buried in an unknown's grave."

---

19 http://www.historynet.com/amos-humiston-union-soldier-who-died-at-the-battle-of-gettysburg.htm.

If you are interested in learning more about Mr. Humiston, I would recommend the book, <u>Gettysburg's Unknown Soldier</u>, again by Mark H. Dunkelman.

Thank you, Amos. I shall remember you and your fallen comrades always.

When judges, elected leaders and everyday folks disregard the founding document so many have died to preserve, I weep for the Amos Humistons and over one million others who have died in combat for this nation. Don't you? If so, help me. Help America recover and take the next and last chapter of this book seriously.

Chapter Eighteen

ONE LAST CHANCE TO SAVE AMERICA

Let's examine the current make-up of the Supreme Court.

Someone has to be in charge, if only administratively. That "someone," currently John G. Roberts, Jr., carries the title of Chief Justice. Justice Roberts is a graduate of Harvard Law School. He was nominated for the High Court (and the position of Chief Justice) by President George W. Bush. He was confirmed by the Senate by a vote of 78 to 22 and took office in 2005. Now serving his 13th year on the Court, Justice Roberts is 63 years of age.

Justice Anthony Kennedy is a graduate of Harvard Law School. He was nominated for the Supreme Court by President Ronald Reagan, was confirmed in the Senate by a unanimous vote (97 to 0) and took office in 1988. Now serving his 30th year on the Court, Justice Kennedy is 81 years of age.

Justice Clarence Thomas is a graduate of Yale Law School. He was nominated for the Supreme Court by President George H. W. Bush, was confirmed in the Senate by a vote of 52 to 48 and took office in 1991. Now serving his 26th year on the Court, Justice Thomas is 69 years of age.

Justice Ruth Bader Ginsburg is a graduate of Columbia Law School. She was nominated for the Supreme Court by President Bill Clinton, was confirmed in the Senate by a vote of 96 to 3 and took office in 1993. Now serving her 25th year on the Court, Justice Ginsburg is 85 years of age.

Justice Stephen Breyer is a graduate of Harvard Law School. He was nominated for the Supreme Court by President Bill Clinton, was confirmed in the Senate by a vote of 87 to 9 and took office in 1994. Now serving his 23rd year on the Court, Justice Breyer is 79 years of age.

One

Justice Samuel Alito, Jr. is a graduate of Yale Law School. He was nominated for the Supreme Court by President George W. Bush, was confirmed in the Senate by a vote of 58 to 42 and took office in 2006. Now serving his 12th year on the Court, Justice Alito is 68 years of age.

Justice Sonia Sotomayor is a graduate of Yale Law School. She was nominated for the Supreme Court by President Barack Obama, was confirmed in the Senate by a vote of 68 to 31 and took office in 2009. Now serving her 8th year on the Court, Justice Sotomayor is 63 years of age.

Justice Elena Kagan is a graduate of Harvard Law School. She was nominated for the Supreme Court by President Barack Obama, was confirmed in the Senate by a vote of 63 to 37 and took office in 2010. Now serving her 8th year on the Court, Justice Kagan is 58 years of age.

Justice Neil Gorsuch is a graduate of Harvard Law School. He was nominated for the Supreme Court by President Donald Trump, was confirmed in the Senate by a vote of 54 to 45 and took office in 2017. Now serving his 1st year on the Court, Justice Gorsuch is 50 years of age.

We discussed in detail five decisions by the current members of the Supreme Court inclusive of Justice Scalia (Chapters Eleven through Fifteen).

In Chapter Eleven (*Plata v. Brown**), we came up **one robe short** of the correct decision and the guilty were freed in California. In order of seniority, Associate Justices Kennedy, Ginsburg, Breyer, Sotomayor and Kagan sold the Constitution short. Dissenting, again in order of seniority, were Chief Justice Roberts and Associate Justices Scalia, Thomas and Alito.

In Chapter Twelve (*United States v. Windsor**), we came up **one robe short** of the correct decision, thus altering the traditional institution of marriage. Guess who comprised the majority? Associate Justices Kennedy, Ginsburg, Breyer, Sotomayor and Kagan. Chief Justice Roberts and Associate Justices Scalia, Thomas and Alito dissented.

In Chapter Fourteen (*National Labor Relations Board v. Canning**), we came up **one robe short** of the correct reasoning, thus unconstitutionally redefining recess appointments and altering the balance of power. This decision pitted the likes of Associate Justices Kennedy, Ginsburg, Breyer, Sotomayor and Kagan against Chief Justice Roberts and Associate Justices Scalia, Thomas and Alito.

In Chapter Thirteen, we had a **one vote victory** for prayer in *Greece v. Galloway**. Those in favor: Chief Justice Roberts and Associate Justices Scalia, Kennedy, Thomas and Alito. Those opposed: Associate Justices Ginsburg, Breyer, Sotomayor and Kagan.

In Chapter Fifteen, we had a **one vote victory** for religious freedom in *Burwell v. Hobby Lobby Stores, Inc.**. Those in favor: Chief Justice Roberts and Associate Justices Scalia, Kennedy, Thomas and Alito. Those opposed: Associate Justices Ginsburg, Breyer, Sotomayor and Kagan.

Do you see a pattern?

Of these five cases, Chief Justice Roberts and Associate Justices Scalia (deceased), Thomas and Alito consistently voted in favor of the Constitution. Of these five cases, Associate Justices Ginsburg, Breyer, Sotomayor and Kagan consistently voted against the Constitution. Three cases came up **one vote short** of victory and two cases were victorious by **one vote**. The **one vote** in each of these

One

five cases that made the difference was always the vote of Associate Justice Kennedy. That is why he is often referred to as the "swing man" or "swing vote" among these nine justices.

Can we draw any conclusions with respect to the four "originalists"?

Chief Justice Roberts was nominated by President George W. Bush.

Justice Antonin Scalia was nominated by President Ronald Reagan.

Justice Clarence Thomas was nominated by President George H. W. Bush.

Justice Samuel Alito, Jr. was nominated by President George W. Bush.

There is no rule that works each and every time. For example, although I am a big Scalia fan, I have not always agreed with his rulings. I haven't always agreed with Chief Justice Roberts' rulings. Hmmm! Does "Obamacare I and II" come to mind?

Nevertheless, it is no surprise that Presidents Reagan, Bush I and Bush II (all Republican conservatives who believed in preserving the Constitution) nominated Roberts, Scalia, Thomas and Alito.

Can we draw any conclusions with respect to the four "whatever-feels-good jurists"?

Justices Ruth Bader Ginsburg and Stephen Breyer were nominated by President Bill Clinton.

Justices Sonia Sotomayor and Elena Kagan were nominated by President Barack Obama.

It is likewise no surprise that Presidents Clinton and Obama (both Democrat liberals who favor abortion, same-sex marriage, "evolving standards of decency" that take "the people" out of their governing role, etc.) nominated Justices Ginsburg, Breyer, Sotomayor and Kagan.

The swing voter, Justice Kennedy, was nominated by President Ronald Reagan. Nevertheless, the only thing consistent about his rulings is his inconsistency.

Justices Ginsburg (85), Kennedy (81) and Breyer (79) are no spring chickens.

D.C. talk has it that Justice Kennedy could well retire in the very near future (and may have done so by the time this book goes to the printer). And, Justice Ginsburg is not in the best of health. In other words, President Trump has already replaced an originalist jurist (Scalia) with one of like ilk (Gorsuch). He has an ever increasing chance of replacing the Court's "swing man" (Kennedy) and one of the Court's "living-breathing-whatever-floats-her-boat" jurists (Ginsburg) with oath-taker robes.

And, of course, the possibilities for replacements of conservative justices if the Democrats regain the Presidency in 2020 or the Republicans do not retain the Senate majority in 2018 are very alarming. If seats do not come open until either of the foregoing potentially occurs, contemplate the likes of Eric Holder or even Barak Obama donning a black robe on the High Court someday! It has happened before. Former President William Howard Taft became a member of the Supreme Court in 1921, eight years after the conclusion of his Presidency.

ONE

Just looking at the ten cases we studied in detail, had there been **one less originalist** and, therefore, **one more liberal** on the bench:

Federalism would have been destroyed (*United States v. Lopez**);

> The slaughter of partially born babies would have been upheld (*Gonzales v. Carhart*);
>
>> Your guns would have been made illegal (*District of Columbia v. Heller**);
>>
>>> Prayer to open city meetings would have been forbidden (*Greece v. Galloway**); and,
>>>
>>>> Freedom of religion would have been reduced to a memory (*Burwell v. Hobby Lobby Stores, Inc.**).

And, had there been **one more originalist** and, therefore, **one less liberal** on the bench:

Government sponsored commencement prayers in public schools would have been allowed (*Lee v. Weisman**);

> Term limits would have been preserved as an option for states to adopt in federal elections (*U.S. Term Limits v. Thornton*);
>
>> Recess appointment power would have been limited (*National Labor Relations Board v. Canning**);
>>
>>> California prisoners would not have been released prematurely (*Plata v. Brown**); and,

>Traditional marriage between one man and one woman would have been preserved in the federal system (*United States v. Windsor**).

Thanks so much for taking this journey - hopefully, an eye-opening one - that will motivate you to motivate others to **E**arn your freedom by **L**earning about your country so that we don't **L**ose it. Becoming a member of **ELL** Constitution Clubs would be a great way to end this first leg of a trip that should last you a lifetime. I need you. Your nation needs you - now!

Please contact the website at ellconstitutionclubs.com, then use the site to contact me. We must educate America. We are out of time.

And, finally, I want to address the millions of good folks who love your country, but have not voted in years because you do not believe your vote matters as well as those who are active, but feel a third party is the only way to go.

Please listen to me very carefully. You hold the key to whether we preserve the Constitution and its principles or whether we sink into a long, dark era when America is completely lost and will not recover for decades. I want all of you to know that if we had time, I could easily see myself joining the third party revolt. But, you know better than most that it would take several elections to gain enough power to overcome the Republican Party as the only real alternative to the Democrats.

There is **one and only one** reason why time is not on the side of a third party revolution: the math doesn't add up!

If we currently had a 6-3 margin of constitutional jurists to policy-making-whatever-floats-your-boat jurists on the High Court or,

One

better yet, a 7-2 margin, I would be much more inclined to begin the long journey it would take to establish a third party in this nation.

But, folks, at present we have only four justices we can almost always count on to live within their constitutional limits (Justice Roberts had a few bad days), we have four justices we can never count on, and we have one justice who is unpredictable.

Therefore, I am confident the fallout from just one more Democratic Party controlled administration (president and Senate or weak Republican controlled Senate), and possibly several such administrations until a third party takes over, would be a devastating blow to our founding principles. The shift of power by **just one** justice in the wrong direction will result in Supreme Court decisions that (1) will spell the end of freedom as we know it and (2) will hasten our ultimate demise. How long do you think it would take if the judicial power shifts the wrong way to (1) vote a third party in and (2) await the tenure of the existing liberal justices lives or retirements, together with new liberal justices work-life span? We could easily see the balance of power shift in the wrong direction that would take 100 or more years to remedy.

In 1969, the then President of the American Bar Association, William T. Gossett, said: "The rule of law can be wiped out in one misguided, however well-intentioned generation. And if that should happen, it could take a century of striving and ordeal to restore it, and then only at the cost of the lives of many good men and women."

We don't have time to experiment with a third party. We are on life support right now. The only way to save this nation is to put presidents and senators in place that will send constitutional jurists to the Supreme Court each and every time a liberal justice dies or retires. If I have not made that clear, I have failed.

Your **one vote** for the next Republican nominee for president and each Republican running for the Senate in your State could be the **votes** that save our nation. Don't waste them! In fact, double them by persuading at least one non-voter or third party advocate to join you. If you can't win them over, encourage them to read this book.

I firmly believe the 2018 mid-term elections and the 2020 elections will be our last opportunities to save America! Don't let Amos down. Don't sit by and watch as our blood-bought freedoms become nothing more than a memory.

VOTE!

NOT JUST FOR ANYONE, BUT FOR

REPUBLICAN NOMINEES ---

BECAUSE A NON-VOTE OR A VOTE

FOR ANYONE ELSE WILL SPELL

THE END OF OUR CONSTITUTION

AND OUR REPUBLIC!

ABOUT THE AUTHOR

A product of the Universities of Illinois and Texas, Tad Armstrong practices law, wrote a monthly op-ed column for the *St. Louis Post-Dispatch*, has taught constitutional law at Greenville College (Greenville, Illinois) and Brookes Bible College (St. Louis, Missouri), and is a frequent guest on talk radio. He founded ELL Constitution Clubs® and has written a three-thousand page treatise on the subject. He authored a book about the religion clauses of the First Amendment, It's OK To Say "God." Tad and his wife, Melody, reside in Edwardsville, Illinois.

APPENDIX

Should you desire to read any of the following cases (designated with an * the first time they appear in a chapter), they can be found on my website: ellconstitutionclubs.com.

Once there, click on the Supreme Court Decisions tab.

First, I would read the introductory material, then scroll down and familiarize yourself with the indexing system. Each light grey row describes the indexing of the cases to follow.

The index number of each case, below, is located in the right column of the Appendix and can be found in the first column of the Supreme Court Decisions page. The second column of that page briefly describes the topic of the case. Then, click on the case name in the third column of the website page and the case will appear.

Abington School District v. Schempp	1A-R-034
Allegheny County v. ACLU	1A-R-085
Boy Scouts of America v. Dale	1A-A-4
Burwell v. Hobby Lobby Stores, Inc.	1A-R-113
Canning v. National Labor Relations Board	2-24
Clinton v. Jones	2-3
District of Columbia v. Heller	2A-4
Employment Division v. Smith	1A-R-087
Engel v. Vitale	1A-R-033
Gibbons v. Ogden	1-14
Greece v. Galloway	1A-R-112
Griswold v. Connecticut	9A-AP-1

Hernandez v. Commissioner	1A-R-084
Kennedy v. Louisiana	8A-CUP-26
Kyllo v. United States	4A-13
Larson v. Valente	1A-R-061
Lee v. Weisman	1A-R-089
Lemon v. Kurtzman	1A-R-042
Lynch v. Donnelly	1A-R-066
Marbury v. Madison	6-2
Marsh v. Chambers	1A-R-065
McCreary County v. ACLU	1A-R-107
McDonald v. Chicago	2A-5
Missouri v. Seibert	5A-SI-5
Morse v. Frederick	1A-S-47
National Labor Relations Board v. Canning	2-26
Planned Parenthood v. Casey	9A-AP-17
Plata v. Brown	8A-CUP-27
Roe v. Wade	9A-AP-4
Roper v. Simmons	8A-CUP-21
Rosenberger v. Rector	1A-R-095
Stenberg v. Carhart	9A-AP-18
Thomas v. Review Bd.	1A-R-058
United States v. Cruikshank	2A-1
United States v. Darby	1-17
United States v. Lopez	1-20
United States v. Miller	2A-3
United States v. Morrison	1-21
U.S. Term Limits, Inc. v. Thornton	1-4
Van Orden v. Perry	1A-R-106
Wallace v. Jaffree	1A-R-068
West Virginia v. Barnette	1A-S-9
Wickard v. Filburn	1-18

INDEX OF CASES

Abington School District v. Schempp: 55-56, 237
Allegheny County v. ACLU: 51, 234, 237, 239
Bowsher v. Synar: 294
Boy Scouts of America v. Dale: 360
Burwell v. Hobby Lobby Stores, Inc.: 317, 319, 357, 370, 373
Canning v. National Labor Relations Board: 266, 315
Clinton v. Jones: 302
Clinton v. New York: 294
District of Columbia v. Heller: 146-147, 172, 373
Employment Division v. Smith: 323, 353
Engel v. Vitale: 55-56, 241, 264
Gibbons v. Ogden: 66
Gonzales v. Carhart: 116, 373
Greece v. Galloway: 231, 370, 373
Griswold v. Connecticut: 22, 26, 342
Hernandez v. Commissioner: 340
Joyner v. Forsyth County: 260
Kennedy v. Louisiana: 361
Kyllo v. United States: 150
Larson v. Valente: 257
Lawrence v. Texas: 207-208
Lee v. Weisman: 46, 241, 249, 258, 264, 373
Lemon v. Kurtzman: 41, 49
Loving v. Virginia: 205
Lynch v. Donnelly: 51
Marbury v. Madison: 5, 71-72, 295
Marsh v. Chambers: 231, 234-241, 243, 245-247, 249-250, 254, 264
McCreary County v. ACLU: 257, 361
McCulloch v. Maryland: 102
McDonald v. Chicago: 146, 172
Missouri v. Seibert: 361

Morse v. Frederick: 360
National Labor Relations Board v. Canning: 266-267, 370, 373
National Labor Relations Board v. Jones & Laughlin Steel: 66
Planned Parenthood v. Casey: 128-129, 139, 142, 351
Plata v. Brown: 174-175, 180, 194, 369, 373
Presbyterian Church v. Mary Elizabeth Blue Hull Memorial Presbyterian Church: 340
Public Citizen v. Department of Justice: 295
Reno v. American Civil Liberties Union: 150
Roe v. Wade: 128-129, 138-139, 142, 226, 356
Roper v. Simmons: 361
Rosenberger v. Rector: 360-361
Stenberg v. Carhart: 116-118, 124-125, 127, 133, 137, 361
Thomas v. Board of Review: 341
United States v. Cruikshank: 152
United States v. Darby: 66
United States v. Lopez: 63, 373
United States v. Miller: 153, 161
United States v. Morrison: 360
United States v. Windsor: 200-201, 225-226, 370, 374
U.S. Term Limits, Inc. v. Thornton: 87, 113, 373
Van Orden v. Perry: 238, 360
Wallace v. Jaffree: 58, 264
West Virginia Board of Education v. Barnette: 53
Wickard v. Filburn: 66
Zivotofsky v. Clinton: 295

CPSIA information can be obtained
at www.ICGtesting.com
Printed in the USA
FFHW01n0104020718
47279816-50219FF